The
Coolest Startups In™
America

Doreen Bloch

BUILDING BLOCH BOOKS

NEW YORK CITY | 2012

A
BUILDING BLOCH BOOK
PAPERBACK

∞

This book is dedicated to my mentors*, past, present and future. Especially you, Mom!

*Those who not only push you to follow your dreams, but who also give you the tools to do so.

Contents

section 11
Lean Machines
Lightening the Day's Toil startups

section 12
Cuff Links
B2B startups

section 13
Apothecary
Apple a Day startups

section 14
Chatterbox
Interaction Meets Information startups

section 15
Cosmetics
Beautify the World startups

section 16
Jobfull
Hire Me startups

section 17
[Not] Made in America
*International Startups
Too Cool to Leave Out*

section 18
Appendices
*New Ways to
See the Coolest
Startups*

List of Defrosts

"Sometimes, the idea of change is scarier than the reality of it."

- Logan Lee Lamson, Filmmaker
(Forward & Gone, 2011)

about this book

I wrote this book for people who want to be the first to discover the best new companies. Maybe you'd like to become an early tech adopter or, if you're hesitant to come down off the bleachers, maybe you'd like to just peer in on what the early adopters are seeing, hearing, sensing, feeling and joining. In other words, *The Coolest Startups in America* is for anyone who wants to know about startups but doesn't read TechCrunch (a top tech blog), expects "Mashable" to be a property of potatoes (it's a social media blog) or thinks foursquare (a cool mobile startup) is just an outdoor ballgame!

This book is your guide to know about the awesome startups in the USA *today* that will be global household names *tomorrow*. It's your definitive, quick-read tour of the most interesting new companies around our great nation. You'll get the trends, know the gadgets and gain the knowledge necessary to make show-stopping dinner conversation about what's coming.

I took the best of the blogosphere, techie conferences and nerd chatter, and added business analysis to present you with the essence of what's cool and how to discuss it, all in a portable book format for easy consumption for the plane, on vacation or around the office.

I wrote this book with the belief that if you don't keep up with technology, you won't realize how fast we're approaching the future. I hope that empowering you with knowledge about these businesses will enable you to decide which of them to embrace. I aim to make these companies' technologies accessible, and give you the power to control your usage and presence. And surely, I aspire to share with you startups that *wow*. The cooler, the better!

Doreen Bloch
New York City
January 1, 2012

why startups matter

Business is a central part of American life. We party with business in good times and, like a good friend recovering from an illness, worry about it in economic downturns. The recession of 2008 and its aftermath have continued to shine a spotlight on the business world. Reporters and citizen journalists talk about Wall Street and *Occupy* Wall Street, but what is more crucial—yet less often discussed—are the businesses working overtime everyday for our families and communities, our nation and the world.

In November 2011, I was invited to the White House for a summit celebrating National Entrepreneurship Month. Ronnie Cho, Associate Director of Public Engagement for the White House, opened the event, and spoke about entrepreneurship in resonating fashion.

"Entrepreneurship is baked into our nation's DNA," he said. "Free enterprise is the most powerful job-creating force in the world and it's our competitive advantage."

In these two phrases, Cho encompassed the important reasons why startups matter to America. First, Americans believe in the risk-reward paradigm as a core value. Americans know that, while success is never assured, building a business is an ideal way to increase personal wealth and quality of life. Second, entrepreneurial ventures drive our nation forward, generating profits by solving problems. Such ventures employ people to unlock this value, which accelerates economic growth.

I spoke with Pravina Raghavan, District Director of the Small Business Administration for New York, who shared with me her views about entrepreneurship in American society. She says 60% of Americans work for small businesses, and that the sector creates the most net new jobs in the US. "It's prime time to start a business," Raghavan says. "In a downturn, people focus on entrepreneurs to get things up and running. It's the time to be more creative and innovative."

It's great then to know that entrepreneurship is more accessible than ever. Scott Gerber, founder of the Young Entrepreneur Council, in his published opinion for *TIME* magazine in January 2012, dubbed this year as the "Year of the Entrepreneur." Christopher Michel, the serial entrepreneur behind Military.com, founding partner of Nautilus Ventures and former Entrepreneur-in-Residence at Harvard Business School, would agree. "There's a national zeitgeist toward entrepreneurship," Michel says. "It's more in people's grasps than ever before."

And why? The answer is that resources for entrepreneurs abound. Knowledge about starting and running a business is being shared more and more, both on and offline. The cost of launching and promoting a new venture has dramatically decreased with the advent of the Web. And investors—at traditional institutional levels and on new "peer-to-peer" funding platforms alike—are hungry for ideas to fund. Meanwhile, labor today is relatively inexpensive due to recessionary pressures leading to job loss and underemployment.

There's a third reason to care about startups: aiming for big dreams brings us closer to them. Startups must matter because the entrepreneurs behind them are an ambitious lot who need support. Economic development and the fulfillment of a core American value are only possible when entrepreneurs are inspired to think big.

It's as if "startups are freedom," Raghavan says. She describes business as a blank canvas. "Entrepreneurs make things work no matter what industry," she says. "They take a blank canvas and start to paint a wonderful picture. Innovation can come at such a level because entrepreneurs have the freedom to think about things never done before. Startups have the freedom to make right and wrong choices, and the freedom to make the future."

what makes a startup cool?

When I began writing *The Coolest Startups in America* as a passion project, I defined a cool startup as any startup *I* liked to share. There's nothing necessarily wrong with that approach. Alex Taub of Aviary, featured in Chapter 61, says he defines a cool startup as any one he'd recommend to friends, particularly any startups that "make me look cool if I know about them before other people."

But once I committed to publishing *The Coolest Startups in America*, I needed a more rigorous definition because people ask me about the characteristics that make up a cool startup. After dozens of interviews and extensive analysis, core characteristics of "cool startups" did emerge. While some of the startups featured in *The Coolest Startups in America* may lack one or two of the qualities, most of them hit these marks. The list serves as an excellent litmus test if you want to join or create a cool startup, or hope to catch my eye for the next volume of this book.

Cool Startups...

1. Solve a Real Problem. "It has to make lives meaningfully better," says Aaron Schildkrout, co-CEO of HowAboutWe (Chapter 36). In the startup scene, people speak often about "pain," and making clear what the "pain point" is that the startup solves. If the startup's mission is vague, it's not likely to be too cool. Sutha Kamal of healthcare startup Massive Health urges founders to "gravitate to real problems." That's how important companies are built, says Michael Sinanian, who reports on startups for VentureBeat, an important technology publication. "If a startup tackles a hard problem and they've accomplished the impossible, they're creating value," Sinanian says.

2. Do It in a Unique Way. Nick Ganju, CTO of ZocDoc (Chapter 55), cites "an overabundance of startups doing something one percent different than a big player. No one will be seduced by a clone." Marc Brodeur, CEO of Brode (Chapter 29), agrees. "If you're going head to head with Facebook, you're not setting yourself up for success."

3. Have Reach. For the purposes of this book, cool startups have already launched and must be scalable. Startups that are pre-product release are too early-stage to be considered cool. Why? There's still so much that can go wrong; fledgling companies are untested by the market forces that set the bar for "cool." "Reach" is one of these market forces because it affects how many customers a startup can amass. Ilan Abehassera, CEO of Producteev (Chapter 49), says cross-platform performance is a bonus because it bolsters customer acquisition when "you're available everywhere and you're able to be accessed no matter what."

4. Are Ambitious. "There are a lot of startups and raising money isn't as hard as it used to be," says Ilya Sukhar, founder of Parse. "Some companies are okay selling out, but cool startups are ones that do something large, bold and successful."

5. Execute. Jeff Fernandez, CEO and Founder of Grovo (Chapter 34), says cool startups "do what they say they're going to do and they do it quickly and efficiently. They execute like hell. When we set a date, we ship the product on that day. The whole team rallies around it."

6. Focus on the Consumer. Schildkrout of HowAboutWe would add that cool startups don't execute arbitrarily; cool startups engage with their consumers to generate products that address consumers' needs. "Their users are constantly delighted by what the company is pushing out and that should never stop," he says. Brodeur of Brode describes that "when you build a company, you're building a relationship with your customers. It's a corporate personality. You need to be consistent and give them something of value."

7. Have Cool Brands. Sometimes, wonderful brands sprout from the compelling personal stories behind them, says Alex Budak, Founder of Start Some Good, the platform that allows social-minded upstarts to raise funds. This storytelling should run through all levels of the organization, Brodeur adds. "Every single time you talk to or email someone, it's branding. Anything that anyone sees is branding. You never cut corners with it." And that includes naming your startup. "If you don't have a cool name, it can kill a startup," says Will Curran, Founder of Arizona Pro DJs. "Flickr changed the game of naming by remove the 'e.'" Nowadays, great design is also critical. Henrik Werdelin of Prehype, a product innovation consultancy, calls design a macrotrend. Products "have to be prettier and prettier," he says.

These traits constitute a fantastic framework to analyze whether a company could be classified as a "cool startup," but that's not to say there aren't other guiding notions. An elegant concept I came across in writing this book was the idea that sometimes, cool startups lead businesses that are so obvious, you wouldn't believe they didn't exist before. The idea came to me as Ed O'Boyle, founder of Fotobridge, described his startup in the digital photo space. "People have hundreds, if not thousands, of images that they want to preserve and share," he told me. "I thought, 'There has to be a company that creates good quality digital images.' But there wasn't, so I created it."

Daryl Bernstein, CEO of RightSignature (Chapter 52), phrased this concept well. "I love smart solutions to obvious problems, especially those that have some degree of 'wow' effect. These are products and services that make their users gasp, out loud or not."

how to read this book

One word at a time, of course! The book is divided into 18 sections, classifying the coolest startups under the industries in which they are innovating. Each section of *The Coolest Startups in America* has multiple chapters, with one chapter for each cool upstart. In between, you'll encounter "defrost" chapters that explain startup terms or trends. If you're looking to start or join an upstart, these sections will be valuable to you.

In each chapter about a startup, you'll see standard headings. **LET'S BREAK THE ICE** is a quick introduction to the startup. **HOW DOES IT WORK** explains the technology or business model backbone of the company. **BACKSTORY** describes the founding story of the startup. **WHY IS IT COOL?** covers the takeaway for the reader about why the startup is impressive or interesting. **LET'S SAY...** gives you ideas on how the startup may impact daily life. **SMOOTH SAILING** details some strengths or accomplishments of the business so far, and **CHOPPY WATERS** sums up some challenges of the startup's business. If the startup piques your interest, **GOT GOOSEBUMPS?** shares tips on how to follow up, learn more or participate (often for free) in the startup's projects.

Remember, the lifetimes of startups can vary, so some companies featured in this volume may have undergone changes since publication. You can always find out the latest about featured startups by checking the outlets listed in this book's Resources Appendix. Chapter-by-chapter sourcing is also available at the end of the Appendices section.

The chapters are not meant to be how-to manuals or serve as FAQ guides. For detailed product instruction or company contact information, check out the startups' corporate websites. If there are any corrections to the text of *The Coolest Startups in America*, they will be announced and listed on the book website at www.CoolestStartups.In.

CASH REGISTERS
Show Me the Money startups

1. Square
2. Lending Club
3. Kickstarter
4. StarStreet

Chapter 1: Square

BEFORE GEEKS INHABITED garages, kids selling lemonade from their front yards was one of the most powerful incarnations of entrepreneurial eagerness in America. In those not-so-distant days, kidpreneurs would scrawl "Lemonade! 25 cents!" on poster paper to advertise their homemade drink, and they'd await kind neighbors who would dig for lost change in between car seat cushions to support their local businesspeople in the making.

This innocent street corner business stagnated at low-tech though, never benefiting from the revolution *en plastic* of the 1960's: the credit card. Lemonade stand operators could only accept dollar bills and coins because there was no feasible way to hook up a credit card terminal outside a store, not to mention get its application accepted for juvenile, seasonal use.

But now, they can accept credit cards, and with ease. The lemonade stand can become a wired, fired-up machine of credit card munching, all thanks to Square, *The Coolest Startups in America*'s first featured upstart-extraordinaire.

LET'S BREAK THE ICE

Square is a mobile device (with a matching mobile app) that revolutionizes how payments are made.

HOW DOES IT WORK?

Square is a small and (you guessed it) square contraption that connects to your mobile device, like an iPhone or iPad, through the headphone jack. After installing the Square app and configuring it with the relevant bank account information, anyone can start accepting credit card payments through his/her phone.

Brian Zisk, a startup expert who runs entrepreneurship events like the annual Future of Money & Technology conference in San Francisco, says Square is "one of the hottest companies" around. "*Anyone*—it could be your grandma—has the ability to process credit card payments with Square for no money upfront and no contract and no termination and no monthly fee," he says.

To do one transaction, type in the desired payment

amount, swipe the paying party's credit card, have the paying party sign above the designated line with his/her finger on the screen, and email or text him/her a receipt. Within minutes, the transaction is complete. Meticulous records are kept, accessible from anywhere with an Internet connection.

Square takes a 2.75% transaction fee, lower than the average most shopkeepers pay using familiar, bulky credit card terminals. Zisk says, "Anytime you have an industry like credit cards that is so huge, it becomes ripe for disruption. Square stepped right into that opportunity."

WHY IS IT COOL?

Square is sleek and simple to use, and it's making tons of money. Ilya Sukhar of Parse, a mobile technology startup, is effusive. "Square is a no-brainer. Square stepped up to the plate and changed how accepting credit cards is done."

LET'S SAY...

I. You own an SAT tutoring business. In the past, you could only accept cash or check to be paid for your services. With Square, tutees can pay by credit card too. The funds go straight to your checking account within a day, saving you trips to the bank and giving you more time to do what you'd rather be doing: teaching and reaping the benefits.

II. You're at a birthday dinner at a restaurant with a dozen friends. Everyone knows restaurants will usually refuse to divide your bill precisely. So (and this is my favorite way to use Square) after the meal, you grab Square from your wallet and plug it into your iPhone, passing it around the table for each guest to pay his/her share of the bill. Then you just put your own credit card down to pay the restaurant, and voilà! It's brilliant because not only is everyone in awe of the helpful contraption at hand, but you'll get a boost in your credit card rewards bonus points too.

III. You want to use Square for a short-term cash advance. This great tip comes from serial entrepreneur and Arizona State University college student, Zach Hamilton. "I love Square," Hamilton says. "Instead of having to pay 20% on your credit card's cash advance, you can get 2.75% through Square by just running your own credit card through the device. If you need a grand, it's a great way to do it."

SMOOTH SAILING

+ Industry heavyweight and CEO of Twitter, Jack Dorsey, is CEO of Square too. How does Dorsey CEO for two frigidly cool startups? It helps that he lives within a few blocks of both companies' headquarters in San Francisco. Fellow startup CEOs dote on his leadership. Michael Karnjanaprakorn of Skillshare (Chapter 33) told me, "I think Jack Dorsey is going to go down as one of the best CEOs in history." Dorsey is a legacy in the making.

+ Square is already processing $3 million in transactions daily as of May 2011. That's remarkable considering that Paypal, the sector's incumbent, does $6 million daily on mobile as of the same month. Square has immense room to grow; the total value of mobile transactions in the US is expected to reach $1 trillion in the next few years.

+ Square's 2.75% transaction fee undercuts current players, taking well-deserved market share.

+ Square gives new insight to business owners at point-of-sale, including transaction records, categorization, business analytics and the ability to track a client's purchases over time.

+ Square has stellar partnerships; the company distributes its device in Apple stores and is formally aligned with Visa.

CHOPPY WATERS

- Surely Square can do more! Similar to the clunkiness of physical credit card processing, online e-commerce is laborious to set up and use, and I think Square could design something more user-friendly.

- Competitors include Google Wallet and Intuit's GoPayment. Google's solution is partnered with Mastercard, and Intuit has relationships with thousands of small businesses, making distribution of its devices easier. Both are formidable competitors, indicative of the ripe opportunities in the mobile payments space.

GOT GOOSEBUMPS?

To learn more about Square, visit www.SquareUp.com today and order one. Doing so is 100% free. I'm sure you'll love it, and I wouldn't be surprised if you start carting it around in your wallet all day like I do. I call it squarevolution.

DEFROST: Starting Up

"I think I had heard the word 'entrepreneur,' but it wasn't a word in my lexicon," says Christopher Michel. The serial entrepreneur who started Military.com is now a venture capitalist, and he recently served as Entrepreneur-in-Residence at Harvard Business School (HBS), his graduate school alma mater. Michel, who had served in the United States Navy and had worked near Washington D.C. on National Security for years before attending business school in the 1990s, first thought seriously about entrepreneurship after hearing a lecture at HBS by Dan Bricklin, the creator of VisiCalc, an early commercial spreadsheet software. Michel shared his train of thought. "Bricklin may not be the wealthiest guy, but he created something that mattered," Michel recalled.

Michel was deeply affected by that lecture, but his transition to entrepreneurship wasn't immediate. "I was a latent entrepreneur. My epiphany was at a patrol squadron," Michel told me. "People were complaining about military benefits and their difficulty connecting with peers and families. I quit my job a month later to start Military.com."

Michel's venture had the potential to affect over 24 million Americans, he says. "I was the least likely entrepreneur, but once I figured out that it was something I could do, it was more straightforward. Entrepreneurship is a vehicle to engage smart people on problems that matter. Confidence makes all the difference in the world. Not intelligence, but confidence."

The opportunity to solve problems that affect society is wholly fulfilling for many entrepreneurs, yet there are other perks of starting up too.

Sutha Kamal, the CEO of healthcare upstart Massive Health, shares that "being an entrepreneur is a blast. I get to wake up and work with a team that is way smarter than I am alone. It's an outstanding privilege to work at a company where the motivation is a noble one and you can go home and say, 'I built that thing. I contributed to something.'"

Rah, Rah, But Isn't It Risky?

Of course it is. Entrepreneurship has rewards, and it has risks. Many startups do fail. There aren't any definitive statistics as to the quantity of failures, but startups can fail for a variety of documented reasons, including lack of capital to reach necessary milestones, errors in gauging market size or technological feasibility, distribution problems, shifts in the competitive landscape, sour team dynamics, or any other number of managerial and business problems.

The risk comes from the uncertainty. At best, entrepreneurship is a guess. It's a gamble that your idea of a successful company can pan out. The entrepreneur can dream, plan, discuss the plans with advisors, recruit an exceptional team, raise funding, execute, and still fail.

Yet people are often successful. There are a plethora of resources today and fantastic startup communities all across the country help to make more entrepreneurial ventures reach successes. And interestingly, even in failure, there's a silver lining.

Liron Shapira, CTO and co-founder of Quixey (Chapter 50), told me about his startup's early-days dilemma. Tomer Kagan, CEO and co-founder of Quixey, came to Shapira with the idea for the company, but asked that Shapira not quit his job so Shapira could still get a paycheck and avoid excessive risk. Shapira's response to Kagan?

"How is this a risk?," he recounted. "It's a good market, and I can always get an engineering job somewhere. I view it as the most harmless thing ever to do a startup. It's not like I'm going to go to debtor's prison," Shapira says. "There's little downside in terms of career development. I can hit the job market and get a boost." Shapira elaborated on this latter point for me. "Some people think that if you take time to do a startup, you would not be on the stable career track to management. In reality, going to do a startup accelerates your career. You do more stuff, take on more responsibility, and experience more ups and downs. That helps your career." Drew Gilliam at HaveMyShift (Chapter 10) agrees.

"There's nothing I should not be doing as a founder," he says. "I've learned to code. I've talked to customers. I've done sales. It enhances my marketability as a business person."

But it can be hard to make the leap, especially if you're in a stable job and have a family to support. That was the situation Sarah McIlroy, CEO of Fashion Playtes (Chapter 26), was in. "Entrepreneurship is a life-changing scenario," says McIlroy. "It's a huge risk. The more you grow in your career, the more comfortable it gets. If you have kids, it's a big challenge to jump to entrepreneurship from having a stable work environment." So why did McIlroy make the leap? "I wanted to do my own thing and personally, I felt passionate about my idea."

Pravina Raghavan of the SBA says, "There's always risk, but entrepreneurs aren't risk averse. Successful entrepreneurs have a handle on how much they're willing to bet. It's part of being a leader. There's risk in everything you do, but betting well has a huge payoff emotionally as well as financially."

That calculated risk is how Marc Brodeur of Brode (Chapter 29) thought about launching his venture.

"How I think about a risk is something that is likely to have a bad outcome," he says. "If the chances of success are 95%, it can still be a good risk to take. Just because you get a failure doesn't mean it was the wrong choice."

Brodeur concluded his calculus echoing Shapira's thoughts on the matter of starting up. "If my goal is to live a successful life, corporate life is a low probability way to get to that place. You're taking a tremendous risk if you go into corporate America with the life goals of being successful. If you want to build something, meet cool people and be part of a community, starting a business is the less risky thing to do." It's all a matter of perspective.

"Friendship doubles your joys and divides your sorrows"*

The idea for a startup may begin with an individual, but startups rarely launch in solitary confinement. Many founders find that taking off with a co-pilot helps.

Jason Shen, co-founder of RideJoy, a Y Combinator-funded travel startup, began the company with his roommates. The roommates lived together for a year, working at separate companies in San Francisco before deciding that it would make sense to start a company together.

"We have a great bond," Shen says. "Part of why we like working with each other is that we may have differing views on small things, but [regarding] the big items like how we treat people or how we spend our money, we're all on the same page." Shen finds that it's easier to make decisions because they have a history of talking out contentions until coming to a constructive solution to which they can all agree.

Jumping In

I caught up with Gulam Sarwar Ansari, the founder of an early-stage startup called Taxo, which aims to make taxes simple. "Since I embarked on the journey, there's no looking back. I only think about Taxo and moving it forward," Ansari says.

We need more people who give their ideas momentum. Henrik Werdelin of Prehype told me about Nicholas Thorne, founder of a startup called Basno. "Thorne was a 25-year-old Yale alum and a Goldman Sachs employee. Then he decided to create a digital goods business. His journey from a set lifestyle with lots of money to moving back to his parents' [house] is inspirational when it comes to innovation," Werdelin shared. "Innovation requires people gambling on something meaningful instead of the straight line everyone thinks to go through."

Once you do a startup, you may not be able to get enough. Bespoke Innovations (Chapter 65) co-founder and serial entrepreneur Dr. Kenneth Trauner told me, "everything about entrepreneurship is fun. For those of us who are inventors, we can spend the rest of our lives tinkering. Startups are an invigorating environment."

Author Unknown

Chapter 2: Lending Club

EXTENDING CREDIT TO people who are in a pinch (or who just like spending) has an ancient existence in human society. Assyrian and Babylonian merchants were the first to make loans more than 4,000 years ago, and if you couldn't get these traders with deep pockets to give you money, friends and neighbors might help out with IOUs. The lending party would set a rate of return (the premium that the borrower would pay in the future for the favor of receiving money now) and personally vet an individual's likelihood of returning the funds.

This community-centric system lasted a long time, but evolved with the advent of banks during the Renaissance. Banks took savers' monies, pooled them together—making anonymous which money belonged to which investor—and sent the funds out to needy people and projects, perhaps hundreds of miles away from where the money originated. Interest rates became the bank's discretion, with the bank taking a large cut because it was the market maker and it had a lot of bricks-and-mortar infrastructure to support.

This paradigm is now shifting by online banks like the well-known Orange ING and, increasingly, a startup called Lending Club.

LET'S BREAK THE ICE

Lending Club is a website for "peer-to-peer" lending.

HOW DOES IT WORK?

Lending Club is like a bank. It has two sides: investors and borrowers. Investors on Lending Club are everyday people who have money to save, beginning with as little as $25. Borrowers join Lending Club when they need a loan, usually to consolidate their credit card debt, fund a small business, or pay for a nonrecurring expense like a house remodeling, wedding or relocation.

Because Lending Club has no bricks-and-mortar bank facilities, the interest rates it can pass on to investors and borrowers are higher and lower, respectively, than those of a traditional bank. A borrower borrows from as low as 6.78%, depending on his/her financial situation. Lending Club only takes a small fee (about 1%), so more of the interest is passed on to investors.

Jim Bruene of Finovate, a Financial Services industry organization, says that the retail banking system was built on a foundation of the bricks-and-mortar approach. According to Bruene there are 100,000 bank branches across the United States. But now, "retail banking is changing to serve *customers* instead of branches," he says. "The change from branch banking to digital banking online and on mobile will drive innovation in retail banking."

WHY IS IT COOL?

Lending Club is a technology platform that puts the power to borrow and lend back in the hands of the people.

LET'S SAY...

I. You've racked up five credit cards, each with an outstanding debt totaling $5,000 per card and set to spiral up your monthly balance between 14% and 19% APR per card. You decide to seek a loan of $25,000 to pay off the credit cards — and pay one balance down—effectively "consolidating" the loan. What better place than Lending Club to get this $25,000 loan? Because there are no bricks-and-mortar stores, Lending Club's investors can give you a lower APR than a traditional bank would give, making you a happy debtor.

II. You have $1,000 to invest. Rather than play the stock market again, you decide to diversify your investments. With Lending Club, you can deposit $1,000 in your account and begin loaning this money for great rates of return. Instead of making 1% or less in interest and being kept in the dark as to where your money is going, Lending Club has you decide where each of your dollars gets invested, and you get much higher returns because of the efficiencies brought about by Internet tech.

SMOOTH SAILING

+ Peer-to-Peer (P2P) lending is way up and consistently growing. As of December 2011, Lending Club has reached a milestone of $1 million in new loans every day, clearing a breakthrough monthly record of over $30 million in new loans.

+ As of January 2012, Lending Club has funded over $390 million in loans and Lending Club's investors have made over $40 million in interest. Those stats lead the P2P loaning industry; Lending Club's closest competitor, Prosper, is booking only about a quarter of Lending Club's new loan volume.

+ Lending Club provides investors with full control over which loans they put their money toward, along with great transparency on the borrower's financial situation and likelihood to repay. Each loan (while never disclosing the borrower's name) includes pertinent details about the borrower like annual income, outstanding debt, place of work and more. Investors can also pose questions to the borrower about use of funds or financial track record if they'd like additional information before making a decision to lend.

+ Investors can put their funds in any number of loans, beginning at $25 per loan. The ability to easily diversify funds across multiple loans helps to diffuse risk.

+ With credit card APRs still way up, Lending Club has a lot of market share to capture among frustrated, underwater borrowers.

CHOPPY WATERS

- Lending Club is not directly FDIC-insured. If something goes wrong, investors could be the ones with tough luck.

GOT GOOSEBUMPS?

I love investing through Lending Club. My portfolio has upwards of 10% returns, easy. Visit www.LendingClub.com to start investing with just $25.

CREATION IS RISKY. How do businesspeople know whether anyone will like or buy what their businesses make? Whether it's a hardcover tome, a technological knick-knack, or a live-music event, in creation lies uncertainty.

LET'S BREAK THE ICE

Platform to raise funds for projects *before* they're created.

BACKSTORY

A live music event was exactly what kicked off Kickstarter. In 2002, Kickstarter co-founder Perry Chen wanted to host a concert but wasn't sure whether anyone would be interested in attending and paying the cover fee. Kickstarter was born as a way to vet projects before investing resources and effort.

HOW DOES IT WORK?

Each project has a description, location, and ticker showing metrics like the number of backers funding the project, dollars pledged, and time left to contribute.

Funders can contribute at different amounts, and depending on how much they give to a project, they can get different gift rewards in return. Kickstarter does not allow cash or equity rewards. For example, if you fund a book and give $5, you might be able to get an autographed copy of the book when it comes out. Or, if you fund at the $25 level, you might get a signed copy with insider photos to boot.

According to Will Curran, CEO of Arizona Pro DJs and student at Arizona State University, "small projects can come out of nowhere on Kickstarter." And that's changing the way businesses are built. "Traditionally, businesses need to get a loan or investment, or they bootstrap. But if you have a brilliant idea and you can market it, you can get tons of money on Kickstarter."

WHY IS IT COOL?

Kickstarter takes the guesswork out of making things, and can help get the creations funded.

LET'S SAY...

You're an engineer with an idea for a really cool gadget, but a few common hurdles get in the way of full-fledged production. You don't know if anyone would actually buy it, nor do you have the funds for development. Get on Kickstarter and complete your project profile, including how much money you're hoping to raise. If the project clicks with people, you're on your way. Individuals will make monetary contributions toward your funding benchmark. If (and only if!) you reach it, those contributions are called in. Gone is the scenario of money wasted on projects terminated in ideation, and therein lies Kickstarter's magic.

SMOOTH SAILING

+ Kickstarter has over a dozen categories for projects, spanning from Comics to Food to Technology.

+ Beyond browsing by category, Kickstarters can navigate by criteria such as project size, funding stage, and location, the last of which can be used to support local creations.

+ Mike Karnjanaprakorn at Skillshare (Chapter 33) points to Kickstarter as "increasing creativity in the world. They're allowing anyone to be creative and realize their ambitions."

CHOPPY WATERS

- Kickstarter is facing a litigious advance by another firm that claims to hold a patent on crowd-funding artistic ventures. The question at hand, of course, is whether one can patent a process. Such a vague and overarching patent may not hold, but this could be a setback for this Coolest Startup.

- Nothing holds project creators to their words, so funders should have their wits about them when deciding to fund projects. Although it's rare, someone could take the money and run. What the money truly goes to and whether the end result is in line with funders' expectations is never guaranteed.

GOT GOOSEBUMPS?

Sign up to receive Kickstarter's weekly newsletter of projects. Support a project you like and rake in the perks, like a credit at the end of the film you sponsored or an exclusive launch party invitation. Don't forget: if the project is a no go, your money stays put!

DEFROST: Legalese

Ah, the early days of a company. Sometimes it's difficult seeing a majestic bird when it's still without feathers. An early-stage startup might consist of a few people meeting at a coffee shop to work together on a project, or it may be a person staying up late on weeknights and sacrificing weekends to take steps toward their dream. Eventually, the hard work may form a company.

Startups can become big business, so it's important to understand the financial and legal levers that make them tick. Most startups begin informally, but as products and responsibilities become more stable, the founders may decide to take the next step to incorporate their business. A corporation, from the Latin word for "body," is a separate legal entity from any of the people who founded it. In the process of creating this new "body," founders need to decide on the ownership structure of the startup corporation. The paperwork is usually handled by lawyers who specialize in startup law, but the decision on how to split up ownership of the firm remains with the founders.

The information about shares and shareholders is delineated in documents that founders sign early on in the incorporation process. The whole company is represented on paper, and its shares can be traded, sold, combined and split.

That idea of the transferability of shares can confuse people new to business terminology. If you know about it, skip the rest of this defrost! For a neat analogy, read on.

Think of an early-stage startup as a seed. The goal of the startup team is to grow the seed into an oak tree. At the moment of incorporation, the seed is inexpensive and fragile. Each of the founders have equal share over the seed. As their efforts to grow the seed into a sapling succeed, the founders' worth increase in equal proportion because the baby tree is bigger and more valuable.

Later, the startup may be faced with the opportunity to double the height of the tree by purchasing some special fertilizer. Unfortunately, the company doesn't have the resources to achieve the milestone on its own, so it accepts funding in the form of an equity investment to pay for the fertilizer. After the transaction and subsequent growth period, the young plant doubles in size due to the beneficial outcome of the investment. Naturally, the founders no longer own all of the tree though. Investors are now part-owners too, "diluting" the share of the tree owned by the founders. While the founders no longer own 100% of the plant, they are still happy because the tree's value has increased dramatically overall.

A neighboring farm then hears about the tree growing nearby and decides that it would like to "acquire" the young tree before it becomes a full-fledged, expensive oak. The farm can "buy out" the existing owners, giving the founders and early investors money in exchange for all the shares of the tree. The shareholders are satisfied because their startup has paid off: a tree is born, its growers are wealthy, and the farm has added a new tree to its business. That's what we call a "win-win-win" situation.

OWNING EQUITY IN companies is pretty straightforward. Just sign up for an eTRADE account and bam, you can own shares in a public company. But what if you could own shares in a person? I joke that if I could have, I would have invested in shares in Lady Gaga Inc. *years* ago. No doubt some of her loyal fans would have as well, predicting it would return several hundred times the initial investment. While the market for shares in pop culture icons isn't around yet, a market for shares in sports stars is. In fact, the rise of the world's next superstar may come hand in hand with a windfall for his/her early believers, thanks to this Coolest Startup called StarStreet.

LET'S BREAK THE ICE
Invest in sports stars (virtually, of course).

BACKSTORY
Founder Jeremy Levine had entertained the concept for StarStreet ever since he was a child. Collecting baseball cards, he'd go for the rookies because he could sell them down the line for more money.

"I had no shot of being on the front of the cards," Levine says. "So I figured it'd be much easier for me to get fame by being rich enough to buy a team."

He's aimed to gain that wealth by putting his card trading experience into practice with StarStreet. After graduating from college, he recruited technical employees to join the company and several months later was accepted into Techstars, one of America's prestigious startup accelerator programs of which we'll hear more in later chapters.

HOW DOES IT WORK?
StarStreet is an investment platform with bids and asks just like any investment system: there's a price at which you can buy shares and another at which you can sell them. An investor joins StarStreet, adds value to his/her account and can begin trading players. Each athlete debuts on the market in a "Player IPO"—not the most creative name, but it says what it must. In the Player IPO (which is announced on

StarStreet and its Twitter feed), anyone can make a bid which, if high enough, acquires shares for the investor's account.

Over the course of the season, points are accrued by athletes in a fashion similar to typical fantasy sports; each action of the player on the court or field results in some amount of points being added or subtracted. For example, in StarStreet's NBA market, rebounds get athletes 1.25 points, steals get 2 points, and turnovers result in 1 point being taken away. When the investing window on StarStreet closes at the end of the season, the final points of each player are tallied compared to the overall pot. The pile of money on StarStreet gets divided up in proportion to the points.

Some investors, actually double their money on StarStreet. If you "get" sports (and don't get esoteric companies on stock exchanges), this is the investment method for you. The framework may be the same, but the subject matter is in a league of its own.

There are 700 active traders on StarStreet, of whom 20% trade everyday (sometimes for up to three hours at a time). StarStreet makes money by taking a 4% commission anytime a trade is consummated—from the seller's side.

They're still at an early stage. "We want to be the stock market for sports," Levine says. "We want to see financial companies trading on it with statistics and doing arbitrage."

And it's all completely legal. "It's a game of skill and not chance," says Levine. "It's not a yes or no bet." Plus according to Levine, many lawyers have vetted the model and the startup even has a license from the NFL Players Association.

WHY IS IT COOL?
Wage real money, not just fantasy points.

SMOOTH SAILING
+ I love the idea that you can invest in people, not just companies. If you're excellent at judging talent, why shouldn't you be able to invest in individuals?

+ The company is a graduate of the TechStars incubator, which Levine called "really awesome, really helpful and really chaotic." StarStreet gained valuable connections and business insights through the program.

+ StarStreet is the way fantasy sports were supposed to be

created. "There's been no innovation in fantasy sports," says Levine. "There are no real-time stats and there's no revenue model. If you think about it, it's the worst designed game. Yet 32 million people play it." That's a huge opportunity for StarStreet. "There's not too much happening in sports gaming or sports prediction. We're doing it better because people want to bet with real money."

+ Levine sees an opportunity to integrate with other content. For example, he's excited about the vision of being able to see trades in real time in the sidebar or ticker of iTV. "When we can integrate with Siri (the natural language processing software now integrated with Apple's iPhone 4S), you can buy shares as fast as you speak," Levine told me.

CHOPPY WATERS

- No personal finance books talk about this as an investment strategy. That's bad news seeing as StarStreet is often erroneously confused as a gambling platform. This startup needs more education out there regarding its business if it's going to be a mainstream success. Fun fact: Did you know that pinball was incorrectly categorized as a form of gaming too? It was outlawed in New York until 1976, when a pinball enthusiast demonstrated the game in front of City Council, who were effectively convinced that skill, not chance, was the driving factor.

- The value of investors' portfolios on StarStreet is modest. Investors have less than $20,000 on the platform in total market value, so compared to hedge funds on the stock market or institutional investors at Lending Club (Chapter 2), StarStreet's market is like looking at a penny from the top of the Empire State Building!

GOT GOOSEBUMPS?

Think you've got a knack for talent scouting? Get off the sidelines and check out the leaderboards at StarStreet.

DEFROST: Can't Anyone Be an Entrepreneur?

Resoundingly, yes! All it takes is an idea and action. But being a *successful* entrepreneur is another story. When an entrepreneur becomes a true master, putting startup expertise into practice over and over again, we call this being a "serial entrepreneur."

Serial entrepreneurship takes time, thoughtfulness and charisma. Serial entrepreneurs are students of the world; they're able to analyze people, businesses, and society's problems. They jump at opportunities that others may not even see. Where there are challenges without solutions, they bring together every part of the playbook to create value. But for those who aren't yet serial entrepreneur samurai, to begin creating those innovative pathways in your brain, start on a small scale, by being more entrepreneurial wherever you currently work or study.

In fact, many startups focus on building entrepreneurs from within. At TaskRabbit (Chapter 48), a quarter of the team members have already been founders of companies, says CEO Leah Busque. "Being entrepreneurial and independent is something we look for," she says. "Eventually those people will want to start another company, and it's fabulous and fantastic. We have a culture that supports that."

Bring Entrepreneurs In-House

Companies are starting to think more like TaskRabbit. Nick Friedman of College Hunks Hauling Junk, a now-national franchise in garbage and moving services, has a tagline that supports this mantra: "Let Tomorrow's Leaders Haul Your Junk..."

Friedman and I spoke in Washington D.C. last year.

"We treat employees as if they're business owners," Friedman said. The company knows that hauling junk is not a life-long pursuit for its employees, and turnover is something that the company embraces.

"There are no barriers to entry in a garage hauling business, so how do we set ourselves apart?" Friedman posited. "What our customers buy is our employees." And he doesn't just mean as eye-candy.

"We hire future leaders of this country," Friedman said. "We have a playful name and a catchy brand, but we build company culture from the inside out."

This was fascinating to me, because College Hunks Hauling Junk is a company that is shaping itself alongside the trend of turnover, rather than fighting against it. What's unique is that instead of giving their high turnover laborers less responsibility, Freidman gives them more of it. He told me that employees at College Hunks Hauling Junk help set pricing, do scheduling and management at their franchises and more. It's smart because it creates buy-in, and now instead of just hauling junk, as the name suggests, it's about molding business leaders who will always remember the brand and their employment experiences with it as a key milestone in their careers. In a time when employees are ever-fleeting and corporate loyalty is in the doldrums, what Freidman's business achieves is no small feat.

Intrapreneurship - The Prehype Model

There are more ways to create entrepreneurs from within. Henrik Werdelin is an expert at identifying and developing "intrapreneurs," entrepreneurial people within companies. His company Prehype works with large organizations to bring innovation to big companies.

"There are two worlds of innovation - large organizations and early-stage startups," says Werdelin, who has seen all sides of the entrepreneurial ecosystem, from product development for MTV to work at startups and venture capital firms. "I thought it was fascinating how separated those worlds were, but also how much they needed each other. What startups do well is understand how to offload risk by building cheaply and quickly, and sanity checking against real users. Large companies have domain expertise that allows them to identify problems and they have distribution and sales teams to get scale." Werdelin helps large companies breach that innovation gap by applying "innovation architecture," or "trying to get people to act in a different way by changing the structure in which they operate," he says.

The first step for Prehype is to identify intrapreneurs, people inside traditional organizations with a penchant for thinking innovatively. Prehype works with them and their organization to build a startup quickly before deciding with the company whether to spin off the business or close it down. Prehype uses three methods to identify intrapreneurs. First, internal venture competitions get employees excited about new product initiatives. These competitions begin with management sending a company-wide email asking if any employee has a good idea or interesting business problem from which the company can benefit in solving. Prehype meets with anyone who is interested, and Werdelin says "it's clear how passionate they are by how many times they follow up with us after our meeting." Second, Prehype asks CEOs "who is most likely to leave within 12 months to set up their own startups?" Most CEOs will know, says Werdelin. These people are often tapped for the special startup project, which often results in retention. Third, intrapreneurs occasionally approach Prehype directly. Prehype then pitches the CEO to set up a startup project.

After identifying intrapreneurs, Prehype works with them one day per week for a few weeks, says Steven Dean, one of the partners at Prehype and an entrepreneur, educator and designer. Prehype uses "lean startup methodology," a strategy many startups use to build minimal products quickly and take them to market for feedback. "If the product fails, corporations didn't take a big risk by devoting a lot of time or energy to the project," explains Dean. "But everyone benefits from the upside if it does generate a new business for the large company."

That's why "all companies should do innovation," says Werdelin. And according to him, there are three ways to do it. First, companies can build new products themselves, which may prove tough because they have rigid structures and have usually scaled their core products in ways unfavorable to the startup environment.

Second, companies can buy startups, which is expensive and has a reduced probability of integration success. Or third, companies can contract new product development to external vendors. Because vendors are often compensated by time spent, their development is far from "lean" by nature.

There are pros and cons to each option. That's why Prehype structures its consultancy in an unusual way. Prehype makes little money in the production of the product (only taking a small management fee to "keep the lights on"), and books an income if there's upside. It's like a venture capital model, Werdelin explains. Prehype is able to solve the issues most firms encounter by incentivizing lean startup methodology (result: no stagnation). Additionally, they work with intrapreneurs in a separate part of the organization, yet under the same umbrella (result: easier integration). So far they've worked with Kaplan, Coca-Cola, and other established firms.

A new product can justify the price, Werdelin shares. It costs about $250,000 to build a startup from scratch, according to Werdelin, but that new business unit can give a company exponential growth. And even if the startup fails, there are gains. According to Werdelin, retention of innovative talent is a key competitive advantage for any firm. Leading an innovative project within the firm also increases capacity. "When you're deep in the process of building a product, you understand the business in granular detail, so you know for the future what to look for when buying or integrating a similar business," he says. Finally, innovative projects help firms test new theses and determine elements to add to existing products. Werdelin points to Google Wave. While the project failed in low consumer adoption, "they saw that real-time collaboration works," Werdelin says.

No Barriers

Innovation can penetrate existing organizations, and it can be found all over America. Will Curran, CEO of Arizona Pro DJs, says that while Silicon Valley has many startups that are Internet-related, "entrepreneurship is bigger than any one industry."

"We're in an amazing time where a lot of big organizations like the government and universities are becoming supportive of entrepreneurship," he says. Curran received a grant from his alma mater, Arizona State University, to help launch his business.

Non-profit organizations are helping too. The Kauffman Foundation is one of the groups at the forefront of promoting entrepreneurship. At the 2012 Super Bowl, its advertisement aired asking "Will It Be You?" to start the next big venture. The organization provides grants for and education about entrepreneurship, and the research reports produced by the foundation are popular and first-rate.

The government is getting directly involved as well. Pravina Raghavan, District Director of the Small Business Administration (SBA) in New York, joined the public sector after a successful career as an entrepreneur. "It sounds corny, but it's true, I really wanted to give back to my country. I'm not an accountant or regulator. I'm a business strategist at heart, so joining the SBA was a way to give back in something that I do well. Rather than just helping companies [through her former consulting work], I help my country and I help businesses grow."

That help is coming from the SBA in the form of new programs for entrepreneurs, like business counseling and training classes.

"You feel like you're on an island as an entrepreneur. You're not going to be an accountant or strategist all rolled up in one, so you need to find resources that complement your skills. The SBA is a free resource and the government has your best interest in mind. Use the resources to help think about business challenges or to bounce off ideas. And it's free, so you can come back. Some of the most successful entrepreneurs use their SBA counselors as an informal advisory board."

Every state has an SBA office, and many have multiple locations. Many people may think of the SBA as a loan guarantor. "That's an important part of what the banks do in conjunction with us, but if you don't have the right business plan, you can't get to the dollar," Raghavan says. "People think of the government as limited, old and unchanging, but now people are finding that there's relevance."

No One Said It Would Be Easy

It's easier than ever to make the leap, but that doesn't mean entrepreneurship is a cinch.

"The barrier to entry has never been lower because you can start meaningful companies with small amounts of capital," says Bill Dwight of FamZoo (Chapter 8). "People delude themselves that small capital means small work. They may underestimate what it takes to create a sustainable business."

Zach Hamilton, a student-entrepreneur, told me about *this* adage. "The hardest working person in the room and the richest person in the room is the same person," he says. "Entrepreneurship isn't for everyone, and if you're not going to work hard, it's not for you."

FINTECH
Main St-reaming Wall Street startups

5. Segmint
6. SecondMarket
7. AxialMarket
8. FamZoo

Chapter 5: Segmint

BANKS ARE BORING. Really. There's little truly appealing about them or their websites. Yet bank websites get mounds of traffic. In recent years millions of people have turned to the Internet to do their banking. 44 million US households use the Web for bill pay, and 62% of Americans say it's their preferred method of banking. From this banking activity online, you could learn a lot about a customer. All of that rich information is lying in wait right there in the website data, but no one has yet done a good job of untangling it. Until Segmint.

LET'S BREAK THE ICE
Segmint brings intelligence about customers to banking.

HOW DOES IT WORK?
Segmint uses its trademarked system of Key Lifestyle Indicators (or KLIs) to categorize consumers and keep tabs on what products the bank would be wise to offer them. Segmint's KLI system is a sophisticated classification about where people spend money. Based on the KLIs, the bank determines who they want to target and what advertising they to expose to these customers. After running an ad campaign, the bank can check on the campaign's success. As simple as it might seem, the opportunity provided by Segmint is unprecedented.

"We have the best analytics in the industry that can anticipate consumer spending patterns," says Rob Heiser, Segmint's CEO and co-founder. "The power of our system is that it helps businesses deliver highly-targeted messaging and the audience can change at any time based on how consumers spend their money."

Without fear of confusing you with Segmint's lingo—as if Financial Services weren't esoteric enough—the startup also has Key Business Indicators, or KBIs. These are categories specifically aimed at small business accounts.

Segmint addresses everyone's priorities. "Consumers and small business owners want to get the information that's pertinent to them. Advertisers and banks want to spend their money wisely and show advertising that's relevant to the person's lifestyle," Heiser says.

"It's like Google showing offers based on your search activity," says Jim Bruene, founder of Finovate, an important Financial Services industry organization. "Banks use your purchasing data to make offers within your banking. If you've been buying at The Home Depot recently then Lowe's can make a significant offer to get that person into their store instead. They can give you a $25 rebate on any purchase, for example, and all you have to do is use your card. It turns the account statement into a profit center for the bank."

BACKSTORY

Segmint's four founders came together after one founder sought to create an online game about spending for bank customers. It wasn't a bad idea, except that the team couldn't find anyone to pay for it.

"We have all this information about someone's shopping," says Heiser. "We have the story of someone's life in their credit or debit card." He knew something powerful could be done with that data. Then the idea came to "help tailor the bank," Heiser says.

WHY IS IT COOL?

Do you know the name of your bank's branch manager? Didn't think so. And, let's face it, they don't know yours. Every facet of modern life is going digital. Segmint helps the bank keep up with your life stage so it can offer you the right monetary products.

LET'S SAY...

You're a representative of a Financial Services institution and you'd like to increase sales (that is why you're in business, right?). Fortunately, you learned way back that a square peg doesn't fit in a round hole: why bombard people with advertisements for products they don't need? There's no need, say, to waste a Home Equity Line-of-Credit advertisement on that 18-year-old with the newly minted credit card. Instead, you want ads that target people at the right stage of their lives. Set up with Segmint's technology and you'll gain the vision to hand-craft campaigns, sending the right advertisements to the right customers based on their actual purchasing activities.

SMOOTH SAILING

+ Segmint keeps decision-making in customers' hands, while enabling "smarter" ads from banks through its technology. By comparison, a Google search can only show so much about what a consumer is in the market for. Actions reveal preferences, economists say, and if someone is shelling out cash for a product or service, it means a lot. Segmint analyzes these transactions (anonymously, of course), gaining a genuine understanding of customers' needs before sending them any ads; banking products are promoted intelligently.

+ Segmint has garnered many patents and trademarks.

+ Segmint's system has exceptional measures for safety and privacy. For its KBIs, each institution using Segmint signs a form guaranteeing that they'll convert the small business client names they work with into anonymous randomized digits—for example, "Bagels & Bagels" could become "Business 327272724"—helping to protect everyone involved without diluting the benefits of the system. "We're privacy and security nuts. Some people call us crazy because we're probably over the top," says Heiser. Security is essential because "it's a conservative industry by nature," says Heiser. "The relationship between the consumer and their bank is one of the most trusted."

+ Segmint is very much a Business-to-Business (B2B) product, but I think it's cool to talk about so that you recognize all the innovation happening right in that age-old bank account of yours. "It's more powerful to the bank than as a direct consumer play. The pain is that the customer isn't getting the right kind of content. We're passionate to help banks understand customers. It's the toughest way to go because building trust with each bank takes time, but we've built a company of long, strong relationships with financial institutions."

+ The company is also innovating with social media. SegmintSocial is a new product that integrates with Facebook and allows banks to interact with customers through their presences on social networks without breaching any security. For example, Heiser shared how Bank of America maintains a Twitter feed and when people have issues with their accounts, they're told to send a Direct Message with their full name and location, which should have security and privacy zealots shivering. "With SegmintSocial, we don't have to ask those questions. We leverage our core Segmint product for online banking with Facebook's application on the page. Banks are afraid of social media because they don't know who they're talking to, but we can guarantee whether it's a customer."

+ The ecosystem is ripe. Heiser says there are a lot of pressures in the finance space today, from changes in overdraft fees to heavy regulation. These pressures have caused revenue generation challenges for banks, especially as consumers look for the best deals. "Understanding your customers better and predicting when they need products so you can promote and cross-sell to them at the proper time is a huge opportunity. Banks haven't embraced it to the extent that they can," Heiser says. That means there's growth ahead in this space. Bruene says that while "big banks have their hands full with consumer backlashes, privacy violations or get skewered in the media," it's tough for them to innovate internally. This makes it an ideal space for a startup like Segmint to flourish unfettered.

CHOPPY WATERS

- Segmint is not a hands-off technology. Banks need to manage the process and cultivate campaigns to ensure success.
- Now all we need is some fun bank advertising, plus the ability to click through a glossary of terms... what's an APR*, you ask?

GOT GOOSEBUMPS?

Segmint does a phenomenal job delineating different situations for which its technology is applicable. These "case studies" go as far as spelling out the bank's dilemma, sampling KLIs, and telling of how Segmint's solution gets implemented. You'd be surprised at your own intrigue reading through the ways Customer X's dog food spending can affect what bank advertisements s/he might see.

*APR is Annual Percentage Rate – usually the interest you'll receive from a savings account or that you'll pay for a credit card expense that goes past due. If you don't know what interest is, you'll need a personal finance book; one of my faves is called "I Will Teach You to Be Rich" from a fellow young author and member of the Young Entrepreneur Council, Ramit Sethi.

DEFROST: Speak G(r)eek

My amore for Square (Chapter 1) is akin to what Apple fanatics feel for the cool white and stainless steel of Steve Jobs's assembly line babies. After falling head over heels for Square, I was not shy to let everyone know. It didn't stop at friends and family; I even talked to taxi drivers and bike shop repairmen about the company. When coming across a cool startup like Square, there are three ways of acting on the adoration: apply to work for the company, invest in it, or sign up for its "Beta."

What does this Greek letter mean? In startup lingo, a "Beta" (or "Alpha") is an indication that a company is in its early stages of conceiving, developing and delivering a given product.

Let's revisit for a moment how startups work:

1. Someone gets an idea. (*Pop!* The lightbulb is lit!).

2. They (should) write a business plan. In reality, this step often gets skipped or completed later.

3. The founder gets a team together. This can be as informal as a "hackathon," where people meet up to patch together some technology, or as formal as incorporation.

4. The team builds.

5. The startup releases a product, often designating it an "Alpha" or "Beta" for a few reasons: the product may be known to have flaws (also called "bugs"), the founders may be actively soliciting feedback, or the team may want to indicate that they are continuing to tweak the product before it is ready for release to the wild that is public consumption.

When I came across Square, the company was in its toddlerhood, or "Beta" stage. Yet already Square was helping vendors (like a glass blower seeking to sell his/her wares to those without cash on hand) and neighborhood stores (such as a local coffee shop wanting to go from "Cash Only" to credit card cha-ching).

Since then, the company has come a long way. A

modest three years since founding, Square is valued at more than \$1 billion. Its ability to nail down and execute an exceptional product—and scale the business—is what lands it in *The Coolest Startups in America*. Although I don't get to be part of that monetary return as an investor or equity-holding employee, signing up for a company's Beta to get first dibs on using the product has other benefits: bragging rights!

STOCKS TRADE EVERY weekday at the ding of the opening bell on the New York Stock Exchange (and dozens of other exchanges around the world). Anyone with a bit of money and access to a computer can participate in the stock market for public companies. But did you know that there are trillions—yes, trillions—of dollars of assets that don't trade on these well-known, transparent public exchanges?

LET'S BREAK THE ICE

SecondMarket is the marketplace for "alternative" investments, including bankruptcy claims, mortgage-backed securities, and private company stocks.

HOW DOES IT WORK?

SecondMarket combines a technology platform with market specialists to facilitate transactions in alternative investments. Buyers and sellers sign up online and indicate their interest in buying or selling an asset, respectively. Based on these indications of interest (or IOIs as they're called in industry parlance), buyers and sellers may be invited into auctions for the alternative assets, or contacted directly by market specialists who can help facilitate private placement sales.

Not just anyone can use SecondMarket's core services, though. Buying an asset on SecondMarket requires you to be an "accredited investor," a term defined by the U.S. Securities & Exchange Commission as an individual with either more than $1 million in assets (not including the value of his/her personal residence), or someone who has netted at least $200,000 in income over the previous two years.

If you fit those qualifications, you can buy interesting, unconventional assets that help diversify your portfolio beyond typical stocks and bonds. Some of these assets include stock in cool startups like those in this book or esoteric investments like collateralized debt obligations.

Why does SecondMarket exist? There are a bunch of factors that have led to frozen markets and the dearth of IPOs* today compared to past decades. Some of the factors include decimalization (the process by which dollar trades were allowed to be broken into fractions of pennies, making margins ever tighter) and high-frequency trading (the use of algorithms to execute trades, rather than fundamental investment analysis).

Jim Bruene, founder of Finovate, an industry organization for Financial Technology, says of SecondMarket's private company market that "the fact that they've brought liquidity to private stock sales has been a huge benefit to everybody. It's the kind of big idea you don't see often. It may be a derivative of a stock exchange, but it solves a big pain point."

Liron Shapira of Quixey (Chapter 50) agrees. "They're giving people liquidity. I'm all for liquidity. Not even speaking as a co-founder of a company, I think people who have shares in a startup should have liquidity for those shares. There has to be some balance, but the idea that a few years ago if you started a company you'd have to make decisions based on whether you either get a lot of money [by selling all the shares in a merger or acquisition event, for example] or no money doesn't make any sense." That's the dilemma SecondMarket solves; firms can host "interim liquidity events" to cash in shares regardless of buyout offers or IPO delays.

WHY IS IT COOL?
SecondMarket makes formerly illiquid (not easily converted into cash), hard-to-trade assets more liquid. Fun fact: SecondMarket is thought to be the largest marketplace for trading shares in Facebook, Inc. How do I know? I worked there as an Analyst on the trading floor for a year!

LET'S SAY...
I. You're an employee at one of the companies featured in *The Coolest Startups in America* (congrats!). It's a startup, so you've been working your butt off for the past four years. In lieu of bonuses or a high income, you received stock in the startup itself, which everyone at the company hopes will be

* *"Initial Public Offerings" enable private company shares to be purchased for the first time by the public on traditional stock exchanges.*

worth a lot of money someday. When you started working at the startup, your shares were worth $1 each. Now, four years later, you think they're worth more. You convince the management of the startup to go to SecondMarket to set up an auction for some of the shares in the company. SecondMarket's private company specialists inform your company that there are buyers interested in your company's shares at a value of $10 per share. It's a jackpot before the startup's IPO and perhaps before an IPO has even been considered!

II. On the flipside, you're an accredited investor. You could invest your money with a hedge fund or venture capital company, but instead you want more direct control over the particular asset in which you'll be investing. You come to SecondMarket and find an atypical asset that you think is priced well and has potential to appreciate in value in the next few years. You buy it, all thanks to the availability granted by SecondMarket.

SMOOTH SAILING

+ Since there are *trillions* of dollars in assets that do not trade in typical public markets, SecondMarket has huge room to grow. It isn't limited to financial assets either. A marketplace for expensive wine? A destination to buy or sell limited edition art? Any non-traditional, valuable asset could be represented.

+ Buyers and sellers include the most prominent institutional investors, banks, venture capital firms and high net worth individuals. These players are usually considered slow adopters of technology, but Eric Slaim, founder of HFIN One, a startup innovating in the hedge fund space, says that is quickly changing. "People in the Financial Services space are starting to get excited about innovation because technologies like mobile phones and social networks have affected people's lives personally so they carry technology adoption into the corporate world too," says Slaim. "Change is happening in this traditional industry and these startups help the change move faster."

+ SecondMarket doesn't take "proprietary positions." In other words, it does not bet its own money from its corporate balance sheets on any of the assets that it helps trade. This eliminates any conflicts of interest.

CHOPPY WATERS

- Because the definition of an accredited investor is so strict, the pool of potential buyers for these alternative investments is relatively small. SecondMarket is vying—on the long-term—to get these definitions loosened so that more people can have access to alternative assets.

- For the private company stock market, SecondMarket limits itself to working with companies who endorse transactions in their private shares. This strategic business move lowers the volume of trades that SecondMarket can consummate.

- These are still illiquid assets, even if SecondMarket is working to make them more liquid by bringing Internet technology efficiencies to the market. Unlike trades on public exchanges which occur almost instantaneously, SecondMarket transactions require much more legal and regulatory oversight, and thus more time for completion. To buy or sell an asset on SecondMarket may still take several weeks, not seconds.

GOT GOOSEBUMPS?

If you're not an accredited investor, you can use SecondMarket to "watch" private companies and other alternative investments you're interested in following. I use my SecondMarket account to follow news on private companies, even if I can't trade in their shares yet.

JUST AS GOLF carts or cupcakes can be bought and sold, golf cart *manufacturers* and bake shop *chains* can be sold and purchased. Yet selling a business requires an ecosystem of players. A business owner interested in selling his/her business must retain accountants, lawyers, and an investment bank or business broker. There is tons of paperwork involved, and the deal-making process is wrought with inefficiencies and uncertainties.

LET'S BREAK THE ICE

AxialMarket improves the process of buying or selling a business because its online system makes it easier for buyers and sellers of companies to discover one another. The company is one of the leaders in "FinTech," with the largest online network of buyers and sellers of private companies.

HOW DOES IT WORK?

Sellers of businesses are able to create their deal "opportunity"—or intent to sell—on the exclusive network, after being vetted by AxialMarket's team to ensure quality. It's easy to create a "teaser" (a quick, informative description of the company to be sold) about the opportunity by using AxialMarket's proprietary tools. As soon as the seller (or their advisor, be it a local broker or big-time investment bank) sends out their opportunity to the list of potential buyers they'd like to engage, those selected buyers can decide to pursue the deal further or decline. The AxialMarket platform is very sleek, and they've had incredible success at intelligently matching parties on mergers and acquisitions (M&A) deals.

WHY IS IT COOL?

When Mom or Pop decide to retire, their corner store need not close down. AxialMarket can facilitate the sale of the business to a great new owner who will care for the organization and maintain its growth.

LET'S SAY...

Your elderly aunt passed away, and she left you with a

factory in St. Louis, Missouri generating $10 million a year in revenues. As enthralling as it may seem to start a new life managing a factory, you live in another state and don't have a hint of relevant experience. You want to sell the business. AxialMarket would help you find an ideal buyer for the company. Having your business on AxialMarket is a stamp of approval—all the more attractive to potential buyers. Who knows from where interest in auntie's old factory may come?

SMOOTH SAILING

+ The management team has a ton of experience building B2B marketplace businesses. CEO Peter Lehrman is an alumnus of the Gerson Lehrman Group, once dubbed "Wall Street's Biggest Secret," the largest network of business experts in the world.

+ There are hundreds of thousands of businesses topping $1 million in revenue per year in the United States, few of which get much attention. When they're ready for it, AxialMarket empowers these businesses with a presence among financial buyers and strategic purchasers of companies.

CHOPPY WATERS

- Although there are hundreds of thousands of "middle market" businesses (roughly defined as companies with $1 million to $100 million in revenues) in the United States, only a handful are being sold *in any given year*. What does that mean? A pool of sales smaller than appears. At the same time, Axialmarket's goal is, after all, to expand that pool by empowering the very businesses that didn't previously consider themselves in the view of business buyers across the country.

GOT GOOSEBUMPS?

If you're in the market for buying or selling a private business, get on AxialMarket as soon as possible! Without it, you may be missing out on deal flow or potential buyers.

If you're curious and want to learn more about the space, AxialMarket has a stellar in-house research team that makes a consistent practice of publishing exceptional thought-leadership, data, and educational pieces on M&A.

"CAN I HAVE five dollars? Pretty please!" If you're a parent you may have heard this whine from your child before. Whatever those five dollars might be going toward, you'd likely prefer to wait for the tooth fairy's visit than be easy picking for cash anytime. Yet the reality is that kids handle money regularly nowadays. Unfortunately, no one really teaches them a thing or two about it! Schools skip out on personal finance classes until high school, if teaching it at all. That might explain why kids grow up and don't know too much about saving, investing or staying out of debt.

LET'S BREAK THE ICE

FamZoo is family-friendly finance.

HOW DOES IT WORK?

FamZoo isn't an actual bank account, but it seems just like one. It's what the company dubs a "virtual bank account." You don't transfer real money and neither do your kids, but it is a place where the kids can track and check the "funds" they gain or lose. Whenever there's a transaction (like babysitting money or allowance coming in or funds taken out to purchase a new must-have), you or your child simply adjust the FamZoo virtual bank account. You can make all sorts of accounts with custom labels like "spending" or "charity." It's a fun way to familiarize kids with the different types of actions that can be taken with money, all in a supervised environment where everything can be done appropriately and safely.

Upon signing up, or opting for a free trial as typically offered by subscription-based businesses, you configure your account for you and your family. Next, start making accounts, setting up goals (yes, you can let your five-year-old begin saving up for a pony), and "depositing" funds. FamZoo founder and CEO Bill Dwight says it's like the "Bank of Mom & Dad." The parents are the bankers and the kids are the customers.

WHY IS IT COOL?

FamZoo helps parents teach the basics of personal finance

to their kids, and may even get kids excited about chores if there's a personal online "allowance" account that they can see regularly growing in value.

BACK STORY

I love telling the story of FamZoo's domiciliary roots. Dwight, FamZoo's founder, has five kids. As his oldest were growing up, he sought a way to help teach them about financial self-reliance. Unfortunately, "personal finance is one of those life skills that isn't taught systematically," Dwight shares. He laments that books and board games seem to be the only options available, while schools have not stepped in to fill the personal finance education vacuum.

According to Dwight, the lack of options for personal finance education is a problem. "There's a huge gap between the piggy bank, which is a neat introductory tool for really young kids, and real banks, which are not geared toward learning and family. FamZoo seeks to fill that gap."

Dwight believes kids should learn that money is a finite resource to be managed, but that mistakes shouldn't be to the bank's delight. "What other skill do we expect people to pick up without practice?" Dwight created FamZoo to help kids practice-to-make-perfect their personal finance activities. "This has transformed how I talk to my kids about money. That's like vitamins for us. It's a simple idea really, that we're going to systematically keep track of how much mom and dad owe you and how much you're using. It's like the parent saying, 'you've got your own online bank too.'"

LET'S SAY...

You're a parent with five kids, reminiscent of this cool startup's founder. You're tired of your kids being blasé and prodigal with their allowances. You'd like to instill in them valuable, life-long lessons about money and financial goals. You'd like to supervise their monetary activity while they're young—who knows what kind of impulse buys would be dragged into the house without your watchful eye. So you create a FamZoo account for your family, fill out the basics, and begin designating certain funds for certain chores and "depositing" regular allowances at the amounts you'd decided. When your child wants to make a purchase, let them check their FamZoo account to see if they have enough.

SMOOTH SAILING

+ FamZoo teaches kids about personal finance in a fun and interactive way. It's an approachable brand with adorable cartoons drawn by Pulitzer-nominated Henry Payne, a political cartoonist for *The Detroit News*. FamZoo certainly kept its demographic in mind: the graphs and charts make for cheerful visuals. Kids may not suspect that graphs in the "big world" are fundamentally the same!

+ FamZoo is a highly customizable website and it's cheaper than breakfast at Starbucks: just $5.99 a month.

+ FamZoo has a smart distribution strategy. They're partnering with credit unions to gain more customers. "FamZoo is a very sticky application because families use it for years," Dwight says. "There's an opportunity for credit unions to get in front of next-generation customers and start building relationships so that when these kids are ready for real-world financial products in adulthood, the credit union will be top of mind."

+ FamZoo was awarded "Best in Show" from Finovate, a Financial Technology industry organization and conference. Jim Bruene, the organization's founder, says "there's a huge trend in providing banking services to the whole family, like how cell phones cater to the family with parental controls." However, many banks can't justify new product development around kids' accounts which "makes this a great space for a startup," Bruene says.

+ FamZoo's subscription model includes a gift option. Forward-thinking grandparents can buy it for their kids and grandkids as a nice holiday present.

CHOPPY WATERS

- Subscription choices aren't built on a "freemium" model, a popular idea in startups today under which people can use a limited version of the product for free. Why not? "We're not interested in catering to people who don't care to teach their kids about personal finance. We'd rather have a smaller, more devoted audience and give them a lot of TLC [tender loving care]," Dwight says.

- FamZoo doesn't work at the touch of a button. It has a

proverbial hand crank; virtual funds in FamZoo must be adjusted by parents digging through online accounts at their official banks, and who needs any more of that in their lives? FamZoo needs automatic updates that reflect real-world transactions. "I look forward to when FamZoo is connected to external bank accounts," Bruene says. "That feature can be put into it eventually."

GOT GOOSEBUMPS?

Take FamZoo for a test ride. The first two months are free, and there's no fear of falling—it's a bank on training wheels.

SILICON PRAIRIE
The Best of the Midwest
startups

FIGURING OUT FUMBLES, grading winning goals, and pumping up players are all in a sports coach's job description. The whistle-toting head honcho of an athletics team can be a vital determinant of whether a team wins or loses, so any tool helping make his or her job more effective is a sure slam dunk.

In the 1960s, video replay and slow motion had just made their appearances on the courts and fields of the sporting world. They were developed to make games all the more riveting for TV viewers, and soon adopted by referees and coaches. Coaches, from the professional levels to the little leagues, began to watch, watch, and watch again the hits and misses of their players, with a distinct goal in mind: prospecting that raw footage for strategies to step up the game.

LET'S BREAK THE ICE

Hudl means affordable advanced video software for sports coaches and their teams.

HOW DOES IT WORK?

Hudl allows coach to easily store video clips, notes on interesting game moments, playbooks, stats and more. You start by opening an account and uploading video footage in pretty much any format, from AVI to MPEG. Hudl offers countless features: tagging video footage, quickly cutting it into clips, and securely sharing it with teammates. And Hudl knows team spirit, speeding up the video editing process by allowing multiple coaches to edit simultaneously.

WHY IS IT COOL?

Used by top NFL franchises, collegiate wrestling teams, and pee wee baseball leagues alike to shave hours off of the tedious work of playing back sports games.

LET'S SAY...

I. You're a high school football coach. After leading another productive practice, you get an email requesting footage of your star player #18, who's always hustling like it matters. Last season you'd have had to burn a DVD and mail it, or invite the coach (or scout) down to your turf to see the player in action. Although a personal visit may be warranted in due time, Hudl makes it easy to edit and send the footage when you want. Within an email moment, #18 may have taken the first step to an athletic scholarship.

II. You're a student-athlete. Between the demands of academia and sports, you're not exactly rich on time. Rather than schlep to the coach's office for a video review session on top of your already demanding schedule, use Hudl to access the video he or she wants you to watch. Anytime, anywhere. But make sure you stay on top of the videos, because Hudl gives coaches the ability to check out the login activity of each player. No slacking on the field, in the classroom, or with your Hudl account.

SMOOTH SAILING

+ Tons of payment options, from the Platinum plan at $3,000 per year (unlimited storage of game video, text messaging, presentation building, and more) to the Youth plan at $29 per month (break down the video and share it with your team).

+ Know your enemy: Hudl allows teams to store opponent footage too. Just be sure to shake hands after the game.

+ Hudl was founded and is managed by a spirited team based in Lincoln, Nebraska. Their love is shared between sports and coding.

+ Hudl's eclectic and star-studded advisory board includes the CEO of the Bill and Melinda Gates Foundation, the Assistant Head Coach of the New York Jets, and a top Product Manager at Microsoft, among others.

+ Hudl doesn't exactly make old-school scouting obsolete: nothing can replace sizing up an athlete in his/her natural habitat, where even the attitude between plays can be a factor. But now it's not always necessary for a remote scout to trek to the local campus just to view players in action. It's all a click away.

+ Beyond reviewing game play to look for opportunities to gain points, coaches and referees could use Hudl to review tapes for injury prevention as well.

+ The software can be tailored to diverse sports, from basketball to wrestling.

+ Hudl successfully pushed into mobile, launching an app for iPad that has earned rave reviews from its users.

CHOPPY WATERS
- Zip, nil, nada. Hudl wins on and off the field.

GOT GOOSEBUMPS?
Hudl offers free trials for all of the plans for its services. Sign up to see if it's a home run for your team.

HEARD FROM A HOT SHOT

"@Hudl just saved my rear end!..."

– Mike Sanford, Running Backs Coach at
Stanford University, @SanfordStanford

DEFROST: Should You Work for a Startup?

Early on in writing *The Coolest Startups in America*, I received a passionate email from Ryan Brown, a Product Manager at San Francisco startup Posterous. He loves Posterous, and his increasingly large relationship with the company helped explain why. "I've evolved from an avid user to an official college campus ambassador to a marketing intern to Posterous's current product marketing manager," Brown shared.

That passion for the product and acceptance of increased responsibility is what every startup founder looks to hire. Alex Taub of Aviary (Chapter 61) says "you can't sit on the sidelines at a startup." He says it's a lot of fun but also a lot of work. "If you spend a year or two at a startup, you'll get more experience than you would get in five years at another place. Startups can accelerate your career like no other career path. And, if your startup is bought or merges with another company, your next job could be as the head of that division."

Startups need top talent—people who are outgoing, resilient and smart—because the last thing any founder wants to fret over is an unhelpful colleague. "The hardest part about a startup is that you really don't know what the uncertainties are," says Ilya Sukhar of mobile technology upstart Parse. "You're staring out into a void and asking 'how do I make this work' and you make that answer more concrete by finding good people. The team is everything."

Bill Dwight of FamZoo (Chapter 8) agrees. "Startups are a rollercoaster. One day you get mentioned in *The New York Times*, for example, and your traffic spikes and you're on top of the world. Then it's crickets. It's hard to control, but the stakes are high and there's a stream of decisions that feel make or break everyday."

It's quite different than working for an established organization, but that's what makes it so fun. Here are some ways to get involved: First, you don't have to work for a startup to use the principles of innovation at your current job. Take the methods and models of startups and apply them to your work. Second, startups love interns. If you want to test the waters and just see what it's like to work for a startup, try a short-term internship with them. Third, if you don't live near any startups but are interested in working for one, many startups are flexible about virtual teams. Don't hesitate to reach out to a startup about a project you feel you could do for them remotely. The worst they can say is 'No, thanks!" Finally, if you want to work for a startup but don't know how to find out about them, check out the Resources Appendix for outlets that regularly publish new startup job listings.

Ante Up

Salaries can be a touchy subject around fledgling startups. Founders may be uncompensated aside from their equity stakes in the company, and may even be contributing to the company funds out-of-pocket to get the product launched. At seed- or venture-funded startups, salaries are less of an awkward topic, as externally backed companies tend to pay comparably to local market rates for every position.

The difference between startups and traditional companies or small businesses is the possibility in the former for employees to receive ownership of company shares that could give a nice boost in payout when a liquidity event comes around. I saw this first hand when I helped with auctions for Facebook's shares as an Analyst at SecondMarket (Chapter 6). Every week I witnessed former Facebook employees or advisors become overnight millionaires as they cashed in stocks through the liquidity mechanisms provided by SecondMarket's platform.

But Facebook is an exceptional situation. The promise of riches is only as substantial as a startup is superb. Taub says "most people who join a startup don't realize that unless you're joining Facebook and are an engineer who can command a lot of equity, even in a big acquisition you won't make that much money."

That's because the employee likely won't own enough of a company where a liquidity event would greatly weigh down their wallet. "Even if your company gets sold for $100 million, you won't make $1 million," Taub warns. Instead, he suggests focus on evaluating who you'll be working under and what you're going to learn. "The only time to think about a big payday with a startup is when you start your own," Taub says. He told me about Jared Hecht and Steve Martocci, the founders of GroupMe, a successful mobile startup that sold for $85 million within about one year of its founding. "Jared worked at Tumblr and Steve worked at Gilt Groupe," Taub recounts. "Gilt and Tumblr were huge businesses already and Jared and Steve weren't going to make money on them because they each had such a small percentage [of ownership] in the firms. They met and became friends and ended up founding GroupMe. Now they have money to pick their next project," Taub quipped.

The lesson? "Don't join a startup thinking you'll have a payday. Join because you're excited about it," Taub says. "Being in the startup space you'll meet new, creative people all the time and you'll talk about ideas and market efficiencies often. Then, start your own thing."

Culture Shock

Joining a startup can be jolting. Human Resources may not be quite as formal as you'd encounter at an established firm, if it exists at all. People work odd hours, doing anything to make deadlines and ship products on time. Conference rooms will tend to have unusual and funny names, and a general informality in dress, speech and corporate activities (Rock Band battle anyone?) may pervade. Plans can seem ephemeral, as any new feedback from customers or investors may warrant shifts in the products envisioned or strategies employed. Sometimes, the most direction given consists of "figure it out" or "make it work." But if you're an adaptable person, startups aren't a stretch.

Paul Murphy, VP of Business Development at Aviary, recently joined the startup from technology behemoth Microsoft. Prior to Microsoft, Murphy ran his own startups, "two of which failed, and one of which had success," he told me. So why did a serial entrepreneur want to join a conglomerate like Microsoft? To gain experience running a business, Murphy answered.

"My plan was to go there for two years, get a different experience [than at a startup] and do it [a startup] again," Murphy recounted. "I got all these opportunities. I went to London, spent time in Asia and India, and ended up being at Microsoft for eight and a half years." Finally he got back to his goal of rejoining the startup community.

His transition back to startup life was easy. "The process of moving to a startup was natural for me because I had worked at a startup before. It didn't feel that different," says Murphy. "People were saying to go to a medium-sized company before a small one, but as long as the startup pays competitively so you can eat and rent, it's not a hard transition."

"In the early days of Microsoft, they had this idea of N-1," Murphy shared. "How ever many people you need in order to do something, remove one person. By and large it's still that way at Microsoft. They don't have enough people, but they do it for the right reasons which is to encourage innovation. Here at a startup, it's N-10." Depending on who you ask, that's either thrilling or stultifying.

WORKING SHIFTS GETS mixed reviews. Most high schoolers have to go through shift-based work, and probably the worst part—aside from endless piles of clothes to fold or wrist aches arising around the time of the 72nd scoop of ice cream—is that dealing with shift changes can be a pain too. Changing shifts may involve massive phone call loops of people trying to rearrange schedules. The stores rarely get involved. Up to the employee to find a cover, or else it's "see you in the morning!"

LET'S BREAK THE ICE

HaveMyShift lets people trade or sell shifts.

BACKSTORY

In 2009, HaveMyShift co-founder Sean Corbett was working on coding web applications, but wanted something new and interesting to work on. One of his friends who worked at Starbucks had tickets to see the Super Bowl, but found himself in the unfortunate predicament of needing to find someone to cover his shift. "It was a big pain in the butt," says HaveMyShift co-founder and Chief Operating Officer Drew Gilliam. "And shift switching happens frequently."

The friend presented the idea to Corbett, who promptly built HaveMyShift, says Gilliam. The product gained "rapid acceptance" in Chicago's Starbucks community and the company was soon thereafter accepted into TechStars Boston, an incubator program, where the startup could develop HaveMyShift's concept and platform further.

HOW DOES IT WORK?

Anyone can post a shift or search for a shift to fill on HaveMyShift. The system uses geo-location to pinpoint nearby opportunities for shift switch-seekers or shift fillers. When someone posts to the site looking for someone to fill a shift, they can search within their network and among others at the same company. Those who really want (or need!) the day off can post a premium on the offer to exceed the usual wage.

After a match is found, the person switching shifts approves the person applying and answers a few contractual questions. These assure the legality of the switch (for example, the person filling the shift can't exceed state laws in the number of hours worked).

Gilliam gives an example of Starbucks locations in Chicago. HaveMyShift has over 1,500 baristas in its network for the region, so "it's virtually guaranteed that you can have someone cover your shifts." If it's a 4:30 AM shift that no one on earth seems to want, with HaveMyShift, you can add a bonus to make the shift more desirable.

"Every major retailer has a solution for workplace scheduling, but the software is old and doesn't work well," Gilliam says. "There's a theoretical statistically perfect schedule. They do this rocket science modeling, but it doesn't account for last minute changes people need to make. That's our opportunity."

Executives care because "how employees are treated results in a better bottom line," Gilliam shares. "Time and flexibility are important commodities, more important than money or prestige." HaveMyShift's strategy is to grow networks of employees that work for the same company nation- or worldwide because it makes it easier for employees to trade shifts due to standardized accounting systems across the firm.

"Our biggest challenge to grow is that people hear our concept and sign up but they think they need their manager's permission. At Starbucks, they encourage their employees to use HaveMyShift to help each other out and make work more flexible. We want to find more companies that support this kind of shift trading and workplace flexibility," says Gilliam.

WHY IS IT COOL?

HaveMyShift addresses a pain point in the hourly worker industry.

LET'S SAY...

I. You're a college student who just found out your older sibling is coming to town for the weekend to hang out with you. No way you want to spend it cooped up at the clothing store with a bunch of tweens just because you have to work the weekend shift! You go to HaveMyShift and post an emergency shift switch in which you decide to pay your shift-switching savior an extra $10 for the favor. Set up the information about your shift, blast it out to your networks (HaveMyShift will list it on theirs too) and wait for the phone call. Given the premium, someone should take the bait. Finish coordinating the shift switch and there you go! Time to catch up with family.

II. You're running a coffee company with a team of employees who often need to change shifts. Midterms may come and go on a fairly regular schedule, but illness and family emergencies don't. In the spirit of keeping a healthy work atmosphere, you seek to avoid calling in employees disgruntled by the lack of flexibility that HaveMyShift so smartly addresses. You hook up with HaveMyShift to allow your employees to swap times. You don't have to be an active part of the marketplace; just give your blessing to it. It solves your problems and theirs, all in the name of keeping the coffee coming!

III. You're the next big Broadway star, who unfortunately hasn't been discovered yet. You're still looking for those scrappy odd jobs between auditions. Check out HaveMyShift to see if there are any you could pick up.

SMOOTH SAILING

+ HaveMyShift has an elegant solution to a long-standing problem of employee scheduling-related discontent and turnover. And there are already some big brands on board, including Starbucks. Over 10,000 Starbucks employees use HaveMyShift, Gilliam says.

+ The startup is now helping out with volunteering shifts. The idea came from a Starbucks branch where a lot of employees also gave their time at a nearby soup kitchen. When the soup kitchen needed volunteers, a message went out to HaveMyShift's local Starbucks community and the shift got covered. That's a wonderful social initiative.

CHOPPY WATERS

- Mainstream social networks may render HaveMyShift redundant. A coffee crew could simply make a private group on Facebook and post exchange requests there, to much the same effect. Gilliam says that the social network approach ends up spamming people. "We work hard not to do that,"

Gilliam says. "Our process is four clicks and you've signed up with the essential details." Also, the peer-to-peer method can have difficulty catching on because of all the noise on social networks. HaveMyShift goes straight to corporate leadership, and enables firms to disseminate HaveMyShift's service for their employees. Far from being a well-kept secret among shift-swapping employees, HaveMyShift works to the benefit of all parties.

- Group texting companies like Beluga or GroupMe could start stepping on HaveMyShift's turf. Just like Facebook, these are avenues for general communication, but people often re-invent existing tools for their own purposes.

GOT GOOSEBUMPS?

Check out HaveMyShift or recommend it to a friend. If only it could work for Management Consultants too—considering all those 80-hour weeks they work, I'm sure some of them would love to catch some Z's in exchange for a few dollars. Not that we feel *too* badly for them.

DEFROST: Eggs & Chickens

Marketplace businesses fascinate me. Both the startups at which I worked after college—SecondMarket (Chapter 6) and AxialMarket (Chapter 7)—have marketplace models. They unlock tremendous value, but the setup is among the toughest models to bring to success. Matching two sides of a marketplace more efficiently is like getting to the equilibrium point of a supply and demand graph; it's the perfect balancing point that creates win-win opportunities.

Marketplace businesses are notoriously difficult to create or grow because they have a chicken-and-egg problem. It differs from having one customer (e.g. Victoria's Secret sells merchandise to an end client), because marketplace businesses have two customers upon which their success depends (e.g. *The New York Times* has to please its advertisers as well as its readers). If you don't have the first side of the business, the second side won't join (and vice versa).

It takes an astute business strategist to decide how best to approach building a marketplace. Leah Busque of TaskRabbit (Chapter 48) shares that "with any marketplace business, there's a side that you can lock down [first]." In TaskRabbit's case, they were able to recruit fantastic couriers (called "rabbits" in this startup's lexicon) who could "spread the joy" of TaskRabbit, making that the place to start. Busque recommends for marketplace upstarts to decide upfront which side of the marketplace to tackle first. This rarely seems to be the buy-side. At TaskRabbit, Busque led by building up the supply of "rabbits" who could complete tasks, and at AxialMarket, RideJoy and other cool startups, supply of the product was cultivated first too.

Jason Shen of RideJoy, a transportation-based upstart that matches drivers with commuters, told me that he advises to look critically at what factors motivate each side of the marketplace. "Ridesharing is something a lot of people think about, but the hard part is getting people to use it," Shen says. "Because ridesharing must match the right someone at the right *time,* the biggest success to date is using events to drive adoption," they discovered. Hence, RideJoy has created buzz for its startup around big gatherings like the Burning Man Festival or Y Combinator's Startup School.

Another tip: many marketplaces format the business organization to match the model. At TaskRabbit, there is a community management team that focuses entirely on the "rabbit" side and another part of the organization that markets to consumers purchasing tasks on the platform. In Busque's words, "I think it's important to have separate teams thinking about each user experience because they're very different. To get the most out of both sides, you need team members empathetic to a particular scenario and use case," she says. Similarly, at AxialMarket, teams are divided into Client Development (supply) and Buy-Side Sales (demand). Having dedicated team members focused on separate sides of the market helps to ensure that the eggs and chickens have advocates for their interests within the organization.

Finally, entrepreneurs should take the time to learn the underlying logistics of a marketplace model early on, Busque advises. TaskRabbit began in Boston, and didn't expand until a year later, when it opened a second marketplace in San Francisco. "For any early stage company, especially for marketplaces, you want the luxury of time to figure out the learnings of what enables an amazing experience on both sides. TaskRabbit took the time which is great."

AIRPORTS ARE LONELY places for business travelers. Even when you've got your routine down to a TSA-worthy pat—you know the timetable for your cross-country route down to the minute, show up 45 minutes before boarding to whizz through security with your frequent flyer pass, and hang around the loyalty suite to snack on tiny sandwiches and cheap box wine—plane travel is still a bastion of strangers.

Why not turn the place into one for professional networking or socializing? After all, your average airport lounge consists of business people standing around missing out on the opportunity to make a (non-flight related) connection.

LET'S BREAK THE ICE

Uppward is a mobile app that allows you to chat with and meet fellow travelers on your flight, and rake in rewards for every flight you take.

HOW DOES IT WORK?

Install the Uppward mobile app and create an account. Then, "check in to flight" when you're at the airport. When you "check in" you're able to chat with fellow passengers and broadcast your flights to your social networks. Don't you want everyone to know what a fabulous jet-setting life you lead? Once you've touched down, "check out," and see the miles add up in your account. The miles are eventually redeemable for rewards.

WHY IS IT COOL?

Makes the friendly skies even friendlier.

LET'S SAY...

You're a business person who flies the same NYC to Miami route once a month. You check in to your flight on Uppward and see that someone else aboard is looking to share a cab to the same hotel at which you'll be staying. You chat back through the app that you're going to the same destination and, sure, you'll split a cab. Save some cash and make a new friend.

SMOOTH SAILING

+ The airport is a beehive of activity, an oft-wasted opportunity for people to connect in a way that would make their travel experiences better and more sociable to boot. It would be neat to see Uppward add points for social interactions by passengers within the app, instead of only giving points for miles flown.

+ This may be something for which airports eventually pay. If business travelers are having more fun at the airport, they'll likely spend more time and money there. Airports won't complain about more $7 lattes sold. Vendors within airports may even pay to advertise on this Uppward network. After all, if travelers want to discover other people at the airport, they may have an interest in getting to know the airports themselves a little better too.

CHOPPY WATERS

- Flying for business can be a relatively dry routine. Are many passengers actually interested in connecting with fellow business travelers?

- And if someone really wants to make a connection, s/he can just turn to their neighbor in the row, stick out her/his hand, and introduce herself/himself. Do we really need an app for that?

GOT GOOSEBUMPS?

If you're an iPhone user, just download the app from the App store and spread your wings!

Chapter 12: Dwolla

THE CREDIT CARD is the most common form of payment on the web. A company called Dwolla (from the words "web" and "dollar") based in Des Moines, Iowa wondered, "what is the equivalent of cash for online payments?"

LET'S BREAK THE ICE

Dwolla believes consumers should have the option to pay with "cash" online, not just credit.

BACKSTORY

Dwolla's founder Ben Milne is a serial entrepreneur. One of the first companies he launched was a high-end speakers design and manufacturing firm that generated millions of dollars in revenue. "It took Ben all over the world and then some," says Dwolla's Director of Communications Jordan Lampe. "As entrepreneurs know, building a company with your bare hands is a very personal experience, and I think it's why Ben took interchange [the fees collected by banks to consummate transactions] to be so offensive."

Milne was paying about $55,000 per year in fees, says Lampe. "You work, the customer pays, and [the banks] get a chunk of every transaction." This frustrated Milne, who figured other entrepreneurs were facing similar tolls. It compelled him to look for a better way, and like many entrepreneurs, "Ben literally became obsessed," Lampe says. "He tore through everything he could read and banged on every door of every industry expert he could find." About a year later, Milne had a solution and decided to sell his speaker company to "focus on creating the new Visa for the 21st century."

HOW DOES IT WORK?

Once you open an account with Dwolla, you deposit money from your bank account into your Dwolla account. From your account, you can then transfer money to other Dwolla users, including merchants like your local participating coffee shop.

It's seamless and it's cheap. Zach Hamilton, a leading

student-entrepreneur at Arizona State University (a school housing some of our nation's best collegiate startup initiatives), says that "Dwolla short circuits the way payments are made because normal bank wires are over $10." Meanwhile, Dwolla enables bank-to-bank transfers for just a quarter. "To charge 25 cents is crazy and it's beautiful," says Hamilton. "They take a traditional business model and flip it upside down."

If you install Dwolla's mobile app, you gain the enhanced service of being able to transfer money on the move, without a computer nearby. In Dwollaworld, there's no need to use your credit card or handle grimy dollar bills.

WHY IS IT COOL?

Dwolla makes it cheap (25 cents cheap) and easy to transfer money over the Internet by email, social networks or mobile phone to friends, family and participating merchants.

LET'S SAY...

You're out for a night on the town, and want to travel light. You leave your clunky wallet at home, go to a restaurant that accepts Dwolla, and pay via your mobile phone. Even at a non-participating restaurant, you can have a friend spot you, with a promise to pay them back with Dwolla right that minute using your phone.

SMOOTH SAILING

+ Dwolla has undergone exponential growth since mid-2011. In June 2011, they processed $1 million per week. Five weeks later, they were processing the same sum *daily*.

+ Dwolla's low transaction fee undercuts PayPal. You're not dreaming that it's 1956, it's really just 25 cents! And, Dwolla makes transfers under $10 completely free.

+ Unlike the flagship offering from Square (Chapter 1), no special hardware is required for Dwolla to work.

+ Dwolla gives you options; money transfers are even possible through Facebook and Twitter.

CHOPPY WATERS

- The big banks (specifically Bank of America, Wells Fargo, and JPMorgan Chase) have developed an interbank peer-to-peer money transfer platform that would be provided to consumers for free. That may effectively behead Dwolla's efforts.

- Dwolla's mobile solution steps on the same turf as Square (Chapter 1), the latter of which has more funding.

GOT GOOSEBUMPS?

It's free to open an account and cheaper than PayPal to transfer money. The next time you need to fulfill an IOU to a friend or buy something online, think about this startup that has a funny name (then again, don't they all?).

MINORITY REPORT
I Swear I Saw that in a Tom Cruise Film startups

Chapter 13: Qwiki

TMI IS DISTRACTING. I don't mean "TMI" as in people over-sharing the intimate details of their lives. I mean that there may literally be "too much information." In 2010, the amount of digital information created in the world exceeded a zettabyte for the first time. That's one *trillion* gigabytes of data. How can we make sense of it all? If a picture speaks a thousand words, perhaps changing information's format from words to visuals can help.

LET'S BREAK THE ICE
Qwiki re-imagines the information experience.

HOW DOES IT WORK?
Qwiki pulls data from websites like Google Images, Wikipedia and more to curate an informative entry about a topic, called a "qwiki." It's safe for work, I promise. When "experiencing" a qwiki, a bionic female voice narrates the text of the entry as videos and images about the topic are presented. When finished, you can click on a related qwiki, share the entry, or bookmark it.

You can learn about virtually any person, place or thing in Qwiki's media-rich format of photos and video, and Qwiki can be accessed online or via its stellar mobile apps. But Qwiki makes it into this avant-garde section of *The Coolest Startups in America* due to the startup's forthcoming products, such as an awesome alarm clock that you'll swear was taken straight from the Jetsons. This gadget awakens you with rich information and graphics about your upcoming day.

WHY IS IT COOL?
Qwiki makes learning beautiful and interactive, all under a futuristic veneer.

LET'S SAY...
You want to learn more about Kansas City before an upcoming trip there. A search on Qwiki for "Kansas" yields many entries from which you could learn, all while enjoying a preview of tourist spots, historical images, landscapes, local

celebs and more. Too bad it doesn't come with a side of barbecue sauce.

SMOOTH SAILING

+ Qwiki thrives on the same addicting phenomenon that plagues users of Wikipedia. Maybe this point shouldn't be a positive...

+ Qwiki's applications will be highly commercial. Many people will pay handsomely for the upcoming Qwiki alarm, which pulls data from your calendar and location to tell you details for the day, like whether you should pack an umbrella, who you're meeting and where, and more.

+ Integrations (with Yelp.com and others) would make Qwiki increasingly oriented toward providing information that aids in decision-making. Learning about a location may grow to be just a few clicks away from taking action, whether that's booking a flight or grabbing a few tickets to the next concert of a band about which you've just learned.

+ Content websites or attractions could pay Qwiki for white-label integrations. For example, a museum or art gallery could pay to pull qwikis into their displays, rather than the static placards they currently use.

+ Qwiki can be an education hub, featuring language translation or expert-curated qwikis.

CHOPPY WATERS

- Qwiki pulls information for entries primarily from Wikipedia. While Wikipedia is popular and robust, it is hardly on the front line of innovation for Qwiki to use just one source.

- The automaton speaker could use work, as she sometimes has trouble with pronunciations. And further, the automaton can speak, but not listen. That makes for a lack of interaction with Qwiki. It could learn a thing or two from Apple's Siri; saying "more" should have the entry expand on a presently displayed fact, photo or video.

GOT GOOSEBUMPS?

Sign up for Qwiki's daily emails. The Qwiki PR team does a fantastic job curating a daily qwiki, always workplace-friendly. If the two-sentence email doesn't catch your attention on a given day, there's always tomorrow.

DNA TESTING IS being elevated from the pits of tabloid talk shows. Ever since the Human Genome Project was finished in 2006, regular old Joes have the option of accessing their DNA sequences, in large part because the cost of "sequencing" has dropped incredibly over a short span of time. Consider this: it cost a whopping $3 million to sequence one individual's genetic map in 2003. In 2011, a company called Illumina reached a milestone low cost of $4,000. By 2014, the National Human Genome Research Institute of the US National Institute of Health hopes that sequencing a human genome will cost a mere $1,000.

While the race continues to quickly and cheaply map the individual genome in its entirety, it turns out that a lot of valuable information is gained from analyzing just the genetic variations of an individual's SNPs (Single Nucleotide Polymorphisms). Biologists-turned-founders Linda Avey and Anne Wojcicki created the company 23andMe (named for the 23 chromosomes in human DNA) to do SNP genotyping for individuals who want to learn about their genetic makeups.

LET'S BREAK THE ICE
23andMe is a personal genetics company.

HOW DOES IT WORK?
Leaving science to the experts, all a consumer needs to do is sign up with 23andMe and pay for a personal genetics kit to be sent straight to his/her home. The kit arrives within a few days: open it, put a saliva sample in the test tube provided (yes, that means spit!), seal it up, and mail the package back to 23andMe. Within a few weeks, you'll receive a private report with all your DNA information, including your estimated likelihood of having various genetic diseases or conditions.

WHY IS IT COOL?
Get to know the inner you.

LET'S SAY...
You're curious about your predisposition for any genetic

diseases or conditions. You decide to use 23andMe to preemptively get educated about your body. Knowing that you have a 70% susceptibility for Parkinson's disease, for example, can help you direct your charity dollars to research for relevant cures. And of course, you'd be sure to adopt activities and habits that proactively mitigate the personal health risks you discover.

SMOOTH SAILING

+ Over 200 diseases and conditions are analyzed for each person, including your likelihood upon conception of having had red hair (a terrible problem, I can tell you).

+ 23andMe's reports are viewable by ethnicity, a useful feature seeing that genetic elements can vary in frequency or prevalence by ethnic group.

+ 23andMe has implemented consistent cost reductions. Its standard kit once cost $999. Now it's just $99 with a one-year commitment to pay $9 per month.

+ The startup has been praised by various media, including a TV feature on Oprah and recognition by *TIME* magazine as "Invention of the Year."

+ 23andMe is also launching an exciting new pilot project called Exome, which aims to provide consumers with affordable access to their entire genomes soon.

CHOPPY WATERS

- Some states ban genetics testing without a permit or authorization from a doctor. For example, 23andMe's product is unavailable to New York residents after a warning letter from the New York State Department of Health. 23andMe is also unable to ship to Maryland, but otherwise the service is available in the States and in 50 other countries.

- There are quite a few competitors in the space of genotyping, including fellow startups deCODEme, Knowe, Navigenics and more.

- Many experts have concerns over a layman customer reviewing his/her own DNA information without the proper academic knowledge or context. Their claim is that simply decoding the DNA without unpacking what that DNA *means* for consumers is frivolous.

GOT GOOSEBUMPS?

Take the plunge and order a kit. It's a bit of an investment, but an investment in something you should love—your body. If you live in a state where 23andMe isn't allowed to test, you're out of luck with this startup, but there are still options with a physician if you're bent on learning more about those A-T-C-G's in you.

JUST AS INK prints layer by layer onto paper, *envision* that plastic, metal, or gold could be printed layer by thin, liquid layer to form a 3D object. Now snap out of that daydream, because 3D printing isn't just for your imagination anymore.

LET'S BREAK THE ICE

Shapeways prints 3D objects.

HOW DOES IT WORK?

Shapeways hooks up to special software programs, including the very ones used by architects to visualize objects in three dimensions. Once the files are prepared, with the push of a button Shapeways prints plastic out layer by layer, from bottom to top, until the object is created. While it may feel strange using the word "print" for physical objects, get used to it! NASA itself dreams of using these "matter printers" in space to replace broken machinery, sidestepping the massive expense incurred by launching anything beyond our atmosphere.

Here on Earth you can use pre-programmed templates to help create various tchotchkes, faux movie memorabilia or figurines. Scott Summit, co-founder of Bespoke Innovations (Chapter 65), a Coolest Startup that produces custom prosthetic limbs, told me that virtually anything is possible with 3D printing. Summit, a 3D printing expert, began his involvement with 3D printing in its earliest days about 20 years ago. "3D printing is mindblowing," he says. "I could go on all day about the stuff you can do. You can create amazing objects and don't need manufacturers in China to do it. You just need to make a phone call and upload a file."

While it's that easy to hit print, the processes in the printers are more complex, including Selective Laser Sintering (SLS), Stereolithography (SLA), Laminate Object Manufacturing (LOM) and Fused Deposition Modeling (FDM)—all of which are too technical for the scope of this book. For those of scientific bent looking to learn more, Shapeways does have informational videos about the ins and outs of the technology.

WHY IS IT COOL?

It's a 3D printer. Enough said.

LET'S SAY...

You're after a one-of-a-kind Halloween costume accessory. You can't find it anywhere (your costume idea is *that* good). Go to Shapeways and design it using their "Easy Creator"—which allows customization of pre-designed objects like cufflinks or figurines—or one of the designated tools for more abstract projects. Once you submit the files, you'll get your neat, new printed item in the mail in about ten days. If that strikes you as too long, the future is sure to see hand-me-down 3D printers coming into homes from specialized businesses.

SMOOTH SAILING

+ Shapeways paves the way for printing other 3D objects, like edible food or body parts (see Chapter 57).

+ People have used Shapeways to make niche craft items that snowball into big business opportunities. Some even make a great living off of creating custom Lego pieces, for example. Henrik Werdelin of Prehype, an innovation design consultancy, told me he's fascinated with the trend of the democratization of business-building. "It used to be that mass distribution and production were how things had to be done," he says. "Platforms are now created for independent people to scale how they create a business, even at home. In order to create these things, you have to build a big business [like Shapeways] to start to deploy hardware. There are a lot of hot world-meets-web companies making this possible."

+ Shapeways is highly customizable, which may lead to other businesses jumping in on the creation of proprietary objects. Michael Sinanian, a reporter for VentureBeat, says, "3D printing will make it easy for young startups to create hardware."

+ Shapeways has a huge global community. Unlike many Americentric Coolest Startups, Shapeways enjoys a loyal following of people from all around the globe. And the number of Shapeways "creators," people who share their 3D designs with others on the Shapeways website, is great. There are tons of inspiring designs to peruse daily.

CHOPPY WATERS

- While virtually any material can be 3D printed, Shapeways is not so unlimited. For the present, the company accommodates primarily plastic prints, with occasional silver and steel.

- It's still far from inexpensive, and hardly comparable with typical prices for objects. But as it *is* a custom 3D print, the cool factor may justify the higher price.

GOT GOOSEBUMPS?

If you're not ready to create a design yourself, browse Shapeways's online shop for items from model airplanes to iPhone cases to pretty necklaces. Now there's a gift with a story to it: "no honey, this wasn't made by hand, it was actually... printed out."

Chapter 16: Word Lens

EVER FIND YOURSELF in the middle of a foreign country, unable to read anything around you? Yes, you came for the novelty of a different culture, a different language, a different script... But the fact of the matter is, you're lost! You need directions. You need the ability to read the words around you.

LET'S BREAK THE ICE
Word Lens translates anything you show it, instantly.

HOW DOES IT WORK?
Word Lens is a mobile app created by the company Quest Visual. Buy the app and use it by pointing the phone's camera to a sign, document or text. The app will display a real-time translation of the words at hand.

It's one of these products you have to see to believe, which is why it's so fitting for this section of *The Coolest Startups in America*. Once you've seen it work, you'll be curious to know how it does so. The company is tight-lipped about its technology, and various members of Quora (Chapter 59) have offered their educated hypotheses. The prevailing idea is that Word Lens works by first identifying the pixels on the screen. It then detects how those pixels are arranged and uses OCR—Optical Character Recognition, a technology also used in making digitized documents searchable and editable—to "understand" the words displayed. From there, it likely uses commonplace translation algorithms to demystify the foreign words. What's remarkable is that Word Lens moves through that process in just the blink of an eye.

WHY IS IT COOL?
An Anything-to-English dictionary, without the dictionary.

LET'S SAY...
You're traveling around Spain, but don't speak Spanish. You'd like to park your rental car on this charming street and explore by foot, but looming over you is an ominous sign that, for all you know, indicates limitations on parking. You have

your phone handy with the Word Lens app open. You hold up Word Lens to the sign and it reads: "Danger! Do not park." Fine averted.

SMOOTH SAILING

+ Word Lens has been downloaded well over 2 million times since its debut. And it doesn't even need connection to the Internet to work, making it perfect for international travelers wary of enormous data roaming fees.

+ Word Lens works on handwriting just as well as on typographic signs. No need to forever wonder what that love letter from your vacation romance says (oh, and Word Lens can keep a secret, too).

+ Aren't there opportunities for other practical applications of this technology, like immediate arithmetic calculations? If the app recognizes the numbers and the operations among them, it could display the correct response. Math teachers, tell those students to put away their calculators *and* their phones.

CHOPPY WATERS

- Word Lens isn't your 21st century Rosetta Stone quite yet; it's currently limited to Spanish and French translations.

- The technology still has a few kinks to it. Cursive handwriting isn't handled too well, and be sure to have a steady hand with the screen, as the translations may bounce in and out of focus.

GOT GOOSEBUMPS?

Download the app, scribble something in Spanish—"Hola!" if you're short on ideas—and watch the magic happen before your eyes.

DEFROST: Hockey Stick in a Haystack

Every startup wants to create products and services that are popular, because a large market reach is one of the cornerstones of a cool company. When investors review startups' growth plans, they call the ideal growth paradigm a "hockey stick," where the shape of the growth curve starts small, but grows exponentially over time.

Easy to picture, hockey stick growth is, in practice, tougher to achieve. Greg Meier, serial entrepreneur and co-founder of the Milwaukee-based startup incubator 94Labs, says that scaling is the most difficult thing for a startup. "You can build anything, but getting to scale is really hard," he says. "You can sell any piece of software to a few people, but can you get a few hundred thousand or a million people to buy it?"

Rising to that challenge requires exceptional marketing strategies in all perspectives, including product, pricing, promotion and distribution. Startups don't have the cash to advertise new products with mass media, so they have to think smarter. For example, when a startup can't reach the end consumer easily, it will seek partnerships. Truequity, a startup making it easier for fellow companies to keep track of shareholders, rarely markets straight to the end users. Instead, founder Hagi Schwartz and his team work with law firms as informal distributors for Truequity's product. "The law firm acts as a channel, with 300 to 600 companies [Truequity's prospective customers] each. By working with law firms, we get access to their client bases."

Making a product synonymous with a process is another idea to gain scale. For example, Schwartz regularly lectures on Capitalization Table Analysis—the format by which firms traditionally track their shareholders—at schools such as Stanford's Graduate School of Business and Tel Aviv University. He builds his exams and curricula on Truequity's system. "Students get used to a product and if they love it, it'll spread in the organizations they join," Schwartz says. "Companies that use the education strategy to market their products have to have patience, but it simplifies their sales processes in the long-run."

Finally, many startups simply hope and pray that their products "go viral." They may network with members of the media or influential entrepreneurship community members so that when they launch, many people will be excited to share the startup's story, making customers eager to try it out. But getting market factors to align is why virality is as serendipitous as finding that needle in a haystack.

While it's ideal for a startup to get lucky and take off, there are downsides to hockey stick growth too, I learned. Paul Murphy, who runs Business Development at Aviary (Chapter 61), says that much of his job revolves around managing the startup's growth. Aviary has about 200 partners, but Murphy estimates it will soon have ten times that amount. "We have to make sure that that doesn't kill us," he says.

What does he mean by death in growth? "I spend a lot of time making sure our systems are robust so we can handle the influx. If partners come on in droves and something goes wrong or we don't have a way to support them, they'll leave in droves. You have to be able to scale, but scale intelligently," Murphy says. This means lining up infrastructure and processes to accommodate a high tide of requests for the startup's technology or support.

Murphy reminded me of startups that had become successful before grinding to a temporary and frustrating halt. Examples include Twitter in its early years or, more recently, Tumblr. "They're amazing companies, but I'm helping [Aviary] to get to a stage of scale before our systems cripple like those did," he says.

Nick Ganju, CTO of ZocDoc (Chapter 55), says that scale can also affect the startup's team. When the startup hits record customers, "it's tempting to say, 'crap! I need 200 more employees!' but it's best to push back and practice self-control," Ganju says. At ZocDoc, there are rigorous hiring processes to ensure that the team stays top-notch. "The number one thing to do in growing fast is not lower the bar when you're hiring," Ganju says. "Be disciplined to turn people down who don't make the bar. It's better to double down on recruiting in order to not miss the hiring numbers. That's why we have a disproportionately huge recruiting team, and we all pitch in to help."

Nihal Parthasarathi of CourseHorse (Chapter 32) says that sometimes limiting the startup's geographic reach can work too. "We have an idea that can go global," Parthasarathi responds when I ask him why they're still only offering CourseHorse's service in New York City. "If you scale a marketplace too quickly there may not be enough support. We want to add value in every market before we push it forward without having a foundation."

ACCORDING TO FAMOUS venture capitalist Yuri Milner, there was more data created in any given two-day period in 2010 than by all of humankind in the last 30,000 years. I don't doubt it considering that Twitter alone emits over 250 million tweets (text blurbs of 140 characters) per day from people all around the world.

The methodology behind data collection is getting better, cheaper and faster. We need a way to quickly process all of that information, properly analyzing the world itself as we do so. The goal? Inform and empower business and government decision-making. That's where Palantir comes in.

LET'S BREAK THE ICE

Palantir makes technology that helps visualize and manipulate huge data sets.

HOW DOES IT WORK?

After importing a large data set, Palantir enables a user to get an all-inclusive understanding of what lies within. Palantir has the tools to make various graphs, histograms and plot charts. It can handle all sorts of data, like maps, geospatial inputs, and structured or unstructured data, and makes every record accessible via search. Finally, its filtering criteria are legion, including time of day, day of week, information type and much more. And while huge data sets are Palantir's bread and butter, a user can always zoom in for a closer look at an individual element in the set.

By the end of even a short analysis, the user gleans deep insights from the data, and quickly. It becomes vastly easier to test hypotheses and, by extension, to concretize solutions to a variety of issues.

BACKSTORY

Christopher Michel, an investor in Palantir and the serial entrepreneur behind Military.com, tells me that Palantir was spun out of Paypal. "Paypal dealt with fraud issues and used algorithms to compensate. The only way to counteract the 'bad guys' was with humans though, so they needed to help people better detect patterns in the world of complexity."

This naturally applies to national security and other government matters.

"Patterns aren't obvious to computers because they're not smart enough," Michel says. Palantir gives people another weapon in the arsenal of data analysis.

WHY IS IT COOL?

Lacing huge amounts of data together in interesting ways to uncover patterns is right out of Law & Order... except better. As if Palantir needs further endorsement, Michel shares that "the former head of the CIA has said that this is an interesting company."

LET'S SAY...

You're a general in the US military who is tasked with improving combat conditions in a conflict zone. Rather than guessing as to what might minimize violence across the board, you input the totality of your research and statistics into Palantir. You're able to map, plot, manipulate and analyze any type of variable, from what time of day brings the highest chance of conflict, to what is available at the local market on the weeks that violence breaks out. As you plot attacks over time and space, and against additional intelligence from other databases, you realize that attacks correlate with a variable you would not have thought about before. Congratulations, you've identified an accessible linchpin to reducing attacks. Palantir did in minutes what may have taken countless wo/man-hours, if analysis without Palantir were even possible.

SMOOTH SAILING

+ Palantir gets that data doesn't empower decision-making. Data analysis does.

+ Palantir has a location in the Silicon Valley for its software development and another in Virginia to boost sales around our nation's government hub.

+ While Palantir is quite secretive about its work, the company is known for hiring exceptionally bright people. Liron Shapira, CTO of Quixey (Chapter 50), says that although Quixey "poached" (the term for taking an employee from one company to another) an engineer from Palantir, he doesn't know much about the startup except that "they do data for the government and hire smart people." Michel would agree, "The team has super smart people that care deeply about creating a great product and company."

CHOPPY WATERS

- Palantir has some nominal overlap with the unrelated Palantir.net. You're reminded on every webpage of this disaffiliation. That's a brand nightmare.

- Aimed at top brass, Palantir doesn't do consumer decision-making solutions... yet? As quantifying the self becomes more popular—hence the coolness of startups like FitBit (Chapter 54)—the ability to analyze personal data can become a massive market opportunity. Presumably, Palantir has helpful technology available. I wish they would unleash it to the rest of us because I would love to plot my caloric intake against my Producteev (Chapter 49) deadlines to find out if I'm really a stress eater. I have a hunch about the answer to that already!

GOT GOOSEBUMPS?

Watch some of Palantir's demo videos to see how the technology is applied. Even the silly, videogame-esque narration sounds like it's out of a utopian (or dystopian?) flick.

Chapter 18: Dekko

A PICTURE MAY explain a thousand words, but sometimes even that's not enough. Transport yourself for a moment to the rustic beauty of the Roman Colosseum. A trip to the monument surely wouldn't be complete without a handsome photo album to go with it, but you won't need to check Wikipedia to share its history with those leafing through it back home. As you're lining up a photo, Dekko could recognize what's in the frame and present you with relevant information: dates of construction and renovation, dimensions, and number of visitors per year. It's what's called Augmented Reality, or AR, and it's fast approaching thanks to this Coolest Startup.

LET'S BREAK THE ICE
Dekko merges technology with reality.

HOW DOES IT WORK?
I'm actually not too sure (I know, no Pulitzer for me for this chapter!). The company is in stealth mode, and you can guess what that means—everyone's being tight-lipped about the technology and its implementation. All we know from presentations that have leaked is that the company believes in a reality "experience" rather than information just slathered onto a picture. Some city-specific AR projects have featured layers of directional arrows strewn on the ground, guiding you to your destination, but it seems Dekko would be much different.

A helpful clue may lie with the founders' former employer, Layar, an AR startup in Sweden. While Layar has released its app already, reportedly the technology doesn't work quite as well yet as its video demos make out. It'll be interesting to see what Dekko showcases when it's out of stealth mode.

WHY IS IT COOL?
Instant information on whatever the eye can see.

LET'S SAY...
You're wandering around Prague. The clock strikes 12 PM and you haven't even had breakfast. You hold up your camera

phone right in front of your eyes, and far from merely relaying the scene before you, the display is overlaid with rich data via Dekko's technology. You can now see that hiding in a shadowy corner is a cafe with four-star ratings. Bon appetit.

SMOOTH SAILING

+ People would pay for this. Information is power. People pay for power.

+ Justin Timberlake has invested, earning Dekko a plus sign for being celebrity cool.

+ Dekko could have fantastic applications for travel, music, sports, art and other entertainment fields.

+ It may be designed for the modern smartphone with a camera, but who knows where we'll see Dekko's technology implemented? Binoculars, glasses, contact lenses, oh my!

CHOPPY WATERS

- They're still in stealth mode, and hype may outshine the end result. Here's hoping that good things come to those who wait.

- Highly-specialized technology demands highly-specialized employees, which in turn means smaller supply and limited scaling. Sometimes that's the price for exploring something as cutting-edge as AR.

GOT GOOSEBUMPS?

The only thing to do is sign up for this company's Beta, and keep your "standard reality" eyes peeled for news.

BUCKLE UP
Startups *in Overdrive*

Chapter 19: Mission Motors

DRIVING IS A unique American pastime. While the modern car was invented in the 1880s by Karl Benz in Germany, Americans patented their own versions shortly thereafter and were the first to mass produce cars. We became obsessed with building infrastructure for these precious toys. Since the 1950s, nearly 50,000 miles of highway have been placed throughout the US, at a total cost of over $125 billion.

We can't get away with such gross last centuryism for long. If we don't clean up our act by scaling back our fling with the pollution machine, someone better start investing in technology that enables humans to breathe smog. Pollution from automobiles accounts for a third of smog-forming emissions in the US, and government agencies, as well as concerned citizens, are hoping for swift change. Thankfully there are companies making no-emissions vehicles. Among them is a startup by the name of Mission Motors, carrying this green trend to... the motorcycle.

LET'S BREAK THE ICE
High-speed electric vehicles.

HOW DOES IT WORK?
Mission Motors currently has two models: the Mission One PLE and the Mission R. The bikes use lithium-ion battery technology, and feature "regenerative braking," which converts kinetic energy from braking into new electricity. All this on a rig that plugs into a standard electrical socket. The typical qualms one might have with electric are thrown out the window: we're looking at high speeds (150 miles per hour) and long run time (up to 150 miles) on a brief, two hour charge.

WHY IS IT COOL?
Sexy speed demons on two wheels with zero emissions.

SMOOTH SAILING
+ Vehicle and ride data can be accessed over Wi-Fi and 3G. In its techie decked-out glory, Mission's bikes are fit for Batman or 007.

+ Famous industrial designer Yves Behar had a hand in shaping the body of the motorcycle.

+ In 2009, Mission nabbed the national AMA (one of the top racing organizations) top speed record for an electric motorcycle, at over 150 miles per hour sustained for one mile.

+ The San Francisco-based company is backed by well-renowned investors, including private equity firm Warburg Pincus.

+ After the successful IPO of Tesla (the electric car company), Mission Motors presumably has great exit options available to it, from being acquired by an auto maker to going public.

CHOPPY WATERS

- At well over $50,000 a pop, these motorcycles are pricey.

GOT GOOSEBUMPS?

Watch the Mission Motors team race at any of the TTXGP competitions. This tournament is exclusively for motorcycles powered without burning carbon-based fuel or generating toxic emissions.

Chapter 20: Better Place

LEGEND HAS IT that inspiration for one of the Coolest Startups came from the World Economic Forum, when the global organization's influential founder and executive chairman, economist Klaus Schwab, asked in 2005, "How do you make the world a better place by 2020?"

LET'S BREAK THE ICE

Better Place is envisioning a radical system for car ownership that dead ends our use of fossil fuels.

BACKSTORY

After hearing Schwab's question at Davos, Better Place founder Shai Agassi pondered, "how can a country run without oil?"

HOW DOES IT WORK?

Better Place will sell 100% electric, chargeable-battery vehicles for around $15,000, much cheaper than current hybrid models like the Toyota Prius. A home outlet will be provided for car owners to charge their cars with 100 miles' worth of energy. Outside the home, users will take advantage of an accessible network of battery replacement facilities located every few dozen miles. These Better Place battery replacement stations will switch your empty battery with a charged one in just one minute (*way* faster than filling up a tank).

The company has already deployed its cars and network of chargers and battery changing stations throughout Israel and in parts of Denmark. Their wheels are starting to turn in the San Francisco Bay Area and Japan as well.

Yes, Better Place is eco-friendly, conducive to reducing America's dependence on foreign oil, and can potentially make car ownership less expensive, but the innovation doesn't end there. Amazingly, the startup's vision demands little change in the consumer's current car-driving experience. Better Place's secretly-guarded technology solution makes battery switching a 60-second affair, and aesthetically, the car holds its own to any conventionally-powered vehicle.

WHY IS IT COOL?

Better Place turns the page on driving. Its dream is to use the revolutionary cars and business model to eliminate dependence on foreign oil while delivering an exceptional direct consumer experience too.

SMOOTH SAILING

+ Better Place counts Renault-Nissan as one of several strategic partners. The car conglomerate is making 100,000 special cars for the startup.

+ The business model for Better Place was adopted from the cell phone business. Cell phones are given to consumers at relatively cheap prices, the networks sustaining themselves with ongoing service rather than one-time sales of telecom time. Similarly with Better Place, car owners pay little for the electric car itself, and more for battery power on an ongoing mile-to-mile basis.

+ It's hard for competitors to follow suit without large capital commitments; the innovative network and charging stations are this Coolest Startup's key strengths, but they're far from inexpensive. Each battery changing station costs half a million dollars to build.

+ Better Place enjoys government support, including from California Lieutenant Governor Gavin Newsom and former Israeli Prime Minister Shimon Peres, and global media recognition, from the World Economic Forum to *TIME*.

CHOPPY WATERS

- There's a long road ahead for Better Place's far-reaching adoption. Sales cycles for auto purchases are lengthy, and the implementation of infrastructure meant to shift the sizeable American driving culture in its entirety will take a while.

HEARD FROM A HOT SHOT

"Better Place is one of the smartest companies I've ever seen"

– Ashton Kutcher, @AplusK

MILLIONS OF CARS sit around idly for hours a day. It's estimated that over 6,000 square miles of land have been paved throughout the US to accommodate car parking alone, a surface area larger than the state of Connecticut.

LET'S BREAK THE ICE

Getaround is car sharing done right. It safely matches people who need cars with people who don't mind being without their wheels for some time.

HOW DOES IT WORK?

Getaround has patented a deviously cool system whereby users can unlock participating vehicles using Getaround's mobile app. Just like that? Hold your horsepower. There's more to how this startup works.

First, car owners sign up and fill out details about their vehicle, set a rental price, and specify time constraints for availability (just to make sure it doesn't play out as a sequel to *Dude, Where's My Car?*). After installing the "Getaround Car Kit," owners use and park their cars as they always have. Prospective renters open the mobile app, within which a map displays their location and nearby cars available for lease. S/ he can sift through information about the cars (decisions, decisions) and rent one out if it's available. The car's owner then receives a notification that someone would like to rent their ride. It's up to the owner to approve or deny the request. If approved, the renter grabs the key from the in-car "kit" and off they go! Just remember to return it. Payment goes directly from the renter's account straight to the owner's. Getaround makes money in the process.

There are two particularly unique pieces in this process. The first is the patent-pending "Getaround Car Kit." The installation process doesn't take long, only about 15 to 20 minutes, Getaround founder Sam Zaid tells me. Zaid says that technically a leaser doesn't even need the kit to participate in Getaround—all it takes is completion of the auto-insurance declaration card—but the kit does make it easier for drivers to exchange keys without the hassle of meeting up.

The second critical element of Getaround's process is its unique insurance product. Getaround's primary insurance policy, which is rated A++, replaces the car owner's insurance for the time of the rental, covering liability, collision and theft. Both the owner and renter are fully covered so risk is taken off of both parties. This luxury for users was of critical importance, and the passing of the "California Insurance Bill AB 1871 on Personal Vehicle Sharing" is part of what made it possible.

The insurance feature helps defray risk, and so does Getaround's renter and owner feedback system. All members can be rated, and evaluations for cars and renters are made visible. Getaround also integrates seamlessly with social networking sites, so eventually owners could limit their leases to friends and family if they so choose.

BACKSTORY

How did Zaid and his co-founders come up with this revolutionary car sharing solution? The story of Getaround begins with Singularity University's inaugural Graduate Studies Program at the NASA Ames facility in California. "SU," as it's dubbed by students and faculty, is a fascinating institution about which I learned a lot from interviews for *The Coolest Startups in America*. Several of the Coolest Startups have roots with the organization. The main takeaway: the people and ideas at SU are visionary.

Co-founder of Bespoke Innovations (Chapter 65) Scott Summit, who teaches at SU describes the student body as "if you took the top 1% of Stanford, Harvard and MIT." Zaid characterizes the institute as "not a school about the past, but about the *next* 30 years." SU is about industries and innovations on the cutting-edge (seems like my kind of place) where the focus is on "where we're going, not where we've been." The curriculum includes genomics, nanotechnology, anti-aging, and self-driving cars among countless other fascinating topics.

It was self-driving cars, in fact, that interested Zaid and his co-founders; they decided to tackle it as a thesis project.

"There's a lot of interesting electronics and artificial intelligence baked into [Getaround]," Zaid says. "We were looking at the future of transportation and thinking about how, if all cars are autonomous, cars become more like software. If cars can drive themselves then you wouldn't park on the street. People will call up their cars on their phones."

When I heard that, I realized that Getaround had gone much further than most startups care to drive. Getaround sets itself up for futuristic success, and solves immediate problems along the way.

"We looked at transportation today and saw that there must be a better way than buying multiple cars [per household]," Zaid says. "There are 250 million cars unused for between 20 and 22 hours each day. We already have way too many cars. They cause a lot of problems." Such as, "after a home, it's people's second most expensive asset at 19% of household income. At a personal financial level, it makes sense to share a car and defray the costs of ownership. Personal vehicles cause 30% of gas emissions so there's environmental impact. Society dedicates so much of our infrastructure for parking, widening roads and traffic management," Zaid says. "At micro and macro levels, Getaround makes sense."

After ideation, the team spent time incubating the startup at SU. Taking the concept from prototype to production took the team about a year and a half, Zaid recounted, and they've gone through three generations of the car kit to date.

Beyond top-notch execution at each stage, Getaround may transform how we think about transportation as a whole. That's because when renting through Getaround, the sticker price of an hour's worth of driving is clear, a number that is opaque when people purchase cars outright. "It's not like you *need* to drive to the corner store to get milk, but if the car is sitting there, you do it," says Zaid. When people rethink transportation costs, "you reduce your driving by about 44% and reduce greenhouse gases."

WHY IS IT COOL?

Who doesn't like seeing one less car on the road? Getaround is great for traffic, air quality and accident safety.

LET'S SAY...

I. You're a lawyer. You work long hours and commute to work through hectic city streets on a daily basis. Tragically, your car just sits around all day, and hey, why not make some cash off the big investment that is car ownership? You decide to sign up for Getaround and get set up on the system quickly.

You allow your car to be rented only between the hours of 9 AM to 11 AM and 2 PM to 5 PM. After work or during lunch, your car's in the same spot (maybe the parking job's a little different) and you've got a few more bucks to your name.

II. You're a young professional who makes do without a car 99% of the time. Your friend calls in a favor to help with apartment-moving. What you need is a set of wheels. You sign up for Getaround and locate a nearby car that's available for a few hours. You use Getaround's app to reserve the car and put it to good use. Payment and key swaps are done by smartphone without ever needing to interact with the car owner directly.

SMOOTH SAILING

+ Most car sharing programs require membership fees. None in sight for Getaround.

+ Car sharing in general is becoming more mainstream. Traditional car sharing is up tenfold in the fleet-based model, according to Zaid. In the US, it's up to 4.5 million members.

+ Getaround differs from centralized fleet systems like Zipcar, implementing a peer-to-peer system instead. Leah Busque, CEO of fellow "collaborative consumption" startup TaskRabbit (Chapter 48), whose mentor happens to be Zipcar CEO Scott Griffith, says that peer-to-peer marketplaces are fascinating. "People are finding interesting ways to share in underutilized assets" like cars.

"Collaborative consumption is obviously something we look at," Zaid says. "It's something that will become more pervasive, largely to do with a shift in consumerism. Millenials and Generation Y don't value *things* anymore; they value experiences and time spent with friends," Zaid describes. "We're in a recessive market where people are under water on their homes. People question ownership. They feel like owning stuff is a burden because we have a hyper ability to do many things virtually and not need a lot of overhead to do it. Owning stuff today is an onerous process, no pun intended."

+ Getaround is also tied in with the trend of the "connected car." Connected cars are one of the hottest trends in automobiles today, Zaid says. "Car dashboards hadn't changed for 30 years, but now we have touch screens and soft displays. When cars become more [Internet] connected, programmable dashboards could connect you with Yelp, Pandora or Facebook. It'll take awhile, but it will enable transportation-sharing too."

+ Getaround boasts incredible advisors, like Simon Rothman, founder eBay Motors, the $14 billion business that pioneered vehicle sales over the Internet.

+ There's support for Getaround from environmental and governmental stakeholders. "Every shared car takes 9 to 15 cars off the roads," Zaid says. "That's why cities and governments support car sharing."

CHOPPY WATERS

- Most people in rural or suburban areas do own cars, so this might be a startup that's confined to the big cities where more people are carless and have reason to rent on occasion. Nick Ganju of ZocDoc (Chapter 55) is a fan in waiting. "Getaround has little selection outside of San Francisco, but I can't wait until they're live in New York," he says. Most Getaround renters would likely walk, bike or commute by train or carpool to access their temporary rental cars. "We're best in the densest areas," Zaid says. "We're available in a broader set of areas than fleet-based car sharing like Zipcar."

- Speaking of fleets, Zipcar is a big competitive player. "In a lot of ways we're complimentary," Zaid says. "There are features we have that Zipcar doesn't, like no membership fees, daily pricing, or diverse car types like a Tesla Roadster or a minivan. There are lots of complementary aspects, but it's not about us competing. It's about both Zipcar and Getaround bringing an alternative to car ownership. As a society, we've spent a lot of time buying cars. What Zipcar pioneered is 'you don't have to do that. We'll put cars everywhere for you to use.' Getaround has the same mission. We spend $2 trillion on owning and operating vehicles when we could get smarter about how we do personal transportation." Regardless of Zaid's words of friendly competition, Josh Abdulla of LetGive (Chapter 43) thinks Getaround is a big step up from Zipcar. "Getaround is disrupting Zipcar, which disrupted rental cars. They're basically doing what Zipcar should have done."

GOT GOOSEBUMPS?

Getaround is up and running in many neighborhoods. Get involved on either side of the equation! Put your car up for rent, or become a responsible renter yourself.

DEFROST: Why Is Mobile Critical?

There are over 5 billion mobile phone connections worldwide. Yup, that's three times more phones than all personal computers. And by 2015, there are expected to be over 15 billion *Internet-connected* devices. Most entrepreneurs follow such trends, and that means technology companies have started thinking seriously about their mobile strategies.

It's not just the sheer volume of devices that interests founders either. "People are attached to their mobile devices," says Eli Portnoy of ThinkNear (Chapter 39). "There's a lot of opportunity to influence buying decisions through it."

The trend's effects are already starting to be felt by existing businesses. Aaron Schildkrout says that mobile is "the most important product for HowAboutWe and for dating in general." Within a year, over 50% of HowAboutWe's traffic will come from mobile and, in two years, it will grow to 80%, Schildkrout estimates. That's because "we're becoming a mobile culture. We use the Internet on the go and we use it in quick spurts between activities. It's a more private device than the computer, which is good for dating. The size of the screen and the bite-size content experience is also beneficial. A user can look at one person at a time and can scroll through a long list of people while the experience remains manageable."

Schildkrout brings up the point that the mobile experience necessitates a different design perspective than what most startups are used to.

"There's a sense that people are trying to take what works on the computer screen to mobile," explains Portnoy. "The same thing happened with TV at first. People took radio shows and started filming them, until they realized that it's a different medium. People are trying to figure out what works for mobile design."

It's already affected development work too, says Ilya Sukhar of Parse, a mobile startup. "The explosion of mobile is a game changer," he says. "Software development practices are changing. They're moving from web apps in HTML and Javascript to native apps that are custom-built and written in different languages." This has created a need for his company, which makes setting up servers for mobile apps a cinch.

The "explosion" of mobile enables new opportunities for entrepreneurs too. Bobby Emamian of Prolific Interactive, a mobile development firm in New York City, says that "Siri [the natural language processor integrated with Apple's iPhone 4S] gives developers a new tool for their minds to run wild with ideas." Being able to command apps through voice is a powerful tool, one expected to lead a new wave of innovation.

Josh Abdulla of LetGive (Chapter 43) believes the technology will be especially transformational in developing countries. "The advent of Siri has shown people's desire to interact with the Web through their voices," Abdulla explains.

Abdulla gave the example of being able to book a table at a restaurant while driving, all through voice recognition through the phone. In the developing world, "they don't have smartphones but they have great cellular service," Abdulla says. "If they can open up the web through the use of voice recognition you'll see a huge explosion of people who never had access to these types of websites. When Wikipedia can be accessed through your voice rather than through typing, it will open up possibilities in Africa or India that never existed before. That's going to bring a whole generation of people online." Factors that would previously bar the approachability of the Web—age, technophobia, even illiteracy—will become non-issues.

Mobile will also be important for the Financial Services space. According to Jim Bruene of Finovate, a Financial Technology industry organization, online banking is already pervasive in 50% to 60% of US households. In the next 10 to 15 years, he believes, it is mobile that will take that crown. "Mobile is smarter," he says, because it will offer geo-stamped transactions and encourage simpler, more intuitive layouts for the smaller size interface. Potentially, banking on the go could replace branches, ATMs and credit cards altogether. Jeremy Levine of StarStreet (Chapter 4) sees mobile as enabling more trading, too. Trading at the touch of a button (or the sound of "Buy" or "Sell" using mobile voice recognition) means sleeker marketplaces. Alexander Graham Bell would be proud.

THE REC ROOM
We Just Wanna Have Fun
startups

TWICE A YEAR, a series of events captivates the attention of millions around the world: Fashion Week. From Milan to New York, people watch gorgeous models modeling gorgeous threads from the best of the globe's design minds. Celebrities and socialites get to try on the latest attire, but what about everyone else? If it weren't for this cool startup, they'd be left scouring the local mall for a look-alike piece of runway style.

LET'S BREAK THE ICE
Rent clothes hot off the catwalk.

HOW DOES IT WORK?
Consumers sign up with Rent the Runway and select a piece of apparel they'd like to rent. The pricing is set at 10% of the retail price of the piece, much more affordable than purchasing the item outright from a store, particularly if you're only going to wear it once.

On the date of your choice, Rent the Runway delivers a piece of sartorial masterclass on your doorstep, along with the same article in an extra size of your choice, just in case. You pick a rental period of four or eight days. After you wear the attire, just send it back to Rent the Runway in the pre-paid envelope provided. The company takes care of dry cleaning, too. Rent the Runway's got you covered, Cinderella.

Julie Sygiel, CEO of Sexy Period, a hosiery startup based in Rhode Island, says that the service works like a charm. "Their story connects with everyone. Everyone wants to wear that designer dress," Sygiel says. "I Rent-ed the Runway for StyleWeek Providence. It was a great experience. I'm impressed if a company gets me on board that fast."

WHY IS IT COOL?
For the first time, designer-label garb is accessible to the mass market, especially useful for memorable events like weddings or holiday parties.

LET'S SAY...
Your graduation party is coming up. Rather than dressing

in low-key mall threads for your special day, you'd love to look like you're on the red carpet. You check out Rent the Runway and find the perfect dress that retails for $600. You rent it for $60. It arrives just in time for the party, and you ship it back the next day. You spent less than you probably would have elsewhere, and got to dress in something far more enviable!

SMOOTH SAILING

+ Rent the Runway's items can be browsed by occasion and trend.

+ Over 95 designers are represented, from Halston Heritage to Anna Sui to Missoni.

+ Rent the Runway has recently carved out a niche in wedding and bridesmaid apparel. With over 2.5 million weddings a year in the US, that's a lot of potential for profit.

+ Rent the Runway recycles a successful, existing business model pioneered by the movie rental wunderkind Netflix.

+ The New York City company is backed by Bain Capital Ventures and other top venture capital firms. The startup is already valued at over $100 million as of late 2011.

CHOPPY WATERS

- Supply and demand for outfits must be optimized. Unlike cheaply acquired DVDs, expensive glamour gear is costly for the company to have hanging unused on its racks.

- There are no menswear rentals at present, although many men reportedly use the site for memorable gifts for the girl in their lives.

GOT GOOSEBUMPS?

Ooh and aah at the inventory on Rent the Runway. If that special occasion is coming up, consider ordering something for yourself. In the paraphrased words of the Men's Warehouse, "you'll like the way you look."

SHOWER SINGING IS fine, but some of us have musical chops to be shared with the world! Unfortunately, getting a band together takes time, effort and money.

LET'S BREAK THE ICE

UJAM is a jam session with just you and the computer.

HOW DOES IT WORK?

Sing into your computer microphone or upload a piece of music, and UJAM will match instruments to your sound. It's remarkable technology that works by decoding the chords around your melody. You can customize the instruments that are playing backup, tune your voice so you sound gagalicious, and even change the quality of your voice from country crooner to Rock n' Roll Hall of Fame-r.

WHY IS IT COOL?

Orchestrate melodies technologically.

LET'S SAY...

You'd love to record an album someday. Since you don't have the money to get recording studio time, you sign up for UJAM and replicate the studio vibe as best as possible. Lay down some tracks, export them and you could actually send them to a producer to see if you make the cut. The quality is good enough. The question is, are you?

SMOOTH SAILING

+ Become your own artist *and* have auto-tune at your fingertips. Look out, Lil Wayne.

+ As the technology improves, the cost to record viable songs goes plunging down like a riff out of Black Sabbath. While nothing replaces record studios and technicians—experts can achieve a level of granularity simply unavailable with UJAM—this startup's approachable software is a great fit for the mass market.

+ The startup is a collaboration by film composer Hans Zimmerman, artist Pharrell Williams, and technologist Peter

Gorges. That's a super and starry team.

CHOPPY WATERS

+ What is UJAM's business model: Premium accounts? Ads for music? Buying credits if you want to keep recording? The startup isn't generating revenue yet, but they are thinking about premium versions and a monetizable API so other websites could integrate with UJAM.

+ Personally, I'm shy to share, so it's a-okay to me that UJAM will help you make the music without the promotion. If you're aiming for the billboards, you may want to look elsewhere for marketing assistance.

GOT GOOSEBUMPS?

Sign up for UJAM and lay down some tracks. You'll get a kick (and maybe a jive) out of this cool pastime.

PSST... EVER MOVIE theater hop? Come on, never gone to see two movies in a row while paying for just one? Well, for those propping up the silver screen it's a bigger loss of business than you might think. Industry estimates are all over the map, yet all sources say that *billions* of dollars are lost due to film piracy. Movie hopping, film piracy... it's but a stone's throw away. MoviePass aims to sidestep watching without paying entirely. You could now pay a low monthly fee to see unlimited movies each month. And we're not talking streaming movies from home. You'll be going to the movie theaters as usual, popcorn and all! Roll out the red carpet for this premiere.

LET'S BREAK THE ICE

Unlimited movies at the theater for a low monthly fee.

HOW DOES IT WORK?

You pay a subscription fee to MoviePass and get, well, a pass to go to the movies all month long. But if only it were so simple. The startup has not had an easy time implementing its elegant idea. The startup is still in "limited release mode," and apparently movie studios aren't over the moon to join. Presumably there would be some arrangement on a price point beneficial to all parties.

WHY IS IT COOL?

I repeat, unlimited movies.

LET'S SAY...

I. Your mom (it's the case for yours truly) is obsessed with movies, assiduously going to every movie upon release. A MoviePass would make the perfect gift for movie-going Mom.

II. Ever have a tough time convincing friends to see the latest flick? Once on board with MoviePass, the boring old expense argument is out the window. Heck, it's reversed!

SMOOTH SAILING

+ The movie industry is big business. According to the Motion Picture Association of America (MPAA), worldwide box office sales are over $30 billion per year. Not to mention there are over 200 million movie-goers per year in the US and Canada alone. Adding cred to MoviePass's solution, "frequent movie-goers," or those who see a movie once a month or more, total 35 million people per year in North America. This is a big market, and MoviePass may help create more repeat customers.

+ Movie theaters make most of their money off of refreshments anyway. Between 10% and 20% of movie theater income comes from selling popcorn, drinks and sweets. Sometimes, the movies themselves are actually loss leaders for the theaters just because of how expensive it is to show them. Concessions are responsible for theater profitability, so MoviePass could help get more people to the theaters.

+ We all know how purchases often go unused. Many people won't obsess over seeing every movie anyway, so the theaters could actually make money from this.

CHOPPY WATERS

- How does the revenue share work? That's what all parties are trying to identify. MoviePass has received a lot of flack in its initial efforts to launch, including from the Chief Marketing Officer of movie megafirm AMC, who said that the startup "does not integrate well into [AMC's] programs." Ouch.

- The proof of concept problem is a concern. Once something is shown to work or have a market, the movie theaters can sell this idea straight to their consumers and cut out MoviePass as the middleman. And tisk, tisk on MoviePass for not trademarking its (awesome) name yet. Any old movie theater could, conceivably, nab the name (not to mention the idea!) to promote that type of monthly unlimited ticket.

- The film industry is a big old business, resistant to change. Maybe it will lend an ear to the startup considering the radical, observable transformations undergone by the music biz. With revolutionary firms like Netflix having once brilliantly disrupted the industry, time to take the power back!

GOT GOOSEBUMPS?

Sign up to be notified of when MoviePass will be available in your town. But if Hollywood won't #SupportMoviePass, I'm not sure there's hope for the rest of us.

JUST BECAUSE CHRYSLER'S executives were guffawed at for flying on a private jet to Washington DC in 2008 when they came to ask for public funds, doesn't mean we must all give up the luxury. Since the 1% of America continues to maintain (and gain?) financially, there is a market for private jet-setting.

LET'S BREAK THE ICE

evoJets specializes in brokering private jet travel.

HOW DOES IT WORK?

You can search through dozens of jet options, like six-passenger Light Jets or Executive Turboprops arranged like mini-offices in the sky. You request a quote and can speak to evoJets agents anytime to book a flight.

"On average, Light Jets [the type of planes most evoJets customers fly] cost between $2,000 to $3,500 an hour," says evoJets CEO Adriann Wanner. That may seem like a big spread, but Wanner says the cost depends on availability and repositioning. She explained this terminology to me. "Every aircraft has a home base. The easy part is finding the aircraft, but the hard part is finding value," she says. "We look to match people with aircraft going in their direction because repositioning the plane back to its home base is a big cost driver. Our goal is to create as much efficiency as possible."

But you can either afford it, or you can't, says Wanner. The people who use evoJets include businesspeople, privately wealthy individuals, CEOs, and entrepreneurs, she says. These clients often fly with their families when going through commercial airports doesn't make sense, like around the holiday season or graduation time when travelers may have kids, nannies, and even the family dogs in tow.

BACKSTORY

Wanner worked in the jet industry in Aspen, Colorado, where her expertise enabled her to quickly move from Marketing to Sales at her prior firm. She was really close with her clients, and "felt that there was more value to be had." She was determined to figure out a way to create more flexibility and better pricing with aircraft selection and timing. At the established firm, "I hated putting clients on aircraft where I knew they could save more," Wanner says.

So she made the leap to become an entrepreneur by founding evoJets with her now-fiance. "We had that unique combination of not being afraid of taking risk and not being tied down. It's the perfect storm that allowed us to take the risk and have the energy and enthusiasm to make it happen."

Now, Wanner's evoJets can help clients to find jets in as few as two hours or to book travel six months in advance. Any way, evoJets finds clients ways to save on luxury air travel.

WHY IS IT COOL?

Come on, need you ask!? evoJets means access to sexy Cessnas, foxy Falcons and alluring Learjets.

SMOOTH SAILING

+ Availability in over 5,000 airports. 90% of evoJets flights are in the US, but they have the reach to broker flights to and from anywhere in the world.

+ Travel on the best private planes money can book.

+ evoJets helps to unlock value by enabling "empty legs" flights, setting up a passenger in an otherwise empty seat.

+ evoJets is a company thinking about its triple-bottom line. They partner with TerraPass to offset emissions from air travels they facilitate. Fly in physical and conscience comfort.

+ evoJets does not own any planes, so there is little risk as the company does not hold these expensive and illiquid assets on its books. They just broker the seating. evoJets concierge services are provided to help you pick the right private jet arrangement at minimal cost. Plus, catering is available!

CHOPPY WATERS

- It's niche.

GOT GOOSEBUMPS?

If you have $10k or so to spend on a private flight, what are you waiting for? And if you don't, well, you can ogle the pretty planes on evoJets's website.

Chapter 26: Fashion Playtes

SARAH MCILROY, FOUNDER of Fashion Playtes, grew up sketching clothing designs, picking out fabrics and trims, and sewing her creations with her mother's helping hands. When McIlroy's own daughter began sketching, McIlroy wondered why there was no community for girls to become fashion designers and actually receive the designs ready-to-wear.

LET'S BREAK THE ICE
Clothes designed for kids, by kids.

BACKSTORY
McIlroy had worked in the gaming industry for a decade before becoming an entrepreneur. She knew of the various online communities for kids, but none brought the online into the real world, which she felt was critical for fashion.

"When I look back at my childhood, designing built confidence and self-esteem," McIlroy told me. "There's pride knowing that you created something no one else has." Once she got the idea for Fashion Playtes, McIlroy ran the idea by her sister, a mother with four daughters. Her sister loved the idea, so McIlroy went on to do research on how to structure a business plan to make her idea a reality. She was not accustomed to the world of investors or startups, so she began networking. "It's uncharted territory if you're not a serial entrepreneur," says McIlroy. Thankfully, she found that fellow entrepreneurs and CEOs wanted to see her succeed and were ready and willing to make introductions, guiding her along the startup path. The networking paid off and McIlroy raised $5 million for Fashion Playtes.

HOW DOES IT WORK?
Girls go online and choose a garment silhouette from the choices provided. After picking from dozens of clothing templates, they can add ribbons and ruffles, trims and graphics. Once done designing, they can even add their own clothing label to the piece. They then order it, and Fashion Playtes deals with the fabrication and shipping.

The garments are made abroad, but all of the customization

is done in the US.

Content is as much a part of the Fashion Playtes experience as clothing e-commerce is. McIlroy says "Fashion Playtes can be a platform for girls to interact and engage, including blogging, contests, trend education and more. It's a bigger experience than designing your own clothes." Fashion Playtes envisions adding games and online community-building too.

"Fashion Playtes is about individuality and self-expression. It's girl-driven design," McIlroy says. "It's about experience more than product. Buying something or not, there's an opportunity to interact and engage around style, fashion and design."

WHY IS IT COOL?
Fashion Playtes dresses mini-moguls.

SMOOTH SAILING
+ Fashion Playtes can be huge for gifting. There are all sorts of outfits from tops to dresses to accessories.

+ It's "parent-approved," and a Mom's Choice Award honoree.

+ Fashion Playtes has fantastic partnerships; they've worked with the Hello Kitty company to create branded kiosks in-store, and among the startup's advisors is Andrea Weiss, former President of peppy retail brand dELiA's.

CHOPPY WATERS
- What about the brothers? I'm pretty sure there are more male designers in the world (and chefs) than women anyway. McIlroy says that there aren't plans to start a boys line yet, but they will likely rebrand a separate site if and when they do. "The site is so girly, it could never translate to boys, but once we nail down the business model, we'll consider expanding," she says.

GOT GOOSEBUMPS?
Make an outfit on Fashion Playtes. You may not be a kid, but designing is fun for kids at heart too.

Chapter 27: ViKi

THE MELTING POT of the world is more than a catch phrase. America is a land of immigrants. At the end of the last decade, the population of legal and illegal immigrants in the US reached a historical record of 40 million people. Around the world, diasporas are larger than ever. The world has 215 million first-generation migrants, so if migrants constituted a nation, it would be more populous than Brazil.

My parents moved here in 1987, and became naturalized in 1995. I had the privilege of being born in sunny California. As such, I came into the world with English all around. But what about expats born in Moscow? Mexico? Dubai? Singapore? Canada? They probably miss getting to listen to movies and TV in their first language, or getting to experience pop culture from the home country. Imagine a world where entertainment and media aren't confined to the places and languages in which they were created.

LET'S BREAK THE ICE

ViKi is a website that collates thousands of pieces of entertainment—TV, film, etc.—in hundreds of languages, for a community of translators with the goal of accessibility for all.

HOW DOES IT WORK?

ViKi has diverse genres of TV shows, films and other content for which ViKi's community creates sub-titles. There are over 150 languages on the system, and more than 200 million words have undergone translation.

For members, ViKi can be used for watching videos or contributing new subtitles. All subtitles are contributed under a Creative Commons license in an agreement between a creator and licensee whereby no monetary compensation is sought for the content. The ViKi technology is advanced, with revision history and user-generated edits.

LET'S SAY...

I. You're trying to learn Spanish for your high school required course. Why not watch your favorite TV show in Spanish? You can brush up on your language skills while watching TV. How can Mom and Dad argue with that? For similarly productive leisure, you could watch Anglophone television with Spanish subtitles!

II. You're an immigrant, and you really miss home. Your sister keeps talking about this awesome new Telenovela, but you can't get it in the US. You check out ViKi.com and find that they have it, pristine and undubbed.

WHY IS IT COOL?

Entertainment *sans frontières*.

SMOOTH SAILING

+ ViKi's set of languages is comprehensive. They even have Klingon! I may not have the nerd cred to hop for joy on this one, but the fact that it's available attests to ViKi's latitude.

+ Startups like ViKi can help make true cosmopolitans of us all. ViKi itself is hard to pin down. The startup was founded as a collaboration across US coasts, with one co-founder at Stanford University and another at Harvard Business School. Now, ViKi has offices in Palo Alto and Singapore.

+ More than 8 million people use ViKi every month, writes Andras Kristof, ViKi's Director of Engineering, on Quora (Chapter 59). That's a huge lead in information, content and community that would be hard for a competitor to match.

+ ViKi gives power to the people. Esoteric or niche results are possible through the ambitions of passionate contributors.

+ The field of translation is a competitive one. It's not enough to be bilingual; linguistic awareness and specializations are also needed. Hopefully Viki will provide opportunity for new talent to take initiative and gain recognition.

CHALLENGES

- There may be piracy concerns, but it appears ViKi is preventing this by working directly with content providers like Yahoo!, Hulu, Netflix and more.

GOT GOOSEBUMPS?

Want to watch the latest music video from Thai pop star Dome Pakorn Lam? Check out ViKi for his channel... including English translations!

NO NEED TO change out of your slippers for this startup. While usually there's much fanfare associated with going out to a club, you can now rock out in one without leaving the comfort of your room. We knew this day would come...

LET'S BREAK THE ICE

Turntable.fm is a digital dive bar, complete with music spun by the people, er, DJs in the virtual "room."

HOW DOES IT WORK?

Logging in to Turntable.fm places you in a room. Each room has five DJ spots and unlimited audience space. Your cute avatar pops up and starts grooving to the beat if you give the current song a thumbs up, "Awesome" vote. Conversely, if enough spectators give the song selection a thumbs down, "Lame" review, the bad-taste culprit gets the boot. Anyone in the room can DJ, if they can find an empty spot on stage.

As a DJ you collect points when your songs are voted up. As you collect more points, you can redeem them for cooler avatars. Stylish clothes mean people dig your taste in music!

WHY IS IT COOL?

It's a virtual music meetup where you get to DJ anything, anytime.

BACKSTORY

This rockin' startup came out of the ashes of a product called StickyBits. StickyBits had the makings of a Coolest Startup, but when traction with customers failed to catch on, the team had to "pivot" and try something new. They came up with Turntable.fm which got fire-bright traction within days of launching.

SMOOTH SAILING

+ Discover new music from fellow music lovers. As the website says, "humans make connections and suggestions that just would not occur with a computer running the show. Chances are that you will hear something great that you have never heard before." That's a gibe at Pandora's algorithmic approach if I've ever heard one.

+ Oh, the "Guilty Pleasure" room is such a trip down memory lane. Britney Spears, Seal, ABBA...

CHOPPY WATERS

- Turntable.fm may encounter business model problems. Understandably, it's quite expensive to license the music that's playing in the rooms, and in my opinion, it's not likely that the product is sticky enough for fans to pay for the service.

- I worry about creepers discovering Turntable.fm and taking over the chat functionality like it's 1998. Thankfully, Turntable.fm finds DJs with reputable histories on the website to serve as moderators, with the power to flag abusive users.

- It's a bummer when you have to wait a really long time to get the shot to DJ. But hey, you can always open a new room.

GOT GOOSEBUMPS?

Log in to Turntable.fm and spend an afternoon living out the party animal in you.

DEFROST: Pivots Aren't Just in Basketball

A "pivot" is a startup term you'll hear techies and venture capitalists throw around. It means that the business, for whatever reasons, isn't working in terms of bringing in money or users. A change of strategy is in order lest you may run out of funds to operate or a competitor should come over and squash you. In business, as in all parts of life, it's important to realize when things aren't working and act on them before it's too late! That's called pivoting.

Michael Karnjanaprakorn of Skillshare (Chapter 33) says two of the best pivots in recent startup history have been at Fab.com and Turntable.fm (Chapter 28). Turntable.fm was launched as a pivot from Stickybits, when that company was almost out of funds and simply couldn't get the product to market well. Meanwhile, Fab.com started out as a gay social network. Aaron Schildkrout, co-CEO of HowAboutWe (Chapter 36) says that Fab's founder made a dramatic pivot after one year to become a design deal site. The best part is that Fab's earliest members have followed the company since launch and through the pivot. "They've had great success and they're constantly innovating in big ways. They're about making people smile," Schildkrout says.

Pivots take perseverance. It can drain a team to have to switch gears or not find traction with idea after idea. But working through it and sticking together can work out in the positive ways that it has for Turntable.fm or Fab. Drew Johnson at mobile development company SuperBoise recounts the story of Rovio, the Swedish company behind the Angry Birds mobile app. "Rovio came up with Angry Birds as the 72nd game they made. People think Angry Birds was their first effort, but in reality they made a whole bunch of games, switched to contract work, then took all that experience from contract work to create Angry Birds."

Pivots shouldn't be viewed as failures, says Marc

Brodeur of Brode (Chapter 29). "Changing your mind isn't a failure, it's a growth experience," he says. Pivoting doesn't have to be driven by new technology or product, either. "We haven't pivoted that much in terms of product, but for strategy and brand we have pivoted. Our first brand was more natural but we found it wasn't the best way to portray the ideas behind Brode. We made a major pivot to a brand that is more sophisticated by totally reimagining the packaging."

But don't feel like you have to pivot.

Liron Shapira of Quixey (Chapter 50), the app search engine, shares that his team "thought about pivoting because it's the thing to do." But they didn't end up budging much from their original concept. "From day one we said the space of apps is a giant mess and we need to help people with it. How much of our product would be browsing versus search, we weren't sure, but our mission was clear." The implementation of strategy can shift, but the greater vision guides it straight.

HANGOVERS AREN'T FUN.

LET'S BREAK THE ICE

Brode is a dietary supplement that people take when they go out drinking to help naturally detoxify the body and keep it hydrated.

HOW DOES IT WORK?

Brode has mastered Hangover Science. "When you drink, a few things go wrong in your body that dehydrate you in a clear-cut way. Brode helps with that," Brode CEO Marc Brodeur says. Brode's product is ⅔ hydration, ⅓ detoxification, and it helps alleviate the symptoms of a hangover. It's not a panacea though. "Remember that no product can help you metabolize alcohol," Brodeur says. "Don't listen to anyone who says their product does, and nothing prevents alcohol poisoning either. Be responsible because Brode just helps with the symptoms."

BACKSTORY

The story of Brode began when founder and CEO Marc Brodeur was out with some friends and drinking. "It was a particularly heavy night," he recalls. "I got home late and didn't remember to drink enough water, and it was awful the next day. I had the cliche moment of 'there must be a better way!'"

"Some people deal with hangovers as part of the going-out equation," he says of his determination. "I got annoyed by hangovers. I'm not going to accept that we have to compromise."

Brodeur was familiar with the importance of hydration from his childhood playing sports, though perhaps he hadn't thought then of its role in a decidedly more adult lifestyle. He sought to enhance his anecdotal knowledge of hangover remedies with some Googling. Brodeur compiled a list of products that could work to make hangovers feel better. The first product he tried was Pedialyte, a grocery store buy meant to rehydrate children. It worked well in reducing hangover symptoms but had an unpleasant taste and, at over $5 a bottle, was too expensive to be used as an off-the-shelf option.

So what did Brodeur do next? "I made my own Pedialyte," says Brodeur. "The components weren't tricky, but the drink was gross. One of the innovations I brought to Brode was putting the ingredients into a tasteless capsule."

Brodeur then reached out to his medical school friends about whether his product was on the right track. They gave further support for the idea since hydration was scientifically correlated with muted hangover symptoms. Brodeur and his team created 1,000 prototype capsules and distributed them to friends for research. While Brode hasn't applied to government boards for approval, the startup has run standard experiments to show that the product works. Brodeur and his team cultivated a relationship with a factory in New York to do the final manufacturing. Once the team had a product they felt was great, Brode began to focus on branding and operations. "One of the things we learned was how important brand is to this product. Our friends trusted the product because they know us, but anyone who didn't know us personally was skeptical. The prototype packaging was unsophisticated, so we focused on branding to address concerns of trust from consumers who don't know us as founders."

Brodeur was able to launch the startup because he saved up from his post-college job. "I've always been an aggressive saver," Brodeur says. "Combining my savings with the ability to use tools like Google Docs and Amazon Fulfillment services multipled our ability to execute." Brode hasn't yet raised external funds.

"If you raise money, it's a news story. If you worked hard and saved, and don't raise money, you don't get a news story out of it," Brodeur says. "But the ability to have complete control over your company is great."

Brodeur will wait until Brode gains traction before looking for funding. "We're not kidding ourselves that we may want to raise a few million to expand quickly, hit other markets or have more presence on the ground, but if we're making great sales, we'll have more leverage," he says. "Bootstraping so far has been a blessing."

94Labs founder Greg Meier echoes Brodeur's criticism regarding the brouhaha of some startup media coverage. "TechCrunch is a distraction," Meier tells entrepreneurs.

"Don't get caught up in the hype. Focus on the business model and customers."

WHY IS IT COOL?

Hangovers are over... or at least not as bad.

SMOOTH SAILING

+ Brode is a lean organization. Brode outsources many of its functions, including FDA compliance and fulfillment. According to Brodeur, "one thing that's fantastic for anyone starting a company these days is that you can do things now that you couldn't have done even five years ago. People starting companies now can latch on to tools that scale." He believes that despite being low-tech, Brode couldn't have been created 10 years ago. "People take Google Apps for granted, but that tool would have cost thousands of dollars before. These tools allow smaller teams to get exponentially more done."

CHOPPY WATERS

- The company hasn't pursued Intellectual Property protection for their product yet. While Brode is a unique blend, Brodeur says that the cost and time associated with getting a patent issue hasn't made economic sense. "The idea we're using is to create lasting value through our brand, rather than using a patent as a crutch," he says.

GOT GOOSEBUMPS?

Order Brode online, and in the meantime, remember to drink enough water along with the good stuff.

ACADEMIC EPIDEMIC
Back to School startups

BACK WHEN YOUTUBE started, there were dozens of video sites vying to become the video platform for the Internet. YouTube won, and has since given us a way to explore a gamut of video content: from five-second memes like a surprised groundhog turning around to dramatic music to powerful political pieces like live interviews with President Obama.

YouTube also sparked a trend of the "sensation"—the everyday person who showcases a talent and rises to fame with millions of video views. Salman Khan is one of those sensations. He didn't belt out Poker Face to a crowd of middle school students, but he did teach them math topics that many had previously struggled with.

LET'S BREAK THE ICE

Khan Academy is an online "school" where hundreds of videos cover topics from Finance to Art History, broken down into discrete, digestible chapters. Watch over and over again until mastery, without shame over the "one more time" question in class.

BACKSTORY

Khan Academy began with Khan posting videos of his knowledge on YouTube, linked to a website he built called Khan Academy. This guy used to have a high-flying career in Finance, so why play teacher? Some of Khan's cousins hundreds of miles away were asking Khan questions about math, and he'd send them videos explaining the concepts. Soon, as grades no doubt started to go up, more cousins wanted in on these tutoring sessions.

HOW DOES IT WORK?

This is how entrepreneurship takes off: the realization that people have pain points you're helping to solve. Khan figured if his cousins could benefit from these videos, why not share them with more people?

"I'm the biggest fan of Khan Academy. When I first saw it, I thought: this is better than college," says Liron Shapira, CTO of Quixey (Chapter 50). "If you're going to class where someone is lecturing at you, you might as well be able to pause and replay them. To me, Khan Academy is reinventing eduction."

Education expert Jeremy Johnson, founder and Chief Marketing Officer of 2tor (an education infrastructure startup that helps top universities build their online degree programs), points to an increasing acceptance of online education as a high-quality medium. He told me about a US Department of Education study that showed online learning students to have better results than their on-campus peers, and mentioned a growing acceptance of the mode among employers. "69% of employers view online learning to be as good or better than on-campus studies," Johnson says.

Another trend contributing positively to the online learning revolution is consumer fluency with the web, Johnson says. Teachers are increasingly coming from the plugged-in generation. "Professors were skeptical at first, and then realized that online is a compelling way to teach."

Further, web technologies enable Khan Academy to create highly personalized teaching programs. Instead of forcing students to the pace of the class, students can move at their own speeds. "It's exciting to watch the way Khan Academy is revolutionizing the way education is delivered," says Nihal Parthasarathi of education startup CourseHorse (Chapter 32). "Remediation and working through actual problems is a step in the right direction versus one-size-fits-all instruction."

WHY IS IT COOL?

Replay (and pause and rewind... or even mute!) your prof.

SMOOTH SAILING

+ Khan Academy betters education. According to Johnson, "non-traditional education programs, like Khan Academy, can drive down the cost of education, and the surplus can be reinvested into financial aid and more teachers. It's a virtuous cycle where schools get better and better."

+ Khan Academy is a non-profit, which aligns well with its K-12 public education work. Supported by the Bill and Melinda Gates Foundation, it hopes to grow world-round to improve educational access and quality.

+ Khan Academy undoubtedly increases access to education. "The web is a great equalizer," says Johnson.

"Education startups begin from a drive to increase equality."

CHOPPY WATERS

- However because Khan Academy is a non-profit, they may not have the same drive for efficiency as a for-profit education firm, says Johnson. Johnson gives a comparison to Coca-Cola, which he explains has made gains in the efficiency of its bottle every year, allowing it to increase its price at about the rate of inflation each year. "If you can't increase efficiency then you increase cost at more than inflation each year," Johnson says. "For-profit education firms can find ways to be more efficient, which is incentive non-profits may not have."

- Khan is usually the only one to be found in the teachers' lounge; can one professor really fit all learning styles?

- It's hard to skip around to parts of the video that you want to hear. Khan's presentation and layout are excellent, but the website may benefit from using its own video player rather than YouTube. Transcripts of the lessons would help too.

GOT GOOSEBUMPS?

Learn something new at KhanAcademy.org.

DEFROST: Who's TED?

Wrong question. "What's TED?" is right. TED officially stands for "Technology Entertainment and Design," but now its mission is broader. TED is about ideas worth sharing (or "spreading," in TED lingo).

Imagine an old-time salon where the world's brightest share their thoughts, latest research, and cool goings-on. Now imagine that you get invited to this salon and, beyond that, can actually participate in the conversations. TED began as a conference in California for this kind of innovative thinking. Every year since 1990, the smartest and most successful minds across diverse industries convene in a highly exclusive venue to share short (about 5- to 18-minute) presentations on a range of fascinating topics. Most TED talks are jaw-droppingly awesome thought-pieces.

Eventually, TED began to see value (and thank goodness!) in opening up their invite-only community to a wider audience. The walls of this 21st century salon turned to glass, as TED started posting videos online and inviting people to join in its forward-thinking spirit. TED eventually spread around the world and into local communities. It launched the TEDx series, where speakers and audiences could converge around topics or locales.

Scott Summit, founder of Bespoke Innovations (Chapter 65), has presented at TED. "The phenomena of a TED talk is entertainment that isn't empty calories. It gives insight into someone who's inspired," Summit says. "Everybody in startups is a TED fanatic. It's the *lingua franca*. People need examples that it's okay to take wild ideas and throw your life into them. I grew up with a father who's an entrepreneur and saw how it could be done. You need that viewpoint of 'This person did it. It's possible.'"

If you haven't already, check out TED videos at www. TED.com and share one you like with a friend. You'll be glad you did; TED is a real dynamo when it comes to enlightening one's outlook on the world.

"Entertainment that isn't empty calories."

- Scott Summit, co-founder of
Bespoke Innovations (Chapter 65), about TED

Chapter 31: Wolfram Alpha

WE DON'T SEE the world in numbers. Humans describe their surroundings with visual language, so it's harder for us to gauge the world from a mathematical perspective. Stephen Wolfram, the scientist and author who founded Wolfram Research, wanted to change that, and came up with the cool tool called Wolfram Alpha.

LET'S BREAK THE ICE

A resource where any input of language outputs math.

HOW DOES IT WORK?

Wolfram Alpha combines human experts' curated contributions with diverse database knowledge to yield arithmetic answers and rich visualizations to people's queries. The technology backbone is built on one of Wolfram Research's earlier products called Mathematica. It works well on computational queries as well as questions phrased with natural language. "It's clearly an engineering accomplishment," says Liron Shapira, CTO of Quixey (Chapter 50), about Wolfram Alpha. "It has street cred."

LET'S SAY...

I. You want to do a quick calculation concerning an attractive discount. Rather than scrambling around the house to locate and dust off the old calc, just turn to Wolfram Alpha and type in "54% off of 36% off of $72" and you'll get the output you're looking for. If Wolfram Alpha needs clarification on your word problem, it'll ask.

II. You want to see your city numerically. Wolfram Alpha makes it possible. Type "New York City" and the tool surfaces quantitative information about the locale like population (8.175 million people), current weather (39 degrees Fahrenheit), median home price ($450,000), nearest waterfall (Roaring Brook Falls is 77 miles Northeast of the city), and much more.

WHY IS IT COOL?

See the world through Einstein's eyes.

SMOOTH SAILING

+ Wolfram Alpha makes math amusing and accessible. Happen to forget how far our moon is from Earth? Just ask!

+ Wolfram Alpha is now integrated with Siri on the iPhone 4S. It's also licensed by various search engines.

CHOPPY WATERS

- Sometimes there's data missing. Urgh.
- Google can do a lot of these basic calculations too.

GOT GOOSEBUMPS?

Do a few searches with Wolfram Alpha. You'll be shocked to see some really neat results. If you're inspired by Wolfram Alpha's mission to quantify the world, you can apply to become a volunteer curator.

Chapter 32: CourseHorse

WHO SAYS OLD dogs can't learn new tricks? Americans of all ages are going back to school in ever-increasing numbers. The National Center for Education Statistics finds that from 2000 to 2009, college enrollment of students aged 25 and over increased 43%, while their under 25-year-old peers-to-be grew only 27%. This makes the case for lifelong learning. Whether you're wanting to pick up or perfect your chops in Cooking, Accounting, or French, the doors of higher education are open.

LET'S BREAK THE ICE

CourseHorse is an online database of courses, searchable by age group, price, location and topic.

BACKSTORY

CourseHorse's founders met at New York University as undergraduate students. After graduation, and seeing an opportunity for a local education platform, they decided to start CourseHorse. "Once you graduate from school, there's no more structured learning," co-founder Nihal Parthasarathi says. "Even people who actively seek it out have trouble finding classes."

HOW DOES IT WORK?

Type in a few topics that interest you at the CourseHorse website, as well as the days and times in the week that you're available. CourseHorse displays all the nearby classes meeting your criteria. You can further filter these results by age group, price, materials required or other parameters. Enroll for the class right through CourseHorse, or sign up to receive alerts about the class (it's filling up!) if you're still undecided.

Get ready to recycle the stacks of continuing ed magazines from all your local community colleges, because CourseHorse is digitizing this content. The result is easier and greener for you and fellow pupils.

The business team at CourseHorse is core to building the marketplace. "Our business is tech-enabled, but it's not a technology business," Parthasarathi says. "Our technology system is a great way to organize a lot of information, but it's not a new technology."

Their value proposition is so strong that schools pay a 15% to 20% commission each time a new student enrolls through CourseHorse—not a shabby margin!

WHY IS IT COOL?

As Henry Ford said, "Anyone who stops learning is old, whether at twenty or eighty." Being in-the-know is always hip.

LET'S SAY...

You're looking for a yoga class. Unfortunately, you have a really busy schedule (who doesn't?) and lament the fact that you'll need to pore over hundreds of Google listings and dozens of yoga studio websites to find the perfect class. Fortunately, you've heard about CourseHorse from *The Coolest Startups in America*. With just one search you'll have a zen time narrowing down to the ideal yoga course.

SMOOTH SAILING

+ CourseHorse is pioneering a centralized space online for "personal interest" education. CourseHorse has thousands of classes listed.

+ Parthasarathi and his co-founder Katie Kapler won New York University's Stern School of Business competition in 2011, beating out over 200 other startup ideas and depositing a cool $75,000 into their bank account in exchange for no equity.

CHOPPY WATERS

- CourseHorse is only available in NYC at the moment. I hope they'll be expanding their regions of coverage soon. "We want to stay focused on the thousands of classes here in New York City. Once we figure out the right levers, we'll build it to scale and can launch in new cities," says Parthasarathi.

- CourseHorse opted not to take venture capital funding; I wish they had in order to fund quicker expansion across the US.

- Skillshare (Chapter 33) is a tangential and successful competitor, cutting into CourseHorse's market. Parthasarathi calls Skillshare a "pseudo-competitor. They're in the P2P space [Peer-to-Peer] and we're in the B2C [Business-to-Consumer] space." It's an important distinction. "Our thoughts are that it's not quite true everyone can be a great teacher. Everyone has something to learn and established schools have proven that they provide high quality education."

GOT GOOSEBUMPS?

If you live in New York City, see if any classes from CourseHorse interest you. If you want to sign up for a class but don't live in the Big Apple, write to CourseHorse about expanding to where you live—they may listen if you plead.

DEFROST: On Competition

Startup founders are fiercely competitive. They may be gracious, but under the surface they're constantly reviewing the competitive landscape to help inform business maneuverings.

Competitive analysis begins far before launching a company. Ed O'Boyle, founder of Fotobridge, a startup that helps consumers digitize and preserve photographs, says that he followed the market for research and product development purposes in the months (and years) prior to customer acquisition. He even sent orders to different services to learn about turnaround times and ease of use. Although Fotobridge didn't reverse engineer competitors' services, they were able to spot opportunities for differentiation.

Competitive analysis is crucial to startups for pricing strategies, too. "When we think about changing prices we go to the competition to see if their prices move and in which directions," O'Boyle says. "It's important to understand the landscape because your customers are looking at your competitors too."

While they're in the game to win, startups tend to view competition as a good thing, mainly because a robust competitive environment is indicative of money to be made in the space. Competitors can even bring promotional value.

Founder of Producteev (Chapter 49) Ilan Abehassera says that "sometimes our competitors attack or tease us, but I get excited when I see new competitors because every time anyone talks about the industry, we show up."

O'Boyle agrees that competitors can shine light on the industry as a whole, which means startups can "not only get a bigger slice of the existing pie, but get a slice of a bigger pie, too." Becoming part of industry organizations can help. In line with the "keep your friends close and your enemies closer" adage, industry organizations can bring companies together to grow the group's success collectively, providing links to potential partners to boot. On the long term, since all industries eventually mature and consolidate, getting to know the competition can help a startup scout out merger or acquisition exit opportunities.

Remember that no matter what a founder says, all startups have competition. It's common knowledge in the startup space to avoid any firm claiming it doesn't have any. That's because competition doesn't necessarily mean a direct copy-cat company. Competition is *any* replacement for or overlap in the startup's product or service. For instance, a startup working on online appointment booking doesn't count only fellow technology startups as competition, but pen-and-paper appointment books as well.

Acknowledging that competition is a fact can help startups stay on the cutting edge, pushing them to adopt unique approaches. Sometimes that drive to be different can generate immensely innovative firms. Scott Summit of Bespoke Innovations (Chapter 65), the upstart that creates custom prosthetics, follows the Blue Ocean Strategy. "Either compete head-on in an area where all the sharks are eating each other, or create your own ocean," Summit explains. "If you invent your own category, you define the conditions and metrics of success, and it's hard for anyone else to compete."

EXPERTISE IS WIDESPREAD. That may sound like a paradox if you think expertise lies only with "experts," but think of how much you know and could share with others. Whether it's how to get over a fear of presenting in front of an audience or how to skin a squirrel, anyone can teach a skill they know, regardless of credential status.

LET'S BREAK THE ICE
People share skills with others, and make money for it.

BACKSTORY
Michael Karnjanaprakorn has a history in the startup space prior to founding Skillshare. He worked at Behance, a company that creates content and products for people in creative careers like design or art, and led the Product team at a startup called Hot Potato, acquired by Facebook. From where did his passion for education innovation come?

"My interests in education stem from my personal journey. I went to college and then to graduate school. I felt like my undergraduate degree was worthless, even though it was from a prestigious school. I had the polar opposite experience in grad school, where they taught shattering the status quo, working in groups, and other skills I honed to shape how I work and think today. Skillshare wouldn't exist without that."

The experience hinted to Karnjanaprakorn that education needn't be synonymous with college. "Education has been around since the beginning of time," he says. "Education is something in which everyone on this planet participates." Skillshare was conceived with this ideas in mind, along with inspiration from a TED talk in which Sir King Robinson challenged viewers to change education with the Internet. "That was the 'ah ha' moment for me," he says. "I decided to take my passion for education and everything I've learned from startups and put it into Skillshare."

HOW DOES IT WORK?
You can browse lessons on Skillshare.com and sign up for someone's class. Teachers can choose their class titles, topics,

ticket fees and location. The caveat is that all classes are offline. Skillshare is about connecting with people in your community. Classes range from "Blind Food Tasting" to "LinkedIn 101" and much more besides.

"Skillshare is not part of the traditional academic world," explains Jeremy Johnson, founder and Chief Marketing Officer of education startup 2tor, which helps top-notch universities develop online degree programs. Typically, education ventures are separated into K-12 learning and higher education. Skillshare doesn't fit either of those buckets. Instead, it shapes a new and growing category. "Expanding the concept of education to include teaching without academia is a healthy thing," Johnson says. CourseHorse (Chapter 32) and Khan Academy (Chapter 30) play a part in this new classification. As do other startups, like UnCollege which publicizes its aim to "challenge the notion that college is the only path to success."

Skillshare's product is impeccable. The website is easy to use and fulfills its mission of getting people *offline* to learn. Josh Abdulla, founder of LetGive (Chapter 43), says "Skillshare is brilliant because it gives people the ability to make money by teaching and gives the students the ability to find out how to do things. It's incredibly simple to use. The simplest ideas are sometimes the hardest to execute, and Skillshare is seamless."

WHY IS IT COOL?
Skillshare democratizes learning and teaching.

LET'S SAY...
You realize you're extremely talented at applying makeup, and notice a bunch of people really need help with that daily skill. You can sign up for Skillshare to teach a class on makeup application. You promote it to your friends across social networks, and Skillshare helps out by featuring your course on its homepage. A bunch of people sign up, and now there are a handful of more well-put-together people in your community.

SMOOTH SAILING
+ Skillshare has gotten a lot of buzz. Karnjanaprakorn is now a TED fellow too, so he'll be invited to share more about

his work and ideas at the next annual flagship TED conference.

+ Lots of people are making money with Skillshare. Alex Taub of Aviary (Chapter 61) teaches classes on Business Development using the Skillshare service. "By teaching business development, I'm making $1,000 a month [charging about $25 per person per class] and it contributes to my personal brand. I know people who are unemployed who use it to make ends meet. Skillshare is going to change the world in the most positive ways."

CHOPPY WATERS

- I know Skillshare is all about connecting offline, but I'm bummed that it does so exclusively. Skillshare could build up online functionality to compete with Khan Academy's preliminary offering and beat webcasting companies for market share. "I don't think we'll ever do full online learning," Karnjanaprakorn tells me. "We may do a hybrid, but the computer is a distraction box. A lot of magical things happen in the classroom when people meet about shared interests. It's something you can't do online. For example, Stanford University live streams classes and a lot of people watch, but people still go to Stanford and show up for four years. We focus on the campus model."

GOT GOOSEBUMPS?

Check out the courses your peers are offering at Skillshare. com. Or if you're a genius in a topic, sign up to teach the rest of us about it.

Chapter 34: Grovo

THE INTERNET NATION surpassed a population of 2 billion people in 2011. While many newcomers are comfortable clicking around until they figure out the lay of the online land, others need a tour guide.

LET'S BREAK THE ICE

Grovo teaches people on the Internet about the Internet.

BACKSTORY

After working for several successful startups as an early employee, Grovo CEO Jeff Fernandez realized that there wasn't a place for Internet education. He was constantly asked about tips and tricks for the web and became (understandably) tired of being asked how to utilize Evernote or Twitter. Fernandez and his co-founders did some research and saw a void in the marketplace. "The quality of education on the Internet *for* the Internet was quite low. Coverage was spotty because no one was focused on it," he says. The stats were clear. According to Fernandez, one in four people worldwide has access to the Internet, but 650,000 new people gain access each day, and 30,000 of these newcomers are in the US.

HOW DOES IT WORK?

Unlike run-of-the-mill online tutorials, Grovo focuses on superb content to teach Internet users about different websites. The content includes introductory material for people who may be logging on to Twitter or Gmail for the first time, or advanced lessons for people who want to do a deep dive into the complex features of foursquare (Chapter 37) or Pinterest, for instance. Grovo has produced over one thousand two-minute instructional videos with glossaries, notes and lessons rolling up into full courses. All of the videos are made in-house; Grovo employs writers and video producers, and content is churned out under a proprietary system that makes the video creation process smooth and speedy.

The value they bring is immense. "[Entrepreneurs] live in the world of the technophile, but the vast majority of the world doesn't. Most people aren't checking in on foursquare or using

Mint to manage their finances. Now when my friends email me asking questions, I can send them a link to the lesson on Grovo." And the lessons themselves are held to a golden standard in regard to quantity, quality and diversity. "We have a vision for what we're building and we're tremendous executors. We're constantly improving and perfecting."

LET'S SAY...

I. You're a grandparent who just got an iPad for the holidays. Now you need to learn how to use it, without nagging your kids for help all the time. You get an account on Grovo and can study all about the iDevice at your own pace.

II. You're a new employee tasked with being your company's social media guru. Trouble is that you only use Facebook socially and don't know a thing about using it for business. You get on Grovo and find a whole bunch of courses about corporate Facebook use. Now you'll be able to help your firm friend away the professional way.

WHY IS IT COOL?

Grovo gets you in the groove of the Internet.

SMOOTH SAILING

+ Every level of Web expertise is addressed. "We cover newbies and technophiles," says Fernandez. Videos on Grovo may be as broad, or as specific—like setting a vacation responder in Gmail—as users need. Hence Grovo's diverse user base, Fernandez says, including tech lovers who want to stay up on sites they use.

+ Grovo is starting to add corporate clients who pay for Grovo so that employees can use it for training, especially when companies transition to new programs. "Many organizations are moving from enterprise to consumer products like Dropbox or Google Apps. They want their employees to know these technologies better so they use Grovo," Fernandez says.

+ Grovo remains completely agnostic. "We aim to educate about products and what they're good for," Fernandez says. "We're techies so of course we like certain products, but we do our best to let you know if there's anything to look out for or to avoid."

CHOPPY WATERS

- There are competitors, like informal YouTube compilations or Linda.com. I love the layout and urgency of Grovo best though.

GOT GOOSEBUMPS?

Do a lesson for free on Grovo. If you can't find the website you'd like to learn about, it's easy to send Grovo a request to create a new video about it.

DEFROST: What Does an Investor Do?

Investments are critical in the entrepreneur ecosystem. While some founders "bootstrap" by supporting their startups on their own, many entrepreneurs need outside funds to help start up their firms. Investors are the people or firms who give entrepreneurs money to grow startups. But they don't do it as a favor. Investors provide funding in exchange for equity in the company. If the company does well, investors will cash out alongside the entrepreneurs.

There's great variability in the types of investors out there. Angel investors are typically one-person shops that put up a few thousand dollars to support an early-stage entrepreneur. On the other end of the scale, venture capitalists might contribute millions of dollars to promising companies. Often, investors of different sizes and firms can work together to "do a deal." For example, one startup seeking $1 million may get $500,000 from a small venture capital firm, with the rest coming from a handful of "angels."

Funding needn't happen just once either. Startups can get new "injections of capital" if they need more cash to progress to higher levels of value. A capital injection, or new "round," might fund an important geographic expansion or new product development.

"When you take someone else's money, everything gets more real," says Ilya Sukhar of Parse. Parse first received funding from a startup incubator, Y Combinator, and then received more from venture capitalists. "We feel a responsibility to keep our investors up-to-date [about Parse's progress] and to make them a lot of money."

The process to get investors isn't easy, says Liron Shapira of Quixey (Chapter 50). "You hear that getting investment is hard and that's totally true." One of Quixey's investors is former Google CEO Eric Schmidt's personal fund Innovation Endeavors. The preliminary connection to Innovation Endeavors happened serendipitously. Quixey happened to move into an empty room in a building at which the Managing Director of Innovation Endeavors had an office. A year and a half later, the connection led to an investment.

When the investment happens, it can be a huge sigh of relief for founders, and a quick moment to celebrate. "For the first year, I was living off my savings," Shapira recounts. "Tomer [Kagan, Quixey's CEO] was living off of nothing. The salary thing is convenient." I badgered him about what it was like to meet Eric Schmidt. "We don't see him often," Shapira says. "But we met him. He likes our business and [Innovation Endeavors] invested more in us. We had a party at the Innovation Endeavors HQ and it was a classy event with everyone involved. At the party was when we looked like a grown-up successful company. I'm glad I put up $5,000 at the start."

Getting funded doesn't end the hard work. Sukhar says, "It takes some risk out of the equation because we can buy ourselves an office and food, and hire people." But it doesn't reduce the uncertainty inherent with startups. "Funding is just a fraction of what you need to be successful, and in some cases it increases fear because it's not just wasting time that's on the line, but also losing someone else's money. Funding compounds the scope of what you're working on."

When investors join, they can greatly impact the course of the product; legally, founders' share of the startup is reduced, while investors are now part-owners with a say in the project's direction. Sometimes that goes for better. For example, the Silicon Valley spirit has now drifted south to Hollywood where celebrities are investing in startups more and more. Ashton Kutcher is a poster child for celebrity tech investing. Sukhar (whose former startup Etacts had Kutcher as an investor) says "It's cool. In the case of Etacts as a consumer product, having someone like Kutcher tweet about it is huge. Celebrities can give startups a lot of horsepower by publicizing them."

Yet investors can also be a big source of tension for founders. Hagi Schwartz of Truequity, a startup making it easier for companies to self-track equity shareholders properly, has not taken VC funding. "Pure bootstrapping isn't easy. There's no replacement for VCs, but when they put money in the company, they want to influence it. VCs care about value creation rather than cash flow. If a VC can find a 4x or 5x return or they reach the end of the life of the fund [the time they have to invest certain buckets of money], they'll rush to sell. Without VCs, you can take your time to build a real company."

At the end of the day, both investors and entrepreneurs hope to see eye to eye and grow the business mutually. The best investors add strategic as well as financial value. Strategic help can include mentorship, a network that can aid with sales and partnerships, and promotional assistance for customer acquisition. Ideally, the investors share the founders' ideologies, says Scott Summit of Bespoke Innovations (Chapter 65). "I'm not driven by the promise of wealth. I'm interested in how can we change the world in tremendous ways. That's shared with our investors. There's a shared ideology to leave the world improved."

Finding the right investor takes time. Some entrepreneurs decide to push forward without. Ed O'Boyle of Fotobridge told me about seeing his competitors raise funding but said, "we didn't have six months doing what I call 'the money hunt'—putting a pitch together, a demo and collateral, and shopping those around to raise money. We wanted to bootstrap it."

Others decide to bootstrap because it makes strategic sense. I was surprised to hear that RightSignature (Chapter 52) was completely self-funded. "It's guided our decision in unique and interesting ways. Without outside flow of money, companies make strategic and careful decisions at each step because they don't have the luxury of an extra $20 million to test and play. Everything has to be proven at small scale for small cost," says CEO Daryl Bernstein who grew his previous company in the same way. "It's an overlooked path. The growth rate may not be the same, but the business has a stronger foundation."

Non-traditional financing opportunities have become a mainstream way to sidestep traditional funding. Kickstarter (Chapter 3) is one example. IndieGoGo,

Profounder and Funding Gates are others. Summit says, "it's never been easier to start a business given that computing power, bank accounts, and business software have gone from expensive to cheap to free."

Paul Murphy of Aviary (Chapter 61), who founded companies in the 2000s, says the caliber of investors seems to have changed over time, for the better. "In the dot-com decade, the bar was somuch lower. People who were investing had no clue. They just wrote checks. Now, most of the top tier investors know what's going on and understand the intricacies. They know how to suss out a team and they focus on it. They focus less on the business model because they know smart people can pivot."

Chapter 35: Codecademy

THERE'S A DEBATE over whether the US has a shortage of engineers. Paul Otellini, CEO of Intel and member of the US President's Council on Jobs and Competitiveness, says that indeed there are too few engineering students graduating each year in America and that it will hurt our innovation edge. Others, like Duke University researcher Vivek Wadhwa, say that because the quality of engineering talent in the US is higher, our competitiveness won't be hurt in any international innovation race.

I'll let the debate rest. From my observations businesspeople looking for technical co-founders are exhausted. It's harder than ever to find engineering talent for projects. If the increase in salaries for engineers in the Silicon Valley is any indication, programming talent is seeing a rise in demand. Why not spend less time searching for a technical co-founder, and more time becoming one?

LET'S BREAK THE ICE

Input: Do I like Code Academy? Output: Yes. It's an awesome startup. Coding is a skill that everyone should begin to know, and Codecademy makes it hands-on easy to learn.

HOW DOES IT WORK?

Codecademy is an online resource for beginners to learn how to program in Javascript, one of the fundamental programming languages used on the web. The co-founders, Zach Sims and Ryan Bubinski, had been developers for several years and wanted to create a tool that would help others learn to code. In fact, they've dubbed 2012 "Code Year" to inspire more people to join their mission. Codecademy's product is accessed online: it's interactive, well-designed and non-threatening for beginners. Students even get badges that they can share with their social networks for progressing through Codecademy's lessons.

The Codecademy headquarters isn't the only place lessons can be designed, as they've opened up the virtual classroom to allow any advanced programmers to create programming courses. This will enable more coding languages to be taught, like Ruby on Rails and Python.

WHY IS IT COOL?
On Codecademy, anyone can become a programming wiz in no time.

SMOOTH SAILING
+ Thousands of people have flocked to learn from Codecademy, and fast. Even New York City's Mayor Michael Bloomberg is a student. The startup is working with the White House to get more adults and kids into coding as well.

CHOPPY WATERS
> "Codecademy".CoolestStartup?
==> Yes, it's 100% cool!

GOT GOOSEBUMPS?
Go to Codecademy and get a feel for the courses. Don't be intimidated! Codecademy walks you through all the steps. If you're enjoying Codecademy, make the pledge to make 2012 your "code year" and get a new lesson each week.

LET'S GET PHYSICAL
Hooking Up in Time and Space startups

ONE IN EVERY six married couples meet online. Usually there's a lot of pomp and circumstance involved: hundred-question surveys and advanced matching algorithms try to replicate what pheromones do in a matter of seconds. HowAboutWe has a different approach. Instead of trying to use characteristics to match people for dates, it just asks them to say what they'd like to do on the date, not just who they'd like to meet. If someone else sees that date as a good time, they can notify the potential match. If sparks fly, great. But it all starts with the fill-in-the-blank "How about we..." go skydiving, have lunch in the park, grab a beer. You name it!

LET'S BREAK THE ICE
HowAboutWe is a unique dating website.

BACKSTORY
Co-CEOs Aaron Schildkrout and Brian Schechter have been best friends since they were six years old. The friend-founders saw a few trends coming together. "The Internet was moving dramatically in the direction of increased authenticity and the merging of online and offline life. It felt like the space where this would have the most profound and meaningful impact was dating. Also, online dating sites were the most ensnared in unnatural tone, banality and 1990s design. We wanted to create a next generation dating site that would revolutionize the way people go online to get offline."

The co-founders decided to launch HowAboutWe in 2010 after a eureka moment. "Let's create a dating site where you actually say the dates you want to go on."

The co-founders came from "non-technology and non-entrepreneurial" backgrounds, Schildkrout says. "This was a new venture. A lot of our founding story was learning how to create a business from the ground." And they've succeeded, says Nihal Parthasarathi of CourseHorse (Chapter 32). "We love HowAboutWe. There's a huge trend in being active and getting out there. HowAboutWe is reinventing the dating space so that it's about shared activities, not just profiles."

At HowAboutWe, the co-founders split the responsibilities

of leading the startup, with Schechter running the marketing organization and Schildkrout running the product division. According to Schildkrout, task completion is faster because the co-CEOs have more bandwidth among more people. What makes the arrangement work well is that the founders have a history of collaboration. "We know how to work together really well," says Schildkrout. "Being a CEO is a wonderful and challenging job, but it can be lonely. To be a co-CEO is a great experience personally and professionally."

HOW DOES IT WORK?

To participate on HowAboutWe, you make a profile of yourself and send out a date idea. Those who fit your overall dating profile can voice their interest if they want to join you for the date. You browse your options and select the person you'd like to invite. If you're a match, great! When you're short on date ideas, don't stray; visit your HowAboutWe account to see the dates others are proposing.

"Chemistry happens offline and in the real world on real dates with real people," says Schildkrout. "Whether you're looking for true love or casual dating, it always starts at the first date. We wanted to make an experience that helps you get offline as fast as possible in a way that's natural with a person who you think you could like. It's through the activity that you decide if you're compatible."

HowAboutWe doesn't go as far as eliminating the stereotypical profile format, Schildkrout says. "Profiles are important and we push people to complete them because you don't want to meet cold. It's not a blind date."

WHY IS IT COOL?

HowAboutWe puts the focus of online dating on the date itself, not just the daters.

LET'S SAY...

You haven't found any matches on Match.com or you're "unable to be matched" on eHarmony. So you try HowAboutWe. You fill out a date idea and see if anyone's interested in joining you. When you post a date idea that you've been lusting for—a helicopter ride over Manhattan—you get a dozen responses, and before you know it, you're over the moon with happiness because your date has turned out to be your soulmate!

SMOOTH SAILING

+ Like a great rom-com, I fell in love with the unique concept for this dating website. It turns the typically awkward experience of online dating into an experience that's fun and breezy.

+ HowAboutWe's distribution is unique. Most dating sites are subscription-based businesses that make you pay to unlock premium features like messaging the cute guy or gal you have your eye on. "The stodgy old dating companies spend huge amounts of money on advertising," Schildkrout says. HowAboutWe didn't feel it wanted or should compete in that way. "We decided that the only way to penetrate the market is to disrupt distribution." They decided to build the technological capacity to white-label and co-brand HowAboutWe. For example, they've partnered with *New York* Magazine and Parenting.com to create branded dating sites. It's HowAboutWe's technology and process, with those communities' dates and daters.

+ "The most gratifying success is when we get emails from people who have met at HowAboutWe and are in love, engaged or getting married, or they're happy in their relationship," Schildkrout says. "It makes the magic of the Internet apparent. These are connections that never would have happened otherwise, and these relationships are deep and true."

CHOPPY WATERS

- Whether good times are to be had is still up to you, your date, and chance... err, Cupid!

GOT GOOSEBUMPS?

Check out some of the date ideas on HowAboutWe. Even if you have a significant other, HowAboutWe may inspire you and your honey bunny for the next date night on your calendar.

DEFROST: Incubation Nation

Many of the Coolest Startups got their starts in incubator or accelerator programs. Incubator programs have become a recent phenomenon in the United States. While incubators vary in structure, the basic premise is as follows: take in a bunch of applications for the incubator, accept the most promising founders, give each team some seed money in exchange for equity, provide a structured program under which to learn and grow, and unveil the startups to the world. It's a win-win for all involved; rather than working in a silo, startups in incubators have access to resources like office space, experienced advisors, investor contacts, a network of alumni, legal services, capital and more. Those funding the incubator are also gaining an advantage. They pay out small amounts of capital to each startup, and end up with a diversified portfolio. If even one or two of the startups take off, they make money back in spades.

One of the most famous incubators—Y Combinator—calls the Silicon Valley home. It was founded by entrepreneur Paul Graham and now has a larger staff and advisory board, accommodating two classes of startups yearly with about 60 to 100 founders a piece. It's abbreviated "YC" by the cool cats around the startup world. RideJoy, an online community for ridesharing, is a YC company. Co-founder Jason Shen says "YC was a huge help to us to refine our idea and stay on track. It gave us a great kick start."

"If you're starting a company there's almost no reason you wouldn't want to do YC if you have the opportunity," he tells me. "Unless you're growing exponentially or have an exit opportunity available, there's so much value." Shen puts the worth of YC into four categories:

1. **Startup education**, like spending time with venture capitalists and serial entrepreneurs, holding "office hours" with mentors like Paul Graham (YC's founder and investor extraordinaire), hearing from incredible speakers like Max Levchin of PayPal or Mark

Zuckerberg of Facebook, participating in panel discussions, and of course...

2. Money. Each startups at YC gets funding to the tune of over $20,000 while giving up only six to seven percent of equity in the firm. In addition, most companies have recently received $150,000 in additional funding from well-known funds off the bat.

3. "Credibility," Shen says. The YC brand itself adds value.

4. Networking. "The YC alumni network is something you can't buy. You instantly have over 100 people who will take your emails. People are super helpful," says Shen. It's a remarkably tight-knit community. I've had several friends at YC who report that everyone keeps in touch via parties, mailing lists, informal meetups and more.

To access all this value, the application process isn't easy. The acceptance rate is around 3%.

Shen gave me a glimpse into the path of a successful applicant. After sending in an application, startups from whom YC would like to hear more are given the opportunity to interview. Interviews last only 10 minutes, and according to Shen, YC decides within five minutes whether it's a yea or nay vote. The renowned incubator calls the startup with the verdict that night. "We were sitting outside and it was getting later and later," says Shen. They had heard that YC calls people who are accepted before those who are rejected, so it worried the team. Around 5 or 6 PM, co-founder Kalvin Wang came out of the house on the phone, and put it on speaker. "'Hey guys, This is Paul Graham. We'd like to offer you a spot in Y Combinator and the terms are ... does that sound good to you?' We thought we would negotiate," Shen told me. "And we all chickened out."

After hanging up the phone, Shen says he had never been more excited about anything in his entire life. Lots of shouting and high-fiving, Shen recalls. "[Co-founder] Randy [Pang] was doing cartwheels to get the energy out!"

Ilya Sukhar of mobile startup Parse also spent time in

YC. "The application process is a bit like applying to college, but it's more interesting," he says. "You have to prove that you're smart, that you get things done, and that you have the right mindset and track record. They evaluate personal characteristics to try to deduce how determined and crafty you are. When they accepted me, they hinted that my startup idea wasn't that great, but they wanted me to be a part of YC and meet other people."

Because founders like Sukhar are green upon entering incubators, there's an understanding that sometimes the startups under which they applied to the program may look wholly different upon graduation. Parse's founders were introduced during YC's program by Graham, and a solid and successful business emerged because of it.

Incubators like YC are important in the US because they can be used to improve the entrepreneur density in a locale, says Greg Meier, the founder of a new incubator in Wisconsin called 94Labs. "Madison, Wisconsin is a behemoth of technology and research, yet we're in the bottom three states for creating startups. The Kauffman Index says that on average in the United States for every 100,000 adults in the state, 0.34% create companies each month. But last year in Wisconsin we were at 0.18%, so we're starting from a low base of economic activity."

A similar philosophy is being applied in Harlem. I skipped across Morningside Park from where I live by Columbia University in New York's Upper West Side to a nice wine bar where IncubateNYC was having its launch party and celebrating a recent vow of support from Google.

"The Web is this generation's steel industry," says IncubateNYC founder Brian Shields. IncubateNYC aims to bring more of those jobs to the Harlem community.

Incubators, a term often used interchangeably with "accelerators," have become more popular in recent years and "have a lot of impact in startup velocity," says Meier. Indeed, incubators move startups rapidly from idea to demo-able firm. At Meier's 94Labs, located on the University of Wisconsin-Milwaukee campus, students get help to transform their ideas into revenue-producing companies. "We have a lot of smart people running around, but we're here to help them organize their ideas and get to a revenue stream," Meier says.

Meier was inspired to create 94Labs by YC. "The model stuck with me," Meier said. "It showed there was an alternative funding process that was lighter on the capital spectrum and that could produce results."

I asked him what he thought about *students* becoming entrepreneurs; some might argue they're too young?

"Most of the people who apply have done pretty interesting stuff by the time they're 18 or 19-years-old," Meier says. "We look at the student's cultural fit in an open and collaborative space, and look at his/her motivational pattern. Are they building something bigger than themselves?"

The open and collaborative environment includes other activities put on by 94Labs, like Hackathons and Business Model-A-Thons, which transition ideas into business templates that can evolve into incubator opportunities. These efforts help to solve against one of the biggest challenges Meier sees today in terms of helping people view "entrepreneur" as a valid professional title. He doesn't believe teaching entrepreneurship in a lecture-format is necessarily the right way to get the word out about the field, and says that activities like Hackathons are better because they enable an engaged process. "Entrepreneurship is a pride profession," Meier says. "It's not something you teach, it's something you do."

Incubators create opportunities for entrepreneurs to engage. In its first year, 94Labs incubated 23 companies and created an estimated 350 full-time jobs. Another famous incubator, TechStars, even got its own reality television show last year on Bloomberg TV, which followed the startups up until Demo Day. There's also excitement about industry-centric incubators, such as RockHealth or Blueprint Health in the healthcare space.

Chapter 37: foursquare

DODGEBALL USED TO be cool. Now foursquare—no, not the playground game we know from grade school—is the game to beat. Millions of people are "playing" on their phones.

LET'S BREAK THE ICE

foursquare (not cool unless you maintain the lowercase spelling) is a mobile phone game application that lets you "check in" to local spots and get points for your loyalty.

HOW DOES IT WORK?

I admit, I don't use foursquare. Certain technologies or apps aren't for everyone. In this case, I find it to be weird to punch in to every restaurant at which I eat. The app allows users to keep their comings and goings private, but something about telling an app where you are and have been feels odd.

That said, foursquare is extremely popular. Users "check in" when at a restaurant (or anywhere, really!). Checking in earns you points and, upon gaining enough points through regular visits, you rise in the rankings, perhaps eventually becoming "mayor" of the place.

Thanks to the business development skills of some stellar members of the foursquare team, members can now breach the virtual realm to collect rewards in the physical one. In one instance, foursquare launched an initiative with American Express to incentivize more consumers to shop local; Amex credited $25 to any shopper who spent the same amount at a nearby small business. The promotion was a great success in publicity and user experience.

foursquare is all about local. You have to physically be at or near the place in order to check in (no cutting corners, as foursquare uses GPS built in to the smartphone to ensure you're not fibbing about your loyalty).

"They clearly are revolutionary. I think they invented the check in. Now, there are check-ins for everything, including TV shows," says Liron Shapira, CTO of Quixey (Chapter 50). It's an engineering accomplishment, too. "The sheer amount of data they're crunching is astonishing," says the CTO of Aviary (Chapter 61) Iz Derdik.

LET'S SAY...

I. You run a popular celeb magazine. You want a fun and engaging way to notify your avid readers of where celebrities were last spotted. Rather than using a Google Map which doesn't quite work for the timeliness of celebrity sightings, you turn to foursquare. Check the celebrities in for them. Maybe the paparazzi can help.

II. You're a regular at the local steakhouse. Start "checking in" via foursquare now, because the house is likely to get on the tech train and start offering deals, discounts and special offers to their most loyal customers. Paper punch cards are so last century.

WHY IS IT COOL?

Anyone can be mayor.

SMOOTH SAILING

+ foursquare experiences incredible user growth driven by social activity. Add friends and colleagues on foursquare and follow them as they hob nob around town, competing for mayorship at your fave local joints.

+ foursquare's founders built a similar product once before; called Dodgeball, this preceding startup was bought by Google in 2005. Google shut down the foursquare-ancestor. foursquare co-founders Dennis Crowley and Naveen Selvadurai mourned the acquisition, but it's all worked out for the better as their new creation has become popular. I always liked four square better anyway; dodgeball was too painful!

+ Developers love foursquare's API. People say that for any geo-related application, foursquare's API is top of the line. CTO of ZocDoc (Chapter 55) Nick Ganju says "they're building an interesting ecosystem upon which new startups like Sonar [Chapter 38] can be built."

CHOPPY WATERS

- Stalker-like feeling.

GOT GOOSEBUMPS?

Get the app. Play the game. If you don't have fun, just hit "uninstall."

DEFROST: Demo Day

The demo, short for "demonstration" of course, is a slightly terrifying yet much revered startup tradition. Like at a science fair, a demo is the presentation in which founders showcase their work. It's often associated with incubator programs' Demo Days, where sometimes hundreds of investors flock to see startup after startup. These spotlit innovators pitch their businesses and show off their products in the hopes of getting funding to grow.

Demo Day is thrilling for startups because it's the moment to impress. It's also a rare opportunity to get in front of so many potential investors at one time. Concurrently, Demo Day is dreaded by startups as a chance that could go squandered (or worse, awry!). Technology can break or get buggy, the founder presenting may contract stage fright, or the pitch itself may simply fail to stir interest.

Nonetheless, "nothing can replace a live demo. When you have a choice to do a Powerpoint versus a live demo, always do the live demo," recommends Leah Busque, founder of TaskRabbit (Chapter 48). "It's riskier because something could go wrong, but showcasing in real-time what your technology is capable of is irreplaceable. We've always incorporated live demos into investor pitches. People get excited to see your technology at play."

Brian Zisk—creator of startup conferences like the Future of Money & Technology and SF MusicTech—says demoing is efficient too. "It's hard to judge a company off a website. Meeting the people or hearing from them is vital to the ecosystem of entrepreneurship these days."

Rather than scheduling meetings with hundreds of people, in a demo the startup can share its product with as many people in a matter of minutes. "It doesn't have to be a theatrical performance, but I don't know anybody who succeeds without demoing in some way." There's also a feedback loop. "Until you're out there, you don't know what people really think," Zisk says. Jim Bruene, founder of Finovate, an industry organization and conference producer for the Financial Services space, reminds that "everyone in the room at Demo Day is a potential buyer, investor, partner or press member who can help spread the word."

Sam Zaid of Getaround (Chaper 21), winner of the demo competition at the TechCrunch Disrupt conference, says demoing is "super intense, in a good way. It brought lots of awareness and was a great launchpad for us." Whatever a startup team's fears or misgivings, a demo is the best way to propel or flop fast.

Zisk's Top 3 Tips for Networking

Most demo opportunities take place at larger events. Here are the Top 3 pieces of advice on how to leave a mark at any networking event.

1. Be a person others want to meet. Don't just jump in thinking solely about your networking goals. Prove that you are there to add to the ecosystem, Zisk advises.

2. Know the roster. Zisk says, "before you go, acquaint yourself with the list of attendees and firms." That will help you to anticipate great connections that can be at the event.

3. Show up, and early. "Remember, if you don't put yourself out there, nothing is going to happen for you!" says Zisk.

Chapter 38: Sonar

NO MATTER HOW affable you are, I'm sure you can relate to times when you just stand around at a bar or conference unsure of who to turn to next. You wish you could effortlessly strike up a chat with the person standing next to you (most likely doing the same, awkward, repetitive email-check motion on his/her phone as you are) or that you had a bird's-eye view of the scene. Surely *someone* around you is game for natural, great conversation—the trouble is who?

Introducing Sonar, a piece of software enabling us information-hungry Americans to lay the virtual social world onto physical space.

LET'S BREAK THE ICE
Meet people nearby.

HOW DOES IT WORK?
Sonar knows your location. It displays the people physically near you with whom you have some degree of connection. The app works by first displaying the people nearby which whom you're already friends on Twitter, Facebook and more. That's useful in itself: grabbing coffee with a friend (on an improvised basis due to proximity) becomes a more common occurrence with Sonar. Beyond that, Sonar shows the people nearby with whom you have mutual friends too. With one click, you can reach out to anyone on the list and send him/her your customized message about wanting to meet.

"It's built on top of foursquare, Facebook and Twitter," says Nick Ganju, CTO of ZocDoc (Chapter 55). "I like Sonar because it's fun. How many times have you been in a bar, starting to talk with someone new and accidentally realizing that you have a mutual friend? Sonar is making that systematic, so it happens anytime."

LET'S SAY...
I. You're at a business conference and you're there to make professional connections. Using Sonar, you see that you have a mutual friend with the CEO of a company you'd like to court.

Send them a message with Sonar and boom, you're foot is in the door.

II. You're at a bar. Rather than staring at your phone awkwardly waiting for someone to strike up a conversation, use Sonar to see who around you might have similar interests or mutual friends.

WHY IS IT COOL?

Sonar is the first mobile app that helps you easily connect with interesting people in your immediate surroundings.

SMOOTH SAILING

+ Sonar puts the "social graph" on the real-time, physical world.

+ Sonar was the runner-up winner at the 2011 TechCrunch Disrupt "startup battlefield" demo competition.

+ Sonar could add customizations (for example, a setting that shows only single people nearby).

CHOPPY WATERS

- Two words: Big Brother.

- Right now you need a foursquare account to sign up or use the application. This limits distribution and could affect Sonar's robustness.

GOT GOOSEBUMPS?

If you have an iPhone 4, install the app and see whether it helps you meet online people in your offline environment.

HEARD FROM A HOT SHOT

"My favorite thing about location-based apps is they encourage us to go outside and explore."

- @AmritRichmond, founder of Magenta Labs

CAN'T WAIT FOR the day I walk by a Starbucks and get a text message saying "get a free cupcake with your latte!" I would backpedal some paces for that deal!

Believe it or not, the technology is now a reality. So why isn't it more prevalent? The marketers in charge are exercising caution; they know that they might have regulatory problems on their hands (and creep people out) if they implement the idea without care. It used to be that deals would be promoted in newspapers, sending penny-pinching moms and dads into coupon-clipping frenzies around the dining table. If it was a good deal, a store could expect to see sales grow appreciably. If it was *too* good, they would possibly run out of inventory.

When you're a service business, these traffic fluctuations are hell. If you have a full house, customers complain about long wait times. If you have too few people, things get stale and you're left strumming your fingers. To avoid either extreme, businesses strive for consistent and predictable customer flow.

LET'S BREAK THE ICE

ThinkNear helps stores smooth out foot traffic by offering targeted, real-time local discounts.

BACKSTORY

ThinkNear's co-founders were working for Amazon.com when they began contemplating the incredible optimization engines that power business decisions at large companies. Why couldn't local merchants enjoy similar help? ThinkNear wanted to offer these sophisticated tools.

Eli Portnoy, one of ThinkNear's founders, knew investors from former startups; it helped jump-start the project. "They gave me a check and said 'Go,'" Portnoy recounts. The co-founders built the prototype and with it applied to the incubator Techstars. Once accepted, they quit Amazon, and within two days were in New York City, fresh to the entrepreneurial life. Portnoy describes it as "by many orders of magnitude the hardest time of my life." He cites countless 18-hour days finally culminating in a successful product that received further funding.

HOW DOES IT WORK?

ThinkNear isn't yet as sleek as its vision. Currently, a business signs up and inputs its typically slower hours manually (so it's not real-time from the business's standpoint). In the future, ThinkNear aims to add more flexibility.

From the customers' perspective, ThinkNear does work in real-time and on location. According to Portnoy, "the big difference" for them between ThinkNear and the Starbucks example from the start of the chapter "is that ThinkNear works with existing mobile apps instead of forcing you to check in or download anything." Hence the absence of "push notifications." Customers simply interact with their smartphone as usual and, if they're near a participating vendor, ThinkNear can showcase an ad approved by the vendor offering 20% off, for example, one item or another.

To do this, ThinkNear works with partners—like companies that build mobile advertising servers—to make the startup work. "We deliver discounts through mobile ad infrastructure. On CNN you'd see an ad for Toyota," Eli explains. "Instead of a big brand ad, with ThinkNear you're looking at local ads on your mobile phone. The merchant is our customer." To sign on merchants, ThinkNear offers a subscription service with a 90-day free trial.

WHY IS IT COOL?

Happy hour isn't confined from 4 PM to 7 PM anymore.

SMOOTH SAILING

+ ThinkNear works with developers to integrate into apps. That's a great way to gain distribution.

+ ThinkNear's ads are well-designed and non-invasive on your mobile screen.

CHOPPY WATERS

- ThinkNear tangentially competes with daily deals sites, of course. Note that there are no daily deal websites in this book—I find them to be quite anti-innovation in their present states. They're just email lists blasting out deals by location. Come on, folks! We can do better in this day and age! It doesn't get much more 1999 than an email list. ThinkNear is 2012 and beyond!

- Marketplace businesses are notoriously difficult to establish. ThinkNear has to bring together merchants *and* passersby to succeed.

- There are challenges with marketing to local businesses. "A lot of them aren't even on email," Portnoy says. It can be tough to communicate with local merchants because of low technology education and language barriers. Thankfully for ThinkNear, "our product sells itself because it so clearly helps them that they do want it," says Portnoy.

GOT GOOSEBUMPS?

If you're a business, get the 90-day free trial.

DEFROST: Going Public

Startups take time, money and effort. Those resources aren't put into companies for nothing. Founders and investors hope their sweat and tears (we hope no blood!) will return big bucks several times over.

When a startup succeeds, there are several ways to get that money back to initial investors: a bigger company could purchase the startup, paying off all the shareholders through a merger or acquisition, or the startup could "go public," in which case the shares are sold to the public at a higher price than what investors initially paid.

What does it mean to "go public?" When any company is founded and incorporated, it is inherently private. Only a few (under 500 in number as required by the Securities and Exchange Commission) individuals or investors own the company. If you want to buy shares, you'd have to find a way to reach out to the company and get them to agree, or you may be able to find a few shares on a "secondary market" like SecondMarket (Chapter 6).

In an ideal scenario, a startup grows and grows until its private shareholders decide to join the big leagues. To raise ever-greater amounts of money, aggregating funds from a ton of smaller investors is virtually the only route. So, the startup goes public. For the first time, its formerly private shares become available for purchase on the public markets, the preserve of anyone with the will (and the wallet) to invest.

IPOs are almost always a cause for celebration at the startup, and means that the startup has left the nest. That's why when you hear about a startup going public or going IPO, people ooh and aah. I don't mind if your jaw doesn't drop, but it's good to know why other people's do.

SUPER HEROES
Social Good startups

ANTOINE DE SAINT-EXUPERY, author of the famous little book *The Little Prince*, once said in his book *Wind, Sand, and Stars* that water was not simply necessary for life, but that water is life itself. While those with the fortune of living in the developed world might just flick open a faucet to get to this essence, many people around the globe struggle to access potable water each day.

LET'S BREAK THE ICE
Mission seemingly impossible: clean water for all.

HOW DOES IT WORK?
Wello produces the WaterWheel, a big yellow wheel with a handle. WaterWheel eases the burden of carrying water long distances. Rather than engaging in the hard labor of transporting water on one's head, the device enables users to carry many gallons of water in a rolling wheel. How do you pay for a device like this when you're already poor and struggling? It turns out that the big yellow wheel is the perfect place to slap on some advertising! And this new contraption is sure to get some eyeballs.

WHY IS IT COOL?
Wello sees a deficiency as an opportunity to do good.

SMOOTH SAILING
+ One Wello wheel holds 25 liters of liquid, five times more than any traditional water carrying method could handle. That's a lot of efficiency gained!

+ Wello contributes to female empowerment. Most people carrying water in the developing world are women; up to 25% of her day may be spent on water transportation leaving little time for education or other labor.

CHOPPY WATERS
- They need to roll (no pun intended) this out faster to more places!

- The Hippo Water Roller is a similar device distributed in

Africa, though it does retail at a higher price.

- Because margins are thin, Wello's founder Cynthia Koenig has said that they're aiming for profitability through scale. If people share WaterWheels (the device is said to be quite durable), it may stunt growth projections.

GOT GOOSEBUMPS?

Donate or volunteer to Wello. Water is in all of our veins; it unites us, so have some humanity and donate gosh darn it.

HEARD FROM A HOT SHOT

"World-changer of the day"

– ABC News, @ABCSaveALife

Chapter 41: Blueseed

MOST AMERICANS MAY not realize that getting a visa for the US is hard. International entrepreneurs really want them. Morgan Dierstein, CEO of RentAStudent—a company founded in France but recently relocated to the US—says that this is because those wishing to change the world "need to do it in the US." According to Dierstein, it's in America that companies flourish. "You meet people who have the financial and intellectual resources to make your project something big and global," he says.

LET'S BREAK THE ICE

Blueseed is an incubator that will *float* off the shore of Silicon Valley, so foreign founders can legally participate in the entrepreneurship ecosystem just a boat-ride away.

BACKSTORY

Blueseed came out of a movement called seasteading, the concept of creating permanent communities on international waters with floating cities outside the jurisdictions of any land-based governments. I've followed the movement with intrigue, but have found that it can be surprisingly divisive due to political undercurrents of Libertarianism. Blueseed, on the other hand, should coast across the political spectrum like a sea otter lounging in the sun.

Blueseed is not a movement, but a startup incubator. The incubator will be on a vessel several miles off the coast of the Silicon Valley so that entrepreneurs from around the world can start companies near the important American startup hub. I spoke with Dan Dascalescu, one of Blueseed's founders and a part of the seasteading movement since its early waves, about this cool startup. It may sound nuts or un-American, but hear this concept out.

The need for an incubator like Blueseed stems from our government's policies on immigration for entrepreneurs. It's well known that the US has some of the most beneficial policies for businesses, as well as the educational and capital resources to make businesses prosper. People from around the world wish to come to America to join and found companies, but not all can do so due to immigration rules. These laws may be in place for good reason, but there are certain practices that many in the startup community hope to see shift.

First, there are obstacles in the way of foreign students studying at American universities founding companies after graduation. Currently, foreign students who graduate from American schools are permitted to stay in the US for work at *established* firms, but if they intend to quit and build a startup, they'll be sent home. Dascalescu points to studies showing that 86% of international student graduates report concern over visas; many, faced with the inflexibility of the problem, simply return to their home countries.

Second, current visa rules bar international workers—no matter how innovative—from founding companies. Dascalescu recounts his experiences from when he worked at web giant Yahoo! Inc. "I interfaced with a lot of cultures at Yahoo!. However, when the company began going through a rough patch, I witnessed colleagues from India who had worked at Yahoo! for three years get cut during layoffs and they had 10 days to find another employer or leave the country. If you had a good lawyer, you could stay a month."

10 days. 10 *days* to keep the life you'd led for three years. It is harrowing to think that those people might have built the next Coolest Startup in the States. There is a piece of legislation sponsored by Senators John Kerry (D-Mass.) and Richard Lugar (R-Ind.), The StartUp Visa Act, currently under review by the government to try to fix the situation foreign-born entrepreneurs face. Unfortunately, Dascalescu says, it isn't making much progress, "despite a lot of lobbying by big names in the startup community like Dave McClure and Brad Feld."

If passed, the bill would increase the number of visas allocated to entrepreneurs, currently set at 10,000. Yet even this legislation doesn't go far enough, according to Dascalescu. "There's significant investment that has to be made by a qualified US investor for each visa," he says. And there's uncertainty besides: "It's hard to make legislative changes. Startups can't take this to the bank. What if the visa doesn't pass?"

Producteev's Ilan Abehassera, who moved to the US from France, agrees that change is needed. "America is rejecting some bright people. It doesn't make sense. We all come from somewhere else and if you block everyone to get a visa, those bright people go back to their countries and they're starting businesses there."

The above challenges in mind, Dascalescu and others of entrepreneurial spirit have taken matters into their own hands. Blueseed counts influential supporters too, like PayPal founder Peter Thiel. "Even if people think Blueseed is crazy, it's more secure than waiting for government legislation to pass," Dascalescu says. And location is key. "We want to allow innovators to bring their ideas to where those ideas have the highest chance to thrive. Other countries don't have tolerance for failure or networks for growth. Silicon Valley is conducive for startups to grow."

HOW DOES IT WORK?

"We want to offer a home to entrepreneurs," Dascalescu says. "If you couple seasteading with what it means to be in international waters and reform entrepreneurship, you get Blueseed. It's outside US jurisdiction and we can legally house it there." This broad, heroic mission and their recent spin-out from Seasteading's 501(c)3 non-profit status is what lands them in the Super Heroes section.

Physically, Blueseed will be located on a cruise ship or barge. The team already has a vessel in mind, unfortunately in use by another customer at the moment. The logistics are immense, calling for environmental analysis, retrofitting of the vessel, and legal and immigration filings. Blueseed plans to launch in 2013, and is already accepting applications.

They've received dozens already. Most of the startups and teams are in the software, IT and electronics spaces, Dascalescu says. There have also been applications for cleantech and greentech startups, and others focused on, naturally, marine innovation. There have also been applications submitted by individuals who are interested in participating in the environment on board, such as fitness or entertainment businesses. "There's even an entire incubator in Texas that wants to relocate," Dascalescu says. Startups looking to innovate in health and medical technologies may face a tougher admissions process due to separate legal issues.

"Blueseed will be a permanent Hackathon," Dascalescu describes, complete with daily seminars, workshops and events. Half-hour ferry rides to San Francisco or Palo Alto will depart multiple times a day, allowing the entrepreneurs to transit easily between the ship and land.

"They'll use a business visa which doesn't allow them to work on land, but they can use it to travel to conferences, trainings, events, meetings and recreational activities." The only restriction? "The total number of days spent on land has to be fewer than 180 days."

WHY IS IT COOL?

Foreign founders must go big or go home, quite literally.

SMOOTH SAILING

+ The Seasteading Institute and Blueseed have split amicably so that the former could further its work with community-building and research; Blueseed, meanwhile, pursues investment opportunities.

+ The idea is already spreading globally. There's interest in Japan for a seastead because of similar immigration problems, Dascalescu says.

+ Blueseed publishes a regular newsletter informing readers of developments to immigration policy and The StartUp Visa Act.

+ Blueseed has incredible backers, including Paypal founder Peter Thiel. "Peter Thiel's idea of innovation is that it's been stagnating," Dascalescu says. "Instead of flying cars we have 140 characters [a jab at Twitter's core product]. He's taking measures to promote innovation and has donated $1.5 million to Seasteading [Institute]. Blueseed is a for-profit venture and he's in a position to invest. He wants Blueseed to pick the best foreign entrepreneurs because one may make a breakthrough. He's investing in his dream of promoting innovation."

CHOPPY WATERS

- Blueseed can be polarizing. Dascalescu says "the message is mistaken by the media sometimes. They believe we're going to hire Americans for low wages, but what will happen is that these startups bring with them funding either from foreign VCs or American VCs so, in effect, they hire themselves. They pay us rent." Apparently, some dissidents warn about pirate attacks too. "Pirate activity has taken place around Somalia. If they make it to California, we'll give them a prize!" he laughs.

GOT GOOSEBUMPS?

If you're an international startup interested in coming on board, Blueseed is accepting applications. Apparently, startups around the US have been applying too. "20% of startups that apply to Blueseed are American. They'd like to be on the ship because of the influx of ideas and the awesome environment, in addition to the bragging rights of being on the ship." A lack of visa is not the only motivation; Blueseed will be the highest density incubator space in the world.

NEWS BREAKS FAST, and now disease *out*breaks can be tracked too.

LET'S BREAK THE ICE

HealthMap is an online space for the spreading of news about potentially infectious diseases.

HOW DOES IT WORK?

HealthMap scours thousands of sources of data from Google News to the World Health Organization (WHO), to place real-time information on a specialized, user-friendly and interactive health map. The data is filterable by number of cases, disease types and more.

There are social elements built in to the website, and education on symptoms for hypochondriac visitors. The website is infectious disease-focused, and seeks to inform international travelers, parents and health officials. They even provide a mobile app called "Outbreaks Near Me."

Dr. Fuyuen Yip of the National Center for Disease Control (CDC) and I spoke about government use of social media. She says there's certainly been an increased use of these tools. "The CDC's communications group is active in promoting the CDC and increasing the visibility of the CDC through Facebook and Twitter. It's exciting because social media can make public health more accessible to a larger audience. It is helpful when asked, 'what is public health?' as social media can help to show how broad public health is."

WHY IS IT COOL?

Since the news media is kept busy reporting on celebrity marriages and breakups, no one seems to spend much time on real issues of public health and wellness. With HealthMap, I now know that there's been a Salmonella breakout a few miles away. That's truly gut-wrenching.

SMOOTH SAILING

+ HealthMap was founded by a highly technical team of researchers, epidemiologists and programmers from the

Boston Children's Hospital. It's funded by Google.org among other flagship donors.

+ HealthMap could be used to target advertising products. If there's an outbreak of flu in one locale, ZocDoc (Chapter 55) may want to look into more promotion in that place.

CHOPPY WATERS

- No nausea about this startup! Just remember to eat an apple a day.

GOT GOOSEBUMPS?

Know about a health scare in your area that could affect others? Log it on HealthMap.org.

Chapter 43: Snooze by LetGive

SLEEPING PAST YOUR alarm in the morning is a bad habit. Donating to charity is a good one. LetGive, the startup behind the Snooze mobile app, figured they could offset snoozing with charitable giving.

LET'S BREAK THE ICE

LetGive is a platform that enables developers to embed charitable giving in applications. Snooze is one such app.

BACKSTORY

The co-founders of LetGive met at New York University. They came up with the idea for Snooze, an iPhone app that anyone can install and use in lieu of their typical iPhone alarm clock. Instead of being able to hit "snooze" without repercussion, with the Snooze app, sleeping in means donating 25 cents to the charity of your choice!

In the first 10 days after releasing the app, Snooze had over 2,000 downloads, and was getting featured in every publication imaginable, says Josh Abdulla, one of LetGive's founders. Now, 4,000 people use it regularly, and over $6,000 have been pledged (that's over 24,000 snoozes!). That may not sound like world-saving sums, but Snooze was actually a gateway to a larger idea. "We're not a money-generating tool," Abdulla says. "LetGive is a larger platform."

It's a platform for embedding charitable giving easily within apps, like Snooze did. LetGive took about six months to build its platform, but now any developer with a mobile app can use the code and integrate charitable giving in his/her app in just four hours, Abdulla says. LetGive is not about any one mobile app, it's about making any and all apps charitable.

LetGive has a network of 25 charities, from shelters to non-profit theaters to nature conservation and ecology. "Virtually any cause anyone would care about we have represented in some manner in our network," Abdulla tells me. When LetGive completes its transition from a for-profit firm to a non-profit, its database will increase to over 750,000 non-profits that developers can help their users donate to."

LetGive started out as a for-profit firm, but is now

transitioning to non-profit status in the interest of flexibility. There are two camps in social entrepreneurship, Abdulla details. Non-profits tend to go after foundation money, whereas for-profits implement social entrepreneurship through typical profit-driven business models. LetGive started as a for-profit business because the team thought it would be a more efficient way to run the business. However, being a for-profit resulted in tremendous legal and regulatory burdens for LetGive, hence its transition to 501(c)3 status.

No matter which route founders take, Abdulla is excited about the trend of social entrepreneurship. Abdulla was one of the first graduates of New York University's social entrepreneurship program that launched about a decade ago. "There's a significantly higher amount of entrepreneurs in the space now versus 10 years ago. When I was at NYU studying social entrepreneurship, the classroom was empty. Now it's almost impossible to get a seat," Abdulla says. "Social entrepreneurship is one of the most requested programs from an MBA school. There's more talent joining the space."

WHY IS IT COOL?

Americans are extremely generous people. According to Abdulla, the market for giving is huge: over $300 billion were donated in 2010, $230 billion of which came from individual donations. Beyond this existing market, Abdulla and his co-founders see an opportunity to bring charity into the lives of digital natives. "Right now, only 8% of donations happen online, but it's growing year-over-year."

HOW DOES IT WORK?

Abdulla describes LetGive as a platform. "Our premise is that anybody who wants to include charitable giving in a website or mobile app should be able to do that. The developer shouldn't have to do anything more than embed 10 lines of code and choose which charities donations will go to."

This is far from trivial work. Apple's Terms of Service have made it hard for charitable giving to be included in apps, Abdulla says. For example, after its success with the Snooze app, LetGive tried embedding a similar charitable element into a memorization game application. In the game, players are given one life, and if they "die," they donate. Apple rejected it. It's not that Apple is against charity, Abdulla explains, it's just that Apple charges developers to list in the App Store, so likely doesn't want to be viewed as making money off of charity-based apps. Hence the ban. LetGive was able to release its game on Android (Google's mobile operating system, for which LetGive also has a software development kit, or SDK). As for Apple, LetGive discovered a workaround: if the donation opens a separate browser window, it gains legitimacy.

Now that LetGive's technology is open to developers, it's actively pursuing deeper relationships with non-profits. LetGive is great for both charities and developers. The latter see embedding charitable giving—in addition to being a force of good—as a great promotional opportunity for the app. According to Abdulla, there are nearly 500,000 apps added to app stores every year, so it's difficult for developers' apps to get discovered. Including charitable giving through LetGive allows them to tap into millions of Facebook and Twitter followers, as well as to email subscribers of the non-profits in LetGive's network. As for charities, integration with gaming and other apps naturally brings in greater funds.

Some companies decide to integrate charitable giving by themselves. Zynga and Eventbrite have done so. But this is made tough by regulatory issues; funds for non-profits must be handled properly lest companies be hit with tax and state registration problems. LetGive bypasses the hassle because it's an API on top of an API from Firstgiving, also a non-profit. "We make it easier for developers," Abdulla says. "We've done all regulatory filings. If a developer wanted to integrate with FirstGiving directly it would take months, not just four hours."

LET'S SAY...

I. You're a new iPhone application developer who wants a fun hands-on project that will help a local charity. You devise a great concept for an app, but aren't sure how to effectively get the money to the charity of your choice. You sign up with LetGive and all of the hurdles are cleared for you already. It's easier than ever for you—and your users—to give back!

II. You're the head of a charity looking to get tech-savvy. You'd love to bring in more donations from web and mobile users, but aren't sure how to get started. Building a mobile or website application would be costly and time-consuming. You sign up for LetGive, and the track is already placed—the developers come right to you!

SMOOTH SAILING
+ The case hardly needs making. LetGive's mission of helping developers and enabling charitable donations is noble.

+ Although LetGive wasn't able to commercialize its business for profit, it's impressive that the team is soldiering on down the non-profit route.

CHOPPY WATERS
- Alex Budak, the founder of Start Some Good (a startup that works with social entrepreneurs) says that dealing with legislation is difficult. "There are barriers to doing good in the world," namely in the form of expensive and time-consuming government paperwork to become a non-profit. Budak says that's why he encourages social entrepreneurs to go the for-profit route. "People used to question revenue-generation for social good ventures, but there's growing acceptance in the social impact space that capitalism isn't a dirty word," he says. It's what LetGive aimed to pursue, until confronted by other regulations making it onerous to transfer funds to non-profit firms without similar tax-exempt status. But now that LetGive is going through the process of converting to a 501(c)3, other developers' loads should lighten. "We'll take care of all the paperwork. Just sign on the dotted line," says Abdulla.

GOT GOOSEBUMPS?
Have you been sleeping in a bit too much lately? Get the Snooze app, and donate some change for those extra Zzz's.

DEFROST: Burn, Baby, Burn Rate

Cash flows in. Cash flows out. That's the nature of running a business. Running a "sustainable" business means that more cash is coming into the coffers than is running out. Yet since they're spending to invest in infrastructure, technology or business systems, young startups may incur high negative cash flows. Their products and services that will eventually generate funds are still in gestation.

Negative cash flow also goes by "burn rate," in startuptopia terminology. Founders of startups are always keeping in mind their burn rates, an important metric reviewed to gauge founders' activities and to determine when more money may need to be raised.

The best practice in the startup world is to keep burn rates as low as possible; the less money spent in the pre-revenue phase, the better. If costs are kept low, it can benefit the startup with more "runway." The proverbial runway is the amount of funding available to the startup for its initial efforts.

There are ideas and methods to minimize burn rate and keep the runway strong, but one size doesn't fit all. It behooves any startup to identify what strategies are right for them, while bearing the standing truth in mind that in business it is by keeping outflows lower than inflows that one proceeds on the route to success.

Chapter 44: Catchafire

SINCE TIME IS money, it would be great for non-profits to get pledges of people's volunteering time, not just monetary donations. That's the idea behind this Coolest Startup.

LET'S BREAK THE ICE

Catchafire connects non-profit organizations to people who can volunteer their skills to benefit charities.

HOW DOES IT WORK?

Catchafire itself is not a non-profit. It's a successful social venture making the volunteer "marketplace" more efficient. Specifically, Catchafire connects professionals—think lawyers, marketers, and more—to organizations that could really use the pro help. For the service, Catchafire charges a membership fee to those organizations looking to gain volunteers.

Catchafire has a database of thousands of non-profits working all around the US. Some of these non-profits decide to list a project on Catchafire. For example, they may need help with a logo or legal advice. Outside of Catchafire, these services may be extremely expensive, and non-profits don't want to use their funds for this type of work when they could get a volunteer to help out. Catchafire makes it easier than ever to get the work done by volunteers.

Anyone can create an account on Catchafire as a volunteer, and indicate the types of non-profits they'd like to work with and the types of skills they can contribute. Professionals can choose from a range of competences including branding work, sales or business development, technology and more. When a project created by one of the participating non-profits opens up, volunteers are emailed based on their preferences. If interested, volunteers complete a short application. If selected, there's a two-week grace period whereby either side can bow out if the match isn't quite right. If it is a match, most projects take between one to three months with about 10 volunteer hours contributed each week.

BACKSTORY

Catchafire's founder Rachael Chong felt the need for a

service like Catchafire during her investment banking days after college. The only volunteering jobs she could find involved manual labor; she felt that for her personally there might be other ways she could contribute at higher impact. Looking for volunteer opportunities, she realized it was difficult for willing professionals to find projects. After helping to scale a non-profit called BRAC several years later, she hit upon a model that worked. She was able to turn to friends and colleagues to help on many projects for BRAC, freeing her time to raise funding for the organization. Several millions of funding dollars later, Chong knew she had a viable model, and built Catchafire to expand the process to all non-profits.

WHY IS IT COOL?

It's a great way for professionals to give back, especially if they'd like to contribute without taking out their wallets. Participating non-profits save time on scouting for volunteers or money required to complete tasks, staying all the stronger to focus on their core missions of helping others.

LET'S SAY...

I. You're a new retiree, just off the job which you've had for 18 years as an editor. You're not able to part with what limited funds you have for retirement each month, but you'd love to give back. You can't do manual work because of a bad back. You discover Catchafire, sign up, and indicate your interest and ability for writing and editing work. Before you know it, you're helping a local group polish up its prose.

II. You're the founder of a new organization helping young kids with learning disabilities, *pro bono*. Like any startup, you have a to-do list a mile long! While you have some supporters, funds are limited. You'd like to have a website created, some photographs taken of your group and the students, and ensure that your contracts and waivers are in order. You join Catchafire and create projects for each of these items. Soon enough, you're working with an established web designer, photographer, and lawyer to get your non-profit up and running! Now you can spend more of your time helping the kids.

SMOOTH SAILING

+ Catchafire uses a process geared toward professionals.

Each project is reviewed by Catchafire's team, and the matching is facilitated in an informed manner. The grace period is also an exemplary part of a thorough process.

+ Most of the projects on Catchafire are meant for the individual volunteer, but corporate project opportunities can be created too, empowering whole companies to give back.

CHOPPY WATERS

- Some early-stage non-profits may have a hard time taking the leap to pay Catchafire. Pricing for each membership is several hundred dollars—great for established non-profits, but hard for smaller groups really in need of service.

GOT GOOSEBUMPS?

If you're a professional who can make a difference, sign up! There's no commitment and Catchafire doesn't bombard you with emails. It's an easy way to give back, without any sweat on your brow.

LEAN MACHINES
Lightening the Day's Toil
startups

Chapter 45: Tout

EMAIL, ONCE BORN, was slow to evolve. It's an *incognito* communication tool, unlike the more public ones of today's Facebook and Twitter. We never know who actually reads our sent mail unless we get a reply, and that opacity can be brutal when cold emailing (the email version of cold calling).

LET'S BREAK THE ICE

Tout gives you analytics on your emails.

HOW DOES IT WORK?

After you sign up for Tout, you hook up your regular email address directly to your Tout account in a few easy steps. As you send emails through Tout's system, they'll appear to be sent through your email address; in actuality, they're running through Tout's system, which is then able to track and analyze the recipient's behavior.

It helps inform you on how best to craft an email. If people aren't opening your emails, maybe your subject line could use improvement. If people are opening them but not replying, maybe it's your request that isn't sinking in right. Whatever the case may be, Tout can help troubleshoot. You can even add a variety of email templates, trying out differing salutations and messages to see which earn you the highest rates of reply.

WHY IS IT COOL?

Know who *isn't* reading your mail.

LET'S SAY...

You'd like a new job. You've gone to networking events and scoured LinkedIn, and now have a list of over 30 contacts to email. You want to ensure that your message is spot on; instead of emailing cold, you sign up for Tout and get smart about your communiques. Tout helps you replicate the strategies of marketing companies to optimize your own emails. Every email sent is a new insight gained on which of your templates resonate. As your emails improve over time, you'll be sure to land a dream job. Sometimes, a bit of email intel goes a long way. No more wondering... Did they get my email? Should I send it again? Or, did they think my subject line of 'Howdy Partner" was a bit much?

SMOOTH SAILING

+ Information is power. Email is ubiquitous. Even some luddites have it. It's a powerful communication mode and Tout helps us know whether (and why!) our e-writing is working.

CHOPPY WATERS

- Analytics could become integrated in every email service provider (like Gmail, Yahoo! Mail and more), which would hurt an external party like Tout.

GOT GOOSEBUMPS?

If you're networking for a job or to gain funding, working in sales, or are generally nosy, sign up at www.ToutApp.com.

Chapter 46: AskSunday

PERSONAL ASSISTANTS AREN'T only for the devils in Prada anymore. We can all have our own! The power to boss around your own underling is made possible by labor price arbitrage. People all around the world are gaining connection via the Internet—Skype is one strong instance of this trend—and this enables a new class of work to be moved overseas.

LET'S BREAK THE ICE

AskSunday connects people with *virtual* personal assistants, or VPAs. Virtual as in not hanging around the water cooler in the flesh.

HOW DOES IT WORK?

AskSunday enables you to sign up for a personal assistant. You pay a monthly subscription fee for a set amount of hours each month, or opt to pay hourly. Assign any task to your VPA, from data entry to research to appointment-scheduling. Your assistant is your assistant, and while they do work on other accounts in addition to yours, they really get to know you quite well. They might call you to make sure the project is delivered to your specifications, but otherwise, they're independent and capable. They're also super friendly and actually help you get more work done by striking out the dry items from your to-do list.

WHY IS IT COOL?

I am a 23-year-old entrepreneur and I have a personal assistant. I don't mean to brag—you can have one too!

LET'S SAY...

You're the author of a book about startups, and need the headquarter location, founding year and amount of funding raised for each startup in your book—truly the stuff of an awesome Appendix. Rather than looking it up one-by-one yourself, which would take hours better spent interviewing CEOs or completing the manuscript, you delegate the task to your VPA on AskSunday. Bam! Overnight, it's all there in a neat Excel spreadsheet, worthy of publication in a book benefitting readers all across America.

SMOOTH SAILING

+ AskSunday is a win-win. Hired VPAs land an enviable job in their home country: it's well-paid and more intellectually stimulating than many other lines of work. Those hiring get more done at a great price.

+ The AskSunday system is built for personal assistance. Time spent is measured and billed in five-minute increments. The system also securely stores relevant passwords for the VPA's work, and facilitates a high degree of trust between the service and its users.

CHOPPY WATERS

- AskSunday isn't without competitors. Among others, Elance, Odesk, or Zirtual can connect people with personal assistance too.

- AskSunday makes you feel bad for scaling back your usage. As I wrapped up writing this book, I simply didn't need personal assistance as much since I wasn't using all of my hours. They hounded me for a week after I unsubscribed. I mean, I know I'm a cool boss, but sheesh, let me be!

GOT GOOSEBUMPS?

Get a virtual personal assistant for yourself or an overworked friend today.

DEFROST: On Optimization

The world is getting digitized and optimized, and the two contribute to one another. Digitization may be obvious, but what's that other one? Optimization is the ever more efficient use of a given and finite set of resources. When things go digital, the data is easier to track, aggregate, manipulate, and... optimize. With digital information, patterns helpful for people and systems to make better decisions can emerge.

For example, technologists optimize online sales webpages to convert more people into buyers. Marketers optimize emails to uncover how to get more people to read what they write. We're even optimizing ourselves! More and more people are joining Quantified Self initiatives through products and services like FitBit (Chapter 54) or Tout (Chapter 45).

Optimization, whether for personal or business use, begins with tracking. Aaron Schildkrout of HowAboutWe (Chapter 36), a hyper metrics-driven organization, says they track the number of new users, total subscribers, dates posted, messages sent, subscription conversion rates, revenues, and hundreds of smaller sub-metrics.

"We want to see clear, month-over-month improvements in the core metrics we focus on, often on the order of 100% month-over-month improvements," Schildkrout says. "It's a reflection of our deep focus on metrics and on the idea that you move the needle when you measure the needle. If you don't measure behavior, it doesn't change."

Chapter 47: Boomerang
by Baydin

EMAIL-LAND IS EASY to get lost in. When your inbox is full to the brim, it can be hard to remember who has gotten back to you and whether it's the right time to follow up.

LET'S BREAK THE ICE

Boomerang brings your email back to you.

HOW DOES IT WORK?

Boomerang is a plug-in for Gmail that creates a secondary inbox and outbox within your account. Instead of sending your email immediately after you press "Send," Boomerang will do so at the time you designate. This has powerful implications for your email usage. You may also decide that you'd simply like to get to a given email at another time; just "boomerang" it for a later date using the product.

Each month, Boomerang users get 10 credits for email sends. Beyond that, users must pay a subscription fee to the service. Thankfully, unlimited usage begins at just $4.99 per month.

WHY IS IT COOL?

Don't just *receive* emails anytime. *Send* them anytime too—even in your sleep.

LET'S SAY...

I. You're a night owl. You happen to be super productive in cranking out emails past midnight. Yet you want to be a smart employee, and seek to avoid giving bosses and peers the impression that you're accessible around the clock. Work-life balance is precious, after all. You install Boomerang, write your emails under the moon per usual but set them to a 7 AM send-off. Now you come off as a morning person, even if you're actually planning on breakfast at noon.

II. You're the opposite: an overachiever who wants to seem accessible 24/7. Startup CEOs might relate to this one. Well, write those emails before bedtime, and tell Boomerang to send them in four hours. Can't believe I'm giving away this secret!

SMOOTH SAILING
+ Send emails in your sleep...

CHOPPY WATERS
- But don't *write* emails in your sleep. Then I'll recommend you get Google Goggles, the product that forces you to answer a math question before sending your email, just to make sure you're not either sleep-walking or inebriated.

GOT GOOSEBUMPS?
Install Boomerang. There's really no reason not to. You don't need to use the "Send Later" button from Boomerang if you don't want. Also, check out the Inbox Game—another product from Baydin—if you want a competitive game that helps you clean out your inbox.

MULTI-TASKING IS great until you realize that even that isn't enough. If only you could actually *be* multiple people. Since clone technology isn't far enough along, this Coolest Startups will have to take mini-Me's place in the meantime.

LET'S BREAK THE ICE

TaskRabbit instantly connects you to local labor for tasks, from picking up groceries to doing data entry.

BACKSTORY

The story of TaskRabbit began when founder Leah Busque, an IBM engineer at the time, encountered a problem: She was about to catch a cab for a dinner (and late already!) while her dog, Kobe, had just run out of food. The predicament ended up being good fortune, as Busque wondered why there was no service for her to be able to get in-person, real-time neighborhood assistance. She created such a network, called RunMyErrand, and it evolved into TaskRabbit.

"Once I had the inspiration, I became obsessed with the idea that we could use technology to build a trusted network online and offline," Busque says. "If you think back to 10 or 15 years ago, there was a neighborhood kid you could pay a couple bucks to mow your lawn or pick up groceries. Today, the Internet has created silos for us. People are closed up in their houses and on their computers, but not really communicating. In the last three years, technology has caught up to where it's mimicking human behavior. We're creating a *service* networking platform, rather than a social networking platform. It's about engaging the neighborhood and facilitating trust. It's a throwback to the age-old 'it takes a village to raise a child' axiom. We're using new technologies to enable that."

She decided to leave IBM to pursue startup life. "I didn't know what was coming but I knew that I can figure it out," Busque says. "It's the attitude I continue to have: trust and confidence in myself."

While family and friends were helpful in getting her company off the ground, Busque says support from fellow Boston-based entrepreneurs helped most. In particular, Scott

Griffith, CEO of Zipcar, was a pivotal mentor for Busque. They were introduced through a "friend of a friend of a friend" (networking is vital in startuptopia). The two shared a common interest in getting people to live efficiently and share together. Griffith joined TaskRabbit as one of the startup's earliest advisors. "I relied on him for guidance, insight and perspective. Without him, I wouldn't have gotten as far as I have," Busque says. The importance of mentors is immense. Founders need others to look up to and rely on in furthering their vision.

In 2011, the startup revised its RunMyErrand branding and took on the cuter moniker: TaskRabbit. "RunMyErrand. com was not the brand I wanted to build because it wasn't big enough for the vision in my head," Busque says. "RunMyErrand was descriptive, but I knew in my gut that we could tackle a larger vision with the branding of TaskRabbit."

HOW DOES IT WORK?

TaskRabbit operates on a city by city basis. Once you sign up for your locale, you can post a "task" with a description of the job you'd like done and the fee you're willing to pay. "Rabbits," or people who have signed up to complete tasks on TaskRabbit, bid on the task based on the fee they are willing to accept. The startup's platform auto-assigns the task to a Rabbit, and it's underway. You then review the individual on his/her performance, and pay them online.

TaskRabbit takes a transaction fee of about 15% per task. The most popular tasks are IKEA furniture assemblies, but tasks run the gamut from dry cleaning pickup to Wi-Fi installation and more.

Busque identifies several complimentary trends to TaskRabbit's business, including the tough job market and a shift in American work culture. "Since three years ago the economy is bouncing back, but a multitude of people are [still] unemployed and underemployed. When I started the company and the stock market was crashing, we had lawyers and pharmacists who wanted to be part of the Rabbit network." Second, people are rethinking what work and careers mean to them, Busque says. "People are looking to integrate this new way of working into their lives, making TaskRabbit a way to become a microentrepreneur. Microentrepreneurship is this idea that you can set your own schedule and be your own boss. It's becoming more and more important, and TaskRabbit provides a platform that supports this trend for more people to pursue work-life balance."

WHY IS IT COOL?
The end of running your own errands.

LET'S SAY...
I. It's your significant other's birthday, and you completely forgot to get him/her a present. You're stuck in back-to-back meetings and won't be able to duck out of the office before the celebratory dinner tonight. TaskRabbit comes leaping and bounding to help you; just set up a task picking out precisely what you'd like to buy and how you'd like it wrapped. The good Rabbit will take care of things to your specifications and drop the gift off at your office. No need to have cash on hand; you'll pay them online later! Crisis averted.

II. You're a recent college graduate who hasn't found a full-time gig yet. You'd like to make some money, but also need flexibility to attend job interviews at a moment's notice. Sign up to be a Rabbit, watch the tasks come through, take up what you will, and earn a few bucks!

SMOOTH SAILING
+ Rabbits are thoroughly screened before being listed on the site. The process involves a video interview and a background check. Plus, Rabbits are evaluated after each task.

+ TaskRabbit is aggressively expanding its geographic reach with service in New York, San Francisco, Los Angeles and other major cities. It also has a strongly-reviewed iPhone app for users to post tasks.

+ TaskRabbit has raised millions of dollars from top VC firms including First Round Capital and Shasta Ventures.

+ The value of people's time is steadily rising, as individuals cram more activities into their already busy days; according to the Bureau of Labor Statistics, average productivity per American has increased 400% since 1950. TaskRabbit is a welcome help for overworked Americans.

+ TaskRabbit is popular for small businesses, which can easily outsource menial and one-off tasks through a business account. Many of the Coolest Startups use them, Nick Ganju's

ZocDoc (Chapter 55) and Eli Portnoy's ThinkNear (Chapter 39) included. The latter shares: "I really like TaskRabbit because they're bringing online marketplace efficiency to the offline world. They make it easier for me to get stuff done in the real world that I just need done. We use them for a whole bunch of stuff."

CHOPPY WATERS

- Running errands through this startup is more expensive than a serendipitous connection due to the premium paid to TaskRabbit, the middleman. The recession may make it hard to scale the business as users worry about justifying the cost for a task; many may stick to doing their own dirty laundry.

- TaskRabbit is reminiscent of Kozmo.com, a startup that flopped miserably in the dot-com bust. Thankfully, TaskRabbit does have a stronger business model and more robust technology.

GOT GOOSEBUMPS?

Check out the types of tasks being completed on TaskRabbit if you need ideas for what to offload, and remember to look at TaskRabbit the next time you need a helping hand.

DEFROST: Getting Culture-d

"Culture" is a term startups love to use to describe themselves. What does this amorphous term mean in practice and how does it get created? The founders weigh in.

"Company culture is one of the most important things that you can build in any startup," begins Leah Busque, founder of TaskRabbit (Chapter 48). "Our team members are here because they believe in what we're building."

You'll be hard-pressed to find a founder who doesn't agree. Michael Karnjanaprakorn of Skillshare (Chapter 33) says, "Culture is extremely important. You can hire the best people and put them in the wrong culture and they're destined to fail. Flat organizations are extremely important for creativity, innovation, productivity, and happiness. Nobody really wants to be someone else's executor; employees want to be involved. The top-down model will become outdated," he says. Skillshare implements this philosophy with a variety of practices. "We take professional development and learning seriously," Karnjanaprakorn tells me. "We do one-on-ones with team members to help them develop personally and professionally. We plan the next three to six months and reflect on the past three to six months at a retreat so we set the company roadmap together. We encourage debating because people want their ideas heard. We're anti-long meetings. We ban them, in fact. It's all these things that reinforce culture."

But Ilya Sukhar of mobile startup Parse may have summed it up best when he told me, "Company culture naturally evolves. At Parse, we're open, collaborative, treat each other as equals, and we like to drink beer a lot."

The development of startup culture begins at the hiring stage. Nick Ganju at Zocdoc (Chapter 55), which offers unlimited vacation and complete health insurance to its employees, says "essentially, company culture is part of setting a high bar for your company. All things come to hiring."

One of my favorite stories on hiring techniques comes from Liron Shapira of Quixey (Chapter 50). He says that Quixey begins by judging candidates on a single qualification. "We have one filter for our engineers: algorithms mastery. We apply it very strictly. It eliminates so many people that the people who are left after the filter tend to be good on the other skills we need."

It's like finding kin. Sutha Kamal of Massive Health describes it as finding "fellow travelers." Sarah McIlroy of Fashion Playtes (Chapter 26) says, "As a startup, one of our biggest challenges is getting the right kind of person. We have crazy deadlines and a crazy amount of work. You accomplish about two times what a normal company might accomplish. We've brought on a lot of people who are passionate about our long-term vision and about what they're doing at the firm. It's hard to probe, but through references and networking it's possible to glean."

Another strong factor in startup culture creation is management. Daryl Bernstein of RightSignature (Chapter 52) supports having a casual culture and flat organization where individual responsibility and creativity can thrive. "Each person's ideas count the same," he says. "We often have business folks suggesting things for software development, and software developers making suggestions for business, marketing, and sales. It's a collaborative environment because we have a clear goal of what we want to be as a company."

IT'S EASY TO get lost preparing for work, rather than actually doing it. For instance, to do this book I've set up interviews with CEOs, gone through companies' PR peoples to get to them, interviewed, talked with publishers and agents, etc. etc. etc. And then, although I feel like the book is coming along, I realize that I haven't done much writing!

Organizing oneself to do work can often be as time-consuming as the work itself. Introduce a team of people and everything gets all the more complex. Who is working on what and when? Did Stephanie get the email with the latest project details? And what the heck is Raul working on?

LET'S BREAK THE ICE

Producteev is a project-management tool for teams.

BACKSTORY

Ilan Abehassera moved to NYC from France seven years ago. He worked at L'Oréal and Georgio Armani ("When you graduate from a business school in France, you go to work in beauty and cosmetics," says Abehassera).

"It was everything I didn't want to do with my life—working for a large corporation in the cosmetics industry. I always had an American mindset. New York was my dream since I was 11-years-old," he tells me.

He made his dream happen by joining a French luxury chocolate company to launch the chocolatier's US operations in New York. Then the Web bug bit him. He worked for two startups and then founded Producteev in 2008. "I knew something would be done in the productivity space. There were lots of task managers out there but I couldn't find any winner. There was nothing that *everybody* was using. When you think of email, you think of Gmail and Outlook. When you think of file sharing, you think of Dropbox. When you think of notes, you think of Evernote. In our space, no products were sticky enough."

Why no winners? "Because most of them are developing a product in a closed environment; you have to go to their website to organize. When you're outside of the office, that approach doesn't make sense. Our idea was to build a productivity platform that can be accessed from any device—mobile phone, web, Gmail, Google Calendar, or Outlook... We want to become the task protocol."

This mission gets accomplished with APIs. In fact, Producteev has an integration partnership with TaskRabbit. "If you have tasks you can't complete by yourself, with one click you can outsource them to TaskRabbit. It's a partnership through an API." Producteev also has API partnerships with Google. "This year we're integrating with Google Tasks. Most of our competitors are looking to be the best productivity tool for web or mobile, but they focus on the product and not on outside services. We focus a lot on outside services because at the end of the day, we don't care if you come to Producteev.com to manage your tasks. We don't care about bringing traffic to the site, we want to make sense as a productivity platform."

Liron Shapira of Quixey (Chapter 50), the app search engine, echoes that the best apps have been aiming to unify their presences across platforms. He gave the example of Yelp. "When most people think of Yelp, they think of Yelp.com, the website. But if you're Yelp, the company—if you think of Yelp as just Yelp, whether it's on mobile, web or other point of access—the trend is to go cross-platform and break down the barriers between platforms."

HOW DOES IT WORK?

After signing up for Producteev, you'll create a "workspace" where you can add tasks, label them, add deadlines, and rate the priority of your to-do items. As you set up tasks, you may decide you want to assign them to another team member (or use it with your family, and assign the latest fridge clean-out to Junior), so you can invite people by email address to join your Producteev workspace.

Producteev will send you reminders, if you want, on items that require completion. As you go along, you can mark items as finished. No longer will you need to track to-dos in your inbox. Now you have a smart system of organizing, and you can better track projects across your work teams, too. The best thing is that Producteev knows you're never completing to-dos only when you're online, so they've created stellar desktop and mobile apps as well.

WHY IS IT COOL?
Stay in the loop on-the-go with your team and tasks.

SMOOTH SAILING
+ Incredible, easy-to-use user interface across all devices.

+ Producteev keeps to-do's in one place, accessible anywhere; if you have multiple projects going on, you can still organize them under your one Producteev account umbrella.

CHOPPY WATERS
- There is a well-funded competing firm, called Asana, created by former Facebook founders. They've lagged behind Producteev in launching their product, but now they're up and at 'em as a formidable competitor. Abehassera isn't too worried. "I had high hopes for Asana. I am very disappointed. The guys behind it are Facebook founders so people were expecting something magic, like create a task on Asana and it gets completed by itself!" he joked. "When you search for task management on Google you find Producteev as #1, way above Asana. It's a well thought out product, but it's complicated too. Product-wise it's not a direct competitor because they target larger groups. You can use it as an individual but it's way more complex [because of advanced setup]. We focus on individuals and small teams." I agree with Abehassera. After trying the much-awaited Asana, it certainly isn't ideal for personal to-do list use in the way Producteev is.

- I wish I could get analytics on my productivity. Following the principles of Quantified Self, it would be cool for Producteev to incorporate personal productivity metrics into its product.

GOT GOOSEBUMPS?
Transition your to-do list away from paper notes or flagged emails. You might even use Producteev to orchestrate household chores with your family.

CONTENT SEARCH IS being perfected by Google. Of the billions of pieces of information out there on the Internet, we can find what we need via a search bar. But now that apps are being used more frequently—not just on mobile, but also on desktops—who is helping us find the apps that we need?

LET'S BREAK THE ICE
Quixey is the app search engine.

BACKSTORY
Quixey co-founders Tomer Kagan and Liron Shapira have been friends since high school. Kagan came up with the idea for an app search engine and reached out to Shapira in mid-2009 to discuss it. Shapira agreed to join the effort. "I wasn't invested in the idea. I was invested in Tomer," says Shapira. "Tomer is a serial entrepreneur. He always started stuff, like a fraternity in college, and a bunch of companies to pay his way through college. CEO is a position he's born to do. He's the number one most strategic person I know. Also, he's a very good socializer. He combines strategy with easily getting people on board with his ideas, and that's an amazing combo." It was the ideal yang to Shapira's technological yin.

The first version of Quixey was consumer-facing. Now the business strategy is getting distribution through existing channels such as mobile phone providers whose clients have a need for great app search. "We don't think the world needs another distribution site as much as it needs someone to clean up the existing endpoints. We did the simple logic that if you make another website, only if you get lucky can you start getting traffic in the millions. Instead, you can go to places where there's a vacuum for a player like us and overnight get hundreds of millions of queries per day. It's a total no-brainer from a business development perspective."

HOW DOES IT WORK?
Shapira says that Quixey is ideal for finding niche apps. "It's the stuff only Quixey can help you with. I recently got ClockDummy because my computer only shows hours and

minutes and I really want to see the seconds ticking by, and it turns out there's no way to configure that in Windows. I searched Quixey for 'configure seconds in my task bar clock' and got this niche app that can do it. Quixey works seamlessly."

How does Quixey chronicle all these apps? "It's pretty hard. It's a big data problem. I was scared about it when we started," Shapira jokes. Wit aside, the process is neat. "We do a strategic crawl of the Web and app stores, and algorithmically get all this data," Shapira explains. "We put it all in a database and apply heuristics [approximations] to clean it up. We're constantly running algorithms to better the data, indexing it as intelligently as we can. It's an extremely interesting engineering challenge. It's where our secret sauce goes. It's why we have a good technological barrier to entry. Our database of apps—our clear model of the functional web—is something no other company is even close to right now. We've had some of the smartest engineers in the world making sense of apps." That's why Quixey is one of the Coolest Startups.

WHY IS IT COOL?

Tell Quixey what you want to do, and it will show you the apps to do it.

SMOOTH SAILING

+ Investors include Google's former CEO Eric Schmidt. This is an example of a strategic investor who can provide assets equal to funding in importance: expertise and networking connections.

+ In addition to its strategy of integrating Quixey as an app search engine for enterprises, Quixey can take other monetization queues from search engines: advertising. Quixey can get advertising dollars from developers who want to promote their apps to people searching on Quixey.

CHOPPY WATERS

- No results returned for this heading! Search again.

GOT GOOSEBUMPS?

Looking for good apps? Try out Quixey's app search. It's not restricted to iPhones either—with Quixey, all apps are represented.

EVER HAVE THAT feeling of "what the heck did I get done today?" or "last week went by fast, what did I spend my time doing?"

LET'S BREAK THE ICE

iDoneThis helps you keep a record of what you've done.

HOW DOES IT WORK?

iDoneThis sends you an email daily to which you simply reply with a list or paragraph about what you've done today. When you sign up, you indicate when you'd like the email to arrive to your inbox.

When the email arrives, just shoot back a response. iDoneThis then keeps your replies in a convenient calendar if you ever need a reminder of what you've accomplished. Sometimes, as part of the daily email to which you reply, iDoneThis will take you down memory lane with a snapshot of your accomplishments from the same day last week or month too.

LET'S SAY...

You're particularly ambitious at work this year, and gunning for a promotion. You do great work day in and day out, but you want to have a record of this productivity. You're on your computer all day, and sign up for iDoneThis for an easy way to track your completed tasks. Just reply to iDoneThis's daily email with your wrap-up.

WHY IS IT COOL?

Keep a diary without the diary.

SMOOTH SAILING

+ Each iDoneThis record is a *tabula rasa*. Don't limit yourself to work-related summaries; you can track diet and exercise accomplishments too.

+ iDoneThis is adding an interesting enterprise tool to its product lineup. iDoneThis can assemble helpful reports for managers with the work-related entries from employees from the previous day or week. This can help meetings skip the awkward "so, what have you been up to anyway?" and get directly into discussions that help projects move forward.

CHOPPY WATERS

- As a Quantified Self tracking tool, iDoneThis is rudimentary. I look forward to when they roll out additional helpful features, like quantifiable elements (i.e. *how many* pages did I write, for *how long* did I run, etc.) and metrics-driven employee iDoneThis reports for business owners.

GOT GOOSEBUMPS?

Sign up for iDoneThis for an easy way to record your achievements.

CUFF LINKS
B2B startups

52. RightSignature
53. Demandbase

LAW IS BILLED as boring, backward and pricey. It may deserve some of those adjectives, but a startup called RightSignature is putting law's inefficiency behind bars.

LET'S BREAK THE ICE

RightSignature makes sharing contracts easy and fast, and makes signing them a digital breeze.

BACKSTORY

RightSignature spun out of a company called ELC Technologies. As the staff and clients at ELC were situated around the world, flow of documents proved complex. The product started as an in-house efficiency tool to solve ELC's internal legal challenges. It was nascent, but got the job done.

RightSignature CEO Daryl Bernstein saw huge potential for the product around the world, from small businesses to enterprise companies. "It felt like the only reason people still had printers was for documents that required a signature. There's a tidal wave of change toward paperless processes, but the last piece to solve was document signing."

Bernstein had the Beta product spun out and rebuilt from the ground up, expanding key features that had proven to be more important than the signature itself, like document generation and data collection in form and text fields. RightSignature also could centralize documents to one secure online archive, rather than messy filing cabinets. Plus, performance metrics give visibility into signing efficiency.

Some people may still wonder whether electronic signatures are even legal. Indeed they are, and have been for quite awhile. According to Bernstein, electronic signature laws were passed in the US and in Europe in 1999 and 2000; e-signatures have been legally binding for over 10 years! The American Bar Association counted itself among those encouraging the legislation, which went on to set low barriers for legality; even an exchange of email approvals can be considered a contract. RightSignature is a huge step. "Pen-and-paper signatures carry more risk than e-signatures. Firms realize that RightSignature will improve their legal stance,"

Bernstein says.

HOW DOES IT WORK?

After signing up for an account on RightSignature, you upload the document you'd like sent for approval. Once uploaded, the user can customize the document with form, text, and signature fields for multiple signatories. When ready for send-off, RightSignature emails the document securely to all participants. The signers are welcome to read, review, and even print the document (if they dare waste paper!). Most importantly, they can sign the doc on the line with their mouse. As soon as this is done, the owner of the document receives instant notification. Thereafter, an executed copy is kept in RightSignature for posterity.

RightSignature's e-signature technology replicates the pen-and-paper signing experience. The person can draw his/her signature on the iPad or iPhone, take a picture of the signature to add to the document, or draw the signature by mouse or trackpad.

RightSignature is hyper-focused on user experience for both the senders and the signers. It's important for RightSignature that direct customers who use the technology enjoy it, and that means the customers' clients too (i.e. the people receiving and signing documents). RightSignature's customers' customers may have no experience with e-signatures, so the company has developed cool proprietary technology to walk people through documents step by step, almost as if the lawyer were sitting across the table.

The startup has made an effort to make the technology "self-service," where the customers won't need high-touch sales people or dozens of how-to manuals to use the product. "There are two camps of software business models," Bernstein explains. "Businesses that are tech-light but sales-heavy, and vice-versa. There's no right or wrong, as there are great businesses in both camps. The traditional technology model is to develop software that isn't particularly beautiful or elegant but gets the job done, then go out and sell it with heavy marketing spend and a big sales force. In contrast, RightSignature is tech-heavy and sales-light. The new model we use is to put resources into beautiful technology that doesn't require heavy-handed selling. Like Dropbox and

Evernote, RightSignature is well-designed and can have millions of people sell themselves by experiencing a free trial and using the service in their own businesses. There's no arm twisting, because users appreciate the value immediately."

WHY IS IT COOL?

RightSignature is a product that delights its users. No longer does a person have to receive a document, print it, fax it, and wait for hours or days to complete a contract. They can do all that in the browser in seconds with RightSignature. And sign with their mousepad.

LET'S SAY...

I. You're a next generation realtor. You use RightSignature for all your client papers. Those house ownership docs can take pages worth of printing, so by using RightSignature, you're tremendously easing the burden on the environment.

II. You're on a team with members across the globe. Shipping or faxing documents for signatures is absurdly time consuming and inefficient. You adopt RightSignature to streamline your team's legal communication.

SMOOTH SAILING

+ RightSignature is an organizational tool in a way, maintaining all documents in one place.

+ The company releases new features often, like in-document e-signatures and analytics.

+ RightSignature is a no-brainer green alternative to printing paperwork.

+ RightSignature is part of a group of startups revolutionizing the legal profession. Michael Sinanian, who reports for VentureBeat, says that "Future Lawyers of America" may not even realize that their industry will be "disrupted," which means to become more competitive and cheaper through new business and technology avenues. "There's a big opportunity to democratize legal access," Sinanian says. "Lawyers will no longer be gatekeepers" for legal work. Sinanian cites a company called LegalZoom, which strives to increase people's access to legal documents, and another company working on discovery processes that make it simpler to search case law. "It's easier to be a lawyer, in a sense, so the prices should come down."

CHOPPY WATERS
- RightSignature doesn't integrate a contacts list, so users have to retype the email addresses of common signatories each time. I'm sure that's a feature they could add soon.

GOT GOOSEBUMPS?
You get a few documents free upfront, so take advantage of them! If you love RightSignature, upgrade to get unlimited document sending each month.

DEFROST: What's This Twitter Thing?

Did you notice the byline on this book's spine? If not, don't go anywhere. I'll fill you in! It's @DoreenBloch rather than By Doreen Bloch. Yeah, that's a Twitter relic.

Twitter is an older upstart that came on the scene like a bird to a branch in 2007. It's what is called a "micro-blogging" platform, allowing posts—"tweets"—of 140 characters at most. Twitter now has many millions of people using the service to either privately update their "followers" on what they're up to, thinking, feeling, eating… or to publicly broadcast news and ideas in a fast-paced format.

Twitter has had some pretty revolutionary impacts on the pace of information travel—earthquake news first broke out on Twitter, it was used extensively in the Arab Spring revolts of early 2011, and celebrity gossip seems to travel faster than light nowadays. Many startups stand on the shoulders of Twitter, including city exploration game-cum-social network foursquare (Chapter 37) to name just one.

Unfortunately, for all its vast social impact, Twitter hasn't been able to monetize too effectively. Brands do spend money to "promote tweets," but effectiveness may be compromised by the rise of white noise (i.e., random thoughts, vague feelings, and rambling words).

Twitter can be contentious. Serial entrepreneur Christopher Michel says of Twitter that "the social media stuff today doesn't matter. It may create some value, but did it create something impactful to the world?" Other founders disagree, saying that Twitter has grown because it's a powerful communication tool. Aaron Schildkrout, co-CEO of HowAboutWe (Chapter 36) says "it's an awesome idea that provides great value. They've had totally explosive, unprecedented growth."

Make your own opinion about Twitter. Sign up and get a "handle," your Twitter name, like @DoreenBloch in my case. You can make yourself anonymous if you'd like;

an acquaintance of mine emits rather raunchy tweets from a pseudonymous Twitter account throughout the day to the LOL (laugh out loud) delight of followers. If you don't feel comfortable having your Twitter feed out in the open, just make your tweets private. But I'll warn you now, Twitter can become a big time suck.

THE INTERNET IS a one-way glass. Any page you access on the Internet may collect information on your activity, like where you click, which web page you came from, how long you've visited, and more. This is all fascinating to see, but what if you want to *contact* the person visiting your site?

LET'S BREAK THE ICE

Demandbase checks website visits against its databases of companies and contacts.

HOW DOES IT WORK?

When a publisher signs up for Demandbase, they install a snippet of code that tracks web visits. That's the easy part. In the background, there are important technologies at work. Demandbase has an in-depth database of firms, including each company's name, location, revenue and more. Then, Demandbase Real-Time Identification surfaces in who is visiting your site. Demandbase gives you the option to see that information in a ticker format across your computer screen if you want. It can be a bit distracting when you're trying to work, but if you're in sales, nothing beats seeing a lead come through the door and being able to (virtually) reach out and shake hands in the moment the lead is hot.

WHY IS IT COOL?

Consumer marketers may need demographics, but business marketers need "firmographics." Demandbase makes it easy to contact executives from firms seeking you.

LET'S SAY...

You're in a company that relies on sales for its livelihood. You'd like to know who's visiting your website in case they don't email or call you after visiting your site. You sign up for Demandbase and can see in real-time who is stopping by your site, and even what pages they're going to (eerie, I know, but cool!). If they don't reach out to you, you could contact them, as Demandbase shows you high-level contacts at the firms.

SMOOTH SAILING

+ Real-time identification isn't all Demandbase offers. They also help companies enhance their online presences through better online sign up forms, improved web pages, and Customer-Relationship Management. It's becoming a one-stop shop for Business-to-Business online needs. All you need to bring is the website!

+ Demandbase has tons of great partners, including Adobe and Salesforce.

CHOPPY WATERS

- It's too expensive for the average website owner to use. It's geared to established businesses that want to take their websites to the next level, with subscriptions to Demandbase in the several thousand dollar range per month.

GOT GOOSEBUMPS?

Demandbase has tons of resources online about B2B marketing, sales and more. Check them out on their website and request a demo online if you think the product is for you. Seeing this technology in action will seal the deal!

APOTHECARY
Apple a Day startups

54. FitBit
55. ZocDoc
56. Asthmapolis
57. Organovo
58. Oasys Water

OBESITY IS HUGE nowadays. We're all sitting around (well, at least I am) in desk jobs that are totally sedentary, and hopefully getting to the gym once a day to at least break a sweat in something other than typing fingers.

At the same time, we're surrounded by ads showing thinness and curves of the flattering variety. We're thrown apps of every shape and size that promise to track calories, pedometers that measure the distances we walk, diets that proclaim to trim waistlines, and personal trainers who yell us into shape. It's so much!

LET'S BREAK THE ICE

FitBit is an all-in-one tracker.

HOW DOES IT WORK?

FitBit uses technology, similar to what's in the Nintendo Wii, to track your movements. FitBit tracks steps taken (and thus can calculate miles moved) and sleep (in five minute increments), and the online site is a personal and social network for tracking caloric intake and other types of activity.

FitBit costs about $100, and gets shipped to you in sleek packaging. After a short setup, it's ready to use right out of the box.

LET'S SAY...

You made a New Year's resolution to get your body moving and your abs flat in time for bathing suit season. You buy FitBit and notice as you're doing your regular activities and tracking them that you're really not getting enough exercise to offset your caloric intake. You use that tracking to change your behavior, and gain the satisfaction of knowing that you're now getting enough exercise.

WHY IS IT COOL?

Your health all in one place.

SMOOTH SAILING

+ FitBit is a part of the Quantified Self movement, quickly

gaining momentum.

+ FitBit is a super sleek device. Dare I say, it's Apple-esque.

CHOPPY WATERS

- FitBit has competition from Jawbone Up, Lark, and other firms. I like FitBit for its integrated online engagement and offline components, and for its brilliant hardware and software designs.

GOT GOOSEBUMPS?

Even if you don't buy FitBit, you can join the online community to track your caloric intake.

DEFROST: Quantified Self

There is a movement for data acquisition on everything about our lives. How many steps did I walk today? How many calories did I consume? How long have I been staring at this computer screen? It used to be quite hard to collect this type of information because data capture instruments were not good or cheap enough, nor was the ability robust enough to analyze the data for meaningful results. That's changed in recent years. The movement to incorporate technology into precisely measuring the actions we take as human beings is called Quantified Self (QS). Just as quantification and metrics can inform our business decisions, the idea is that making ourselves data-driven can help our personal lifestyles.

Henrik Werdelin of innovation consultancy Prehype says QS is about "digital tools to monitor yourself and become better at the stuff you do." There are tons of interesting applications. Some of the Coolest Startups are QS-related, including FitBit (Chapter 54), Asthmapolis (Chapter 56), Tout (Chapter 45) and more. Michael Sinanian, a reporter for VentureBeat, shared with me one of his favorites: WakeMate, a wristband for your iPod that you wear at night, programmed to analyze your sleep state so you're woken up to feel less groggy. WakeMate looks for an ideal time in which to wake you based on the depth of your sleep within a chosen 20-minute window. QS was niche in Silicon Valley geek circles, but Sinanian says it's now going mainstream, helped by accessible and easily understood devices like WakeMate.

Nevertheless, QSers have a reputation for being fastidious. Sutha Kamal, CEO of Massive Health, says QS is too specialized for the average person. "We can have devices stuck to our bodies at any time, but how do we really understand how this fits into the life of a normal person? QS folks are by definition early adopters, whereas we're building products to integrate into daily lives." His company created the popular mobile app Eatery, which prompts the user to snap a picture of his/her dish and *approximate* its healthiness on a more qualitative scale.

Friends can then weigh in on it (no pun intended). The idea is that if the user thinks about snapping a picture of the chocolate cake intake to share with friends, they'll be less likely to follow through on the craving. Startup expert Brian Zisk says "Eatery is brilliant because consumers focus on the wrong things. Measuring calories is a tedious task. Massive Health incorporates psychological feedback mechanisms."

I spoke with Steven Dean, who facilitates QS meetups in New York City. He says the movement originated from the ideas of cardiologist Dean Ornish, as well as Kevin Kelly and Gary Wolf who began organizing local meetups in the San Francisco Bay Area for people to come together and share experiences about personal tracking.

I asked Dean why rigorous QS sometimes gets a bad rap. Is it really possible to track all aspects of one's life, from sleep and diet to exercise or productivity? Dean, who completed the Ironman World Championship in 2007, says QS isn't necessarily a new idea; athletes have been doing self-tracking for a long time. "We try to remind people that what we do in QS is episodic for when you're trying to reach a goal," Dean says. "QSers go through quiet periods. For example, I was actively tracking when I was training for Ironman. I would track morning resting heart rate, exercise routine compliance, mood, energy and sleep. It was for me to make sure I was healthy before going into the race. Once the race was done, I pulled back on tracking."

The application to the field of healthcare is immense because QS is particularly useful for solving problems. Dean shared his troubleshooting through QS for an odd dermatological outbreak he experienced. "I started to track what the breakouts were like—redness, itchiness, intensity. I built my own self-tracking tool to understand how the symptoms evolved. The goal was to look at the symptoms and the different treatments. QS works well when someone has a specific goal." This approach could revolutionize healthcare, empowering society to move from the traditional top-down approach to "self-care," whereby people access real-time feedback and shift their lifestyles accordingly.

People have used the QS methodology to improve cognitive abilities for Jeopardy, to cure Crohn's Disease, to lose weight and more. Marc Brodeur, CEO of Brode (Chapter 29), uses foursquare (Chapter 37) to put to practice QS principles. He uses it for analytics on where he has been and how much he has spent in different categories. Josh Adbulla, founder of LetGive, shared a do-good QS app, called Nexercise, which uses the accelerometer on the iPhone to measure fitness goals, and allows you to donate to charity if you don't reach the goal or get rewarded if you do.

QS is about comparing the current state of the data to the ideal state; the better devices get, the better people can reach their goals. Dean says there are now hundreds of mobile apps for data capture. There are also dozens of sensors, like FitBit or Jawbone Up. Dean says the proliferation of consumer-oriented QS has come about because the sensor size has decreased and the cost for an accelerometer has come down to under a dollar. Next up: making sense of all the data that's captured. "[Raw] data is not very interesting to most people. Data in itself *isn't* interesting. Most people don't open Excel spreadsheets and just find meaning," says Dean. "Data visualization is in its infancy and it's a critical component to closing the feedback loop in QS. Charts and graphs add context to activities."

QS reflects, in Stephen Hawking's words, that "humans are entering a stage of self-designed evolution." I believe QS will only become more and more popular. Scott Summit of Bespoke Innovations (Chapter 66) agrees. "Computing is getting exponentially faster, smaller, cheaper, and better. We've seen that over 10, 20, 40, 50 years in nanotechnology, biotechnology and energy. We're turning our lives into an information property."

A BROKEN ARM is a serious injury, beyond doubt warranting a trip to the emergency room (no surprise there!). But what if you have something more benign and less painful, but you don't want to wait days for your appointment to come around? You call various medical offices, seldom knowing the true quality of each doctor, or if they'll even take your insurance. Welcome ZocDoc to the picture.

LET'S BREAK THE ICE

Did you know the average wait time to see a doctor is three weeks? ZocDoc is a powerful platform for patients to make appointments with doctors faster—search by specialty, insurance type, availability, location and more.

BACKSTORY

This Coolest Startup was born when CEO Cyrus Massoumi was on a flight and his sinuses congested, giving him severe ear pain. He tried finding a doctor and ended up unable to find one on such short notice. Yet in the moment, surely some doctor, somewhere close by, had a cancellation. That led to the idea for ZocDoc, like an "OpenTable for doctors."

HOW DOES IT WORK?

ZocDoc is free for patients to use. Find a doctor based on your location, the specialty you need and the insurance you carry. From dieticians to prosthodontists, ZocDoc's databases of docs should have your body covered.

You can browse through doctors and check their ratings and availabilities before booking an appointment. ZocDoc will send you friendly reminders by text or email before the appointment. That means that if you discover a funny bump on your skin at 2 AM, you can get onto ZocDoc within minutes and into a doctor's chair within hours to get it checked out.

So, who pays for us to get the wonderful joy of efficiency in this aspect of the medical experience? Doctors. While doctors are responsible for a lot of life-saving good in the world, they're small business owners in most cases as well. They pay ZocDoc about $200 per month for a spot on the listings. The sum pays for itself; reportedly, doctors who use ZocDoc get many new patients in the door because of the service's efficiency and reach, and one to two new patients per month more than covers the cost of a ZocDoc subscription. It's a win for patients, for doctors, and for ZocDoc.

The startup's subscription model was born in part due to legal obligations which effectively bar doctors from profit-making through publicizing appointments. "It works better to do a subscription anyway," Ganju tells me when I asked why they don't pursue a transaction-based revenue approach. "It's not just sending doctors new patients, it's enabling their existing patients to book online." A transaction-based model, where doctors are charged for each new patient acquired, may drive doctors to only encourage existing patients to book online so doctors wouldn't be charged more. Instead, ZocDoc's pricing approach conveys "use it as much as you want."

WHY IS IT COOL?
ZocDoc anesthetizes the formerly painful process of medical appointment scheduling.

LET'S SAY...
I. It's Halloween, and you've decided to dress as a zombie. By a strange and unwelcome coincidence, you discover an unusual skin rash on your shoulder. Gasp! Were you bitten? You can't recall, but you're not about to take any chances. You visited a doctor to check it out. You didn't book with ZocDoc though, so you went to a random dermatologist in the basement of a building on the edge of town just because the doctor could see you immediately. The doctor tells you he'll need to cut out five inches of skin (eek!). While the doctor is encouraging you to give the green light to the procedure, you get the ZocDoc app in the waiting room and see that there's a five-star rated MD a few minutes away who can see you in an hour. You book the appointment and drive off to your second opinion. This doctor also recommends an incision, but thankfully has better scalpels, taking out only a few millimeters of skin. Thankfully, your biopsy came back negative. Happy Halloween!

II. You're a doctor. You realize that, as a doctor, you're not just a lifesaver but a businessperson too. There are books to manage and insurances to bill. You're pretty cutting edge (insert surgical joke here), and want to encourage new patient visits. You know about Yelp.com for reviews, but that's geared toward revelry, not surgery. Angie's List has reviews, but they're more for consumer protection than business promotion. You've already invested in building a welcoming website for your practice, but you'd like to do more. You hear about ZocDoc from *The Coolest Startups in America*, and sign up to try it. ZocDoc integrates with your current scheduler and you can control it fully. After adding the ZocDoc link to your website, you see more appointments coming through, and your receptionist is now spending less time saying "please hold!" because everyone's booking directly online.

SMOOTH SAILING

+ Ganju says ZocDoc's membership grows by leaps and bounds every month, mainly by word of mouth. "If a user has a good experience with ZocDoc, it's natural to recommend it to a friend," he says.

+ Could ZocDoc deal with medical records next? Having to update one's information every time one visits the waiting room is a hassle. ZocDoc could store it all and send it to the doctor ahead of the appointment. This paves the way for a fully integrated Customer Relationship Management (CRM) system for follow-up appointments, compliance with medication and more.

+ The healthcare space is "blowing [up]," Ganju says. It's the US economy's biggest sector and "gets entrepreneurs salivating." Health insurance legislation will drive further growth for ZocDoc. "There's going to be a lot more demand because of [30 million] more insured patients. The jump in demand makes ZocDoc invaluable because now it's that much harder without ZocDoc to find doctors with free time."

+ ZocDoc does a phenomenal job moving offline inventory online. "It's an immense engineering effort," says Ganju. "We integrate with dozens of practice management systems." It's not just Outlook or Google Calendar, but specialized software that needs to be synced to ZocDoc's servers. ZocDoc has engineers who hone in on coding these integrations.

+ ZocDoc's management team is med-centric. Both the CEO and COO are doctors. Ganju's parents are both doctors.

"The whole medical industry permeates our lives, so we knew about the problems," Ganju says. "Every year reimbursements go down on a per appointment basis, pushing doctors into seeing more and more patients to break even. ZocDoc becomes immensely valuable because we're sending new patients to doctors. Doctors are normal people like any other small business owner. They don't want to be slowed down. ZocDoc isn't computerizing some arbitrary aspect of their business."

CHOPPY WATERS
- Nothing. I give this startup a clean bill of health.

GOT GOOSEBUMPS?
For your next doctor appointment, try using ZocDoc. It'll take your breath away. Don't take that literally, hypochondriacs.

DID YOU KNOW that almost 10% of the US population has asthma? Shocking, right! It's also a leading public health issue, accounting for 1.8 million emergency room visits per year.

LET'S BREAK THE ICE

Asthmapolis equips asthma inhalers with GPS-enabled devices to help monitor asthma attacks, eventually collecting enough data to learn about asthma and to help prevent attacks.

BACKSTORY

Asthmapolis founder and CEO David Van Sickle says he never thought he'd be an entrepreneur. Van Sickle had studied asthma his whole life. He spent time in the public sector at the Center for Disease Control (CDC) as well as in academia before embarking on his startup journey. After leaving the CDC to go to the University of Wisconsin School of Medicine, he found that, as in the public health records, there was a glaring information gap about asthma occurrences in academia too.

I like this startup backstory because it raises an important point about founder backgrounds. We hear a lot in the media about young entrepreneurs, but research shows that most successful entrepreneurs are actually quite seasoned in their careers. In fact, according to The Founder Institute, age has shown to positively correlate with success up to the age of 40, after which there is no correlation. This makes sense. Startups are about finding problems and implementing revenue-generating solutions. Opportunities don't just fall out of the sky; it often takes years of domain expertise to identify a critical issue or inefficiency that could use innovative action.

Van Sickle is one of those startup founders who spent years understanding an ecosystem—asthma prevention and control, in this case—and saw an opportunity to help. "Public health data was out of touch with what is possible in today's world," Van Sickle says. "We were getting data that was years old, and only a fraction of available asthma attack events." Van Sickle's had an inkling that with electronics on the asthma inhaler, you could "see how the patient is doing in real-time. If you aggregate the data for public health, it's the first real-time view of what is happening in the asthma community."

Asthmapolis's first batch of sensors was built in 2008, after which they received funding from the CDC to conduct an evaluation with 40 patients. Evidence showed that the Asthmapolis device reduced uncontrolled asthma by 50%, and that 75% of the patients improved their level of control. The next iteration of the technology was similarly effective and, in late 2010, the team moved off of the University campus and started a company to commercialize the technology.

It can make a remarkable difference to the lives of asthma patients. "Day to day symptoms shouldn't happen," explains Van Sickle. "Most people with the disease are not well-controlled. Most people don't realize that they could be doing way better." Asthmapolis helps patients and doctors better understand the illness.

I spoke about Asthmapolis with epidemiologist Dr. Fuyeun Yip of the Air Pollution and Respiratory Health Branch of the CDC in Atlanta. The branch includes the National Asthma Patrol, a program overseeing 36 asthma programs. One of the biggest challenges with asthma according to Dr. Yip is the management of the disease. "Management of asthma is important in terms of having the proper medication and knowing your triggers to minimize your exposure to them. Proper asthma management is a key area that we're trying to promote. We believe that emergency visits and hospitalizations can be reduced if asthma is managed more effectively." She says Asthmapolis's work is relevant to that goal. "We're excited to collaborate with [Van Sickle]. Our group conducts research to look at the relationship between air pollution and asthma."

Triggers are important, says Dr. Yip, because they vary from person to person. While exposure to air pollutants are a well-documented trigger, others might include Ozone sensitivity, pollen, and animal dander. "Having a GPS attached to a rescue inhaler is extremely innovative because we are able to obtain the information on when a patient needed to take the medication as well as where they took the medication."

HOW IT WORKS

Asthmapolis's product combines hardware and software. The former (called a SpiroScout) is a device, connected to a typical asthma inhaler, which clocks the time and place of inhaler usage. The latter helps make sense of these data inputs.

Design plays a huge role for Asthmapolis. "At a basic level, inhalers are well-designed. It's an awesome drug and delivery device combination. They're virtually indestructible. They're waterproof. Medications last a month in a tiny canister," explains Van Sickle. "If we want to attach onto it—from the industrial mechanical side—we have to be adaptable, portable, last a long time, and can't mess up the use of the device." Design is critical for the software side too, he says. "Most mobile health solutions translate a pen and paper system to electronic screens. That's a recipe for failure. The design has to make management of asthma more effective with less effort. If we make it more complicated or time consuming, we write our own obituary as a company. It's the force multiplier—do better with less. Like a lever, take whatever effort the patient applies and through your tools amplify it. It's about not tolerating an approach that puts burden on the patient."

Because it's in the healthcare space, Asthmapolis has to deal with regulations, long-thought to be an anathema to startup culture. Van Sickle doesn't view it as a massive burden. "It's like preventative medicine for a company. It forces us to go through processes that result in a better end product. In a lot of ways it can be a barrier to entry. To me it's not a negative or positive, but it's there and it's a system that's well-documented. It's like going through TSA; as long as you understand what's involved, it's not a big impediment."

LET'S SAY...

I. On the Island of Hawaii is a new volcanic vent spewing high levels of sulfur dioxide. This chemical compound is a known lung irritant, thought to cause asthma symptoms. Instead of speculating, Dr. Yip explains, "we're using the SpiroScout to understand the potential impact of volcanic emissions on individuals with asthma" and provide data regarding frequency, location, and time of inhaler use.

II. You live in the rural Midwest, where asthma is not thought to be commonplace. Unfortunately, there have been reports of increased cases. The CDC used Asthmapolis's device to see if it was true, says Van Sickle. They gave the sensors to a bunch of rural families with asthma, and indeed there were more frequent symptoms than expected. It surprised everyone, given asthma's label as "an urban disease."

WHY IS IT COOL?

Asthmapolis links data sets together. "There are not many tools developed that can link environmental exposure information and health outcome data in time and space," says Dr. Yip. "The Asthmapolis tool has been instrumental in providing this information."

SMOOTH SAILING

+ There is a financial risk for people with asthma. Uncontrolled, it can cost $3,000 to $4,000 a year. "That's a strong rationale for management," says Van Sickle. Asthmapolis helps patients better manage the disease through the education the data capture and analysis provide. It's part of the QS community, but "it's passive and ambient," says Steven Dean, a leader in the QS movement. "Asthmapolis doesn't require that people be self-trackers in the way that QSers are. Asthmapolis creates facts. There used to be little recall of when asthma attacks occur, but now people can see their behaviors and frequency of medication usage, and correlate it with how well they've been taking action."

+ Government-to-startup partnerships aren't common, but Asthmapolis has one. This is Dr. Yip's first foray into such a collaboration. "We thought it was a great opportunity to collaborate with David. I believe that there is a push to identify innovative efforts and tools, such as David's, to help us develop a better understanding between the environment and health."

CHOPPY WATERS

- Breathe easy. It's a smog-free startup.

GOT GOOSEBUMPS?

You may not have need for an Asthmapolis-bedazzlered inhaler, but you can learn a lot from the QS movement for helping with healthcare issues in general. Watch Quantified Self videos at www.QuantifiedSelf.com. "The stories are very personal," Dean says. " They focus on something the QSer has done to know themselves better through QS tools, methods and data."

Chapter 57: Organovo

NOW THAT IT is possible to print 3D objects, like blocks or jewelry, why not print biological ones like organs? Just replace inanimate plastic with living cells!

LET'S BREAK THE ICE

Organovo prints human tissue on-demand. It's not just any printer: it's a bio-printer.

HOW DOES IT WORK?

Organovo builds 3D inkjet-style printers that shoot out cells instead of ink. After a layer of cultured cells is printed, there's hydrogel added to create a 3D structure.

The technology is still in development, but progressing steadily. It was developed by Gabor Forgacs at the University of Missouri, and Organovo was founded to commercialize the technology. "Gabor and I have formed a great partnership in moving this technology forward," Organovo CEO Keith Murphy tells me. "Gabor had the vision for the science, and I brought the business side. We have complementary skill sets."

Because the technology is still in progress, Organovo has smartly created some interim products and services. In the short term, Organovo is working with pharmaceutical companies to print diseased tissue. Pharmaceutical firms can use these pieces of readily available tissue to test drugs more effectively. "As a company, we had to focus on how we deliver something of value to people in a time frame that can support a return on investment," Murphy says. "We found quickly that we were able to solve a very real problem for a very important customer. By making human tissues in 3D structures, we can make a dramatic impact on the insights researchers have into drug behavior. Based on this, we can grow the company and push the technology to develop more and more complex tissues over time. We always have the long term vision—bioprinted human organs—in mind, but we can't run before we can walk."

For the long-term, Murphy sees academia and non-profit centers helping Organovo lead the charge. Murphy even founded a non-profit group called the Human Organ Project to bolster these efforts. "After founding Organovo, I sensed that investor funding, even to companies with great technology, wasn't enough to achieve the long term dream," says Murphy. "While anyone would support the idea of printing organs, we quickly realized that the best way to push forward is to partner with great academic centers that can use public and non-profit research funding to spur progress with our bioprinters." Harvard Medical School, The Scripps Research Institute, Salk Institute, and more have already installed the NovoGen MMX Bioprinter and "are becoming bioprinting centers of excellence," says Murphy.

WHY IS IT COOL?
Organs need not be in short supply anymore. Bye bye, black market.

LET'S SAY...
You suffer the misfortune of a serious burn, and have only a few days to get new skin lest the damaged skin gets infected. Organovo could print new skin cells that overlay the damaged skin, and you'll heal Superman fast. Of course, that availability might well be years away, so for now, stay away from pyrotechnics.

SMOOTH SAILING
+ Entrepreneurs who shoot for the moon are invaluable. Finding a way to supply living cells to doctors in a sustainable way is called dreaming, but working, as Organovo does, to make it happen is called innovating.

+ Organovo has been able to delay taking venture capital thanks to high demand for its interim technology. Organovo could generate enough revenues from pharmaceutical firms to put off giving away equity for capital. That's the sweet spot in which every startup founder wants to be.

+ They've done blood vessels. Next up are full-on kidneys, livers and more. Drink on, fraternity brothers. You may be able to order a printed replacement from Organovo in a few years. And, there's little chance of rejection as the technology uses your own cells. Organovo may even be able to print directly into the body someday.

CHOPPY WATERS
- There are other approaches, like pig bladder powder for growing back body parts (not kidding) and skin cell guns.

GOT GOOSEBUMPS?
Use cool new words like Bioink and Cell-Friendly Biopaper. Also, try asking your local college about majoring in Tissue Engineering.

Chapter 58: Oasys Water

ONE BILLION PEOPLE lack access to clean water. It's an issue that donations can make a dent in, but what's really needed are solutions. One place people have looked is the vast blue ocean. Unfortunately, desalination of saltwater requires a lot of energy; commercial solutions require the burning of gas to get pure water. Oasys Water founder and former Navy man Robert McGinnis decided he'd find a better way.

LET'S BREAK THE ICE
Oasys Water can turn salty water into drinking water.

WHY IS IT COOL?
McGinnis served in the US Navy in the Persian Gulf during Operation Desert Storm, and saw massive oil rigs working on desalination but with huge energy costs and emissions. After completing his service, he went on to undergraduate studies at Yale University, where experimenting with desalination led to the founding of Oasys Water. That's a cool startup story if I've ever heard one.

HOW DOES IT WORK?
Traditional desalination techniques revolve around two methods. One is to heat saltwater to boiling point, capturing the vapors in a separate chamber and cooling it again to liquid water. The other is to push the water through an osmotic membrane (think of it like a filter) that effectively separates the salt from the water.

Oasys Water's innovation lies in combining the techniques, making the process much faster and cheaper than dams, aqueducts, or traditional desalination stations, all the while creating lower emissions and demanding less fuel than nearly any other water sourcing process.

This combinative method is done by *adding* carbon dioxide and ammonia to the water, which helps it pass faster through a membrane that traps the salt, sources say. It's then heated to about 50 degrees Celsius (a much less energy-demanding temperature than is required for boiling pure water) in order to expel the earlier added ammonia and carbon dioxide. By adding to the water, Oasys Water is able to reduce the time, cost and energy of the desalination effort, in a field where the holy grail was thought to be reduction. This startup demonstrates the success born of a unique outlook. The water never has to change physical states (into steam) to reach greater purity. Instead, the startup effects desalination by changing salt into gasses, rather than water into steam. Rather than the typical reverse osmosis used, Oasys Water uses "forward osmosis" in a re-engineered, re-invented manner.

LET'S SAY...

You're a farmer in Gujarat, India. The water shortages in your region are felt in the face of a growing need for crops. Enter Oasys Water, which will help you responsibly tap the nearby ocean for fresh water.

SMOOTH SAILING

+ Oasys Water's technology addresses hot topics in water management today, including water reuse, energy through osmotic power, wastewater recovery, energy storage and hydroelectric power. Its techniques result in better resource usage and carbon footprint reduction. Al Gore would be impressed with this sustainable business.

+ This startup's product will be imperative on a large-scale considering the many drought-prone regions in our nation and the world. Successful implementation of Oasys Water would also reduce transportation costs for fresh water.

+ Could Oasys Water become solar-powered? The method's lower energy demand makes it a realistic possibility.

CHOPPY WATERS

- Pun alert: There's no damming this startup! The universal need for a solution like the one Oasys Water provides means this startup must next find how to scale its technology globally.

GOT GOOSEBUMPS?

If you're fascinated by water desalination, the first (free!) thing to do is get more educated about water waste. Stop using plastic water bottles to start; remember, blue (water) and green (eco-friendliness) go well together.

CHATTERBOX
Interaction Meets Information
startups

59. Quora
60. Disqus

SOMETIMES YOU DON'T want to search through dozens of webpages for the answer to your question.

LET'S BREAK THE ICE

Quora aims to be the best Q&A website ever.

HOW DOES IT WORK?

When a user joins Quora they can follow a variety of topics, add questions, answer existing queries, comment or edit responses to questions, and upvote answers. It's a community-driven site that operates on transparency and honesty. Users are allowed to ask and answer questions anonymously, but many users also use the site as an opportunity to showcase their expertise on certain topics.

Michael Sinanian, a reporter for VentureBeat, raves about Quora. It's a sleeper for now, he says, but a soon-to-be mainstream hit. Even professional articles are beginning to use Quora as a source because of the candid responses from subject-matter experts, he says. "Google did a huge service when the Internet was the wild west. They could corral information when it was getting out of control," says Sinanian. "Google is still kind of a mess, and Quora can help reel it in."

Questions range from amusing (e.g. "Why are the birds so angry in Angry Birds?") to pragmatic (e.g. "Where in Indiana can I buy a canary?"). It's a neat way to communicate online when you're looking for a specific answer to an equally specific question.

WHY IS IT COOL?

"Quora is like the cracks between Wikipedia articles," describes Liron Shapira of Quixey (Chapter 50). "It's like a country club where you can gossip about topics and ask people questions. Anytime I want an opinion on something, I go to Quora. They're like my country club buddies."

SMOOTH SAILING

+ Quora's user base has seen great growth and they've gone mobile with an iPhone app. Sinanian says Quora has a top-notch team, and believes the team will continue to make the product better.

+ People can use Quora to get a sense of responders' personalities, almost like a blog, suggests Shapira.

CHOPPY WATERS

- Quora's Q&A tends to be tech-heavy, since most of the users are early adopters from the startup space. Join up and change that ratio! Contribute on whatever topics you're curious about or know everything on.

- Quora doesn't currently monetize. "They don't make a cent, but what they're doing is huge because it's a go-to for high-quality information," Sinanian says. "Some people feel overwhelmed by Google search, but introduce them to Quora and there's a quality answer."

GOT GOOSEBUMPS?

Have a burning question? Pose it on Quora. If you're a know-it-all, answer other people's deepest questions.

DEFROST: What Is an API?

No website, network or app is isolated nowadays. Websites "talk" to one another through Application Programming Interfaces (APIs), sets of rules that developers use to facilitate communications among different platforms to share data structures, protocols, and more.

A simple example of an API is from Yelp.com, the old startup that now boasts millions of restaurant reviews. Yelp has an API that allows other developers to "call" the restaurant data. A mobile app devoted to sushi could showcase nearby Japanese restaurants using Yelp's database API.

Another example is Facebook, which has two particularly popular APIs. The first is Facebook's "Single Sign On" API, which allows other websites to enable new members to register using a Facebook login, rather than creating a new username and password. The second popular API Facebook offers is for developers. Facebook's platform API allows developers to tap into Facebook's massive databases to build games and apps for the Facebook online community.

Why would any website want another website to tap into its data?

"Building a platform allows you to allow the next big thing to be built on you, not away from you," explains Alex Taub of Aviary (Chapter 61), which has three APIs. "Zynga [an online gaming company that went IPO in 2011] could have been built somewhere else, but it was built on Facebook because Facebook allowed it through its APIs."

API usefulness can be summed to four benefits:

1. Spreads the word. If your company has a well-crafted API, other developers will likely use it: free promotion!

2. Makes your application more useful. When your company's API becomes the dominant one in the industry (like Yelp for its dining-related listings) and lots of people start building fun and useful applications "on top of" it, the value of the code increases because so much more is now being done with those assets.

3. Saves Time and Resources. If others are building new features using your API, that's work your team doesn't have to do.

4. Stimulates Innovation. If more developers build on top of your application or data, that means more startups. More startups means more innovation... or so we hope!

ONLINE, CONVERSATIONS AREN'T really conversations. They're broadcasts, followed by a bunch of comments. Now that the Internet seems to be here to stay, wouldn't you want to see all the comments you've ever left, across all websites, in one place?

LET'S BREAK THE ICE

Disqus is an easy-to-implement comment system for websites.

HOW DOES IT WORK?

As a publisher (that's what industry insiders call anyone who maintains a website or blog), you can easily sign up to get Disqus by dropping in some code on your website. Or, if you're using an integrated publishing platform like Tumblr, just grab your Disqus unique ID (which is a string of numbers and letters identifying your account) and input it into the appropriate setup field. Most of the best publishing platforms created partnerships with Disqus to make this a cinch.

If you're a user, you'll come across Disqus discreetly embedded as the preferred commenting system on websites. You use it just like any other commenting system, except that you can now log in and have your comment associated with past comments and online presences. If you want to comment anonymously, you can do that too. Disqus effectively aggregates a given user's comments in one place, and makes it easy to share comments across the social web.

Disqus makes money with its really awesome premium services, working on a "freemium" model. Its core features are provided to publishers for free, but its add-on elements, such as in-depth analytics and real-time updating, are only available at a priced subscription level.

"When I first saw Disqus, I couldn't believe no one was doing this yet. So many people need deep commenting. It's a slam-dunk idea. They have totally amazing traction in the hundreds of millions of users. They have a good thing going," says Liron Shapira, CTO of Quixey (Chapter 50).

Chapter 61: Aviary

I HAVE PHOTOSHOPPED since the 8th grade. The original Adobe program is a powerful tool, so I was skeptical when I heard about a potential, *free* equivalent. Aviary ended up being awesome and, I soon discovered, more than just a Photoshop mimic.

LET'S BREAK THE ICE
Aviary's online image editor eliminates the cost of Adobe Photoshop. Being web-based, the program and your files are accessible from anywhere, anytime.

BACKSTORY
Aviary's story began when Avi Muchnick had the idea for an online Photoshop contest website. He wasn't a programmer, but took the idea to his friend Iz Derdik, who was able to launch the site. The image contest website got hundreds of thousands of views. Yet Muchnick wanted to do more than Photoshop contests, keeping in mind that many people were pirating Adobe's staple software, an expensive image editing program. That's when he got the idea of building a set of image editing tools that would be less expensive and complex; Muchnick wanted to democratize creation, says Derdik.

Muchnick and Derdik first released a screenshot technology product, and then an HTML5 and Javascript web-based image editor. Since people responded so well to the online editor, Aviary next rolled out an image editor for publishers to embed on their own sites. They expanded to different types of editing, like audio, music and effects too.

The success continued, and Aviary now sees mobile as the frontier. "We've moved away from competing with Adobe," says Alex Taub, a member of Aviary's Business Development team. "Instead of taking a picture and uploading it, people take photos in apps and can click to edit with Aviary right there on the device," says Derdik.

HOW DOES IT WORK?
First, Aviary has its original "Advanced Suite" of editing tools, like image editing, audio editing, and more. These web

tools open a Flash-based editor to which users can upload files and edit them. The tools have similar efficacy to the advanced features of Photoshop, but are provided at no cost, and images are edited "in the cloud." Thus, no space is taken up on the computer unless the user deliberately downloads the image.

Second, Aviary has shifted its focus to APIs. Aviary has three APIs: Web, Mobile, and Cloud. These allow developers to embed Aviary's image editing tools on their own websites and apps. The company puts a strong focus on exceptional customer experience—they have dozens of clients utilizing the APIs, which are well-supported and easy for developers to integrate and customize.

WHY IS IT COOL?

Play doctor to your photos, whether you're on your phone or at your computer.

SMOOTH SAILING

+ Aviary helps photos become more beautiful. You can even add virtual stickers to photos! Paul Murphy, Aviary's Head of Business Development, is well aware of the popularity of photo decoration. Hearts, stars, rainbows, you name it. There's a lot that can be done with this market; Murphy says that Japan alone holds an $8 billion mobile content market.

+ Aviary is addressing a massive market with its mobile strategy. "iPhonography" is more popular than ever. Facebook alone has 60 billion photos. With so many cameras in people's hands (via their phones), this number is set to balloon.

+ Jeff Bezos, founder of Amazon.com, is a fan and investor.

+ Aviary has taken a strategic route of powering apps and websites' photo editing through APIs. Rather than going direct-to-consumer, the APIs allow Aviary to gain more distribution through its partners. Aviary's technology enables the editing of millions of photos every month.

CHOPPY WATERS

- There is a lot of competition in the mobile photo editing and sharing space, from Instagram to Color and beyond.

GOT GOOSEBUMPS?

The next time you'd like to crop, rotate or color, try Aviary.

Chapter 62: Quirky

YOU COULD HAVE the next big idea, but not want to develop it. If that's the case, don't just lock your brilliant idea away in a drawer just because of the long and scary route to realization. Come over to Quirky, a community for innovation, where idea makers always get a cut of the action, but diffuse the cost and time of development.

LET'S BREAK THE ICE

Quirky is about cool concepts for new products. Submit an idea and it may get made. If it gets developed, you get proceeds. If it's not deemed worthy enough, try again with another idea.

HOW DOES IT WORK?

Quirky calls itself "social product development." Members participate in all aspects of developing the next great product. Anyone can submit an idea, about which the Quirky community—anyone can participate—deliberates and votes.

If they don't deliver enough progress or success at a given stage, products might be phased out or reworked. Many projects do eventually make it out and onto shelves, from where they can be purchased and used by anyone.

Great ideas that have made it through to development and sales include the "Bobble Brush," a device that keeps toothbrushes upright and grime-free, or "Wrapster," a clip-on for headphones that keeps the cords untangled.

WHY IS IT COOL?

Be the next Edison. "It puts the power in the hands of the consumer to design something and have it produced," says Sarah McIlroy of Fashion Playtes (Chapter 26).

SMOOTH SAILING

+ Quirky provides a rigorous framework for successful product design, beginning in ideation and ending with sales.

+ Quirky brings together the wisdom of people through crowd-sourcing, and pairs it with an incredible team of experts armed with specific product development expertise.

+ Everyone who is involved in the development of a

product gets paid. Because it's easy to track people's feedback submissions and product participation with Quirky's platform, everyone who helped shape the final retail form of the product gets compensation. Even if you help 0.00018%, you'll get your fair share of payout from product sales!

+ Submissions cost $10, a sweet spot: the fee will weed out people who aren't serious about their inventions, and is a super cheap investment in your own great viable concept. The cost has come down since the startup first launched, too. In all other aspects of product development, Quirky foots the bill.

CHOPPY WATERS

- Idea marketplaces out in the open mean the ripest melons may be taken! While it's a risk, Quirky prevents idea theft in a few ways. First, the costs and expertise related to product development are prohibitive. Second, Quirky does ensure the products are properly protected with patents or other intellectual property protection—although the rights get assigned to Quirky, not the original inventor.

GOT GOOSEBUMPS?

To start, check out the ideas already on Quirky and vote for your faves! Only the best ideas survive and thrive.

Chapter 63: COLOURlovers

THE WORLD HAS a grand design. Whether you think it was the result of a higher power a couple thousand years ago or of apes running into an evolved state, design is all around us. Color is an important part of the picture, because it's what our eyes connect to instantly. We can register a clash of colors quickly, and feel calm when presented with a pleasant halcyon spread.

Color has the power to change how we feel about something. The cover of this book is bright yellow because yellow is the color of eccentricity and creativity—evocations I knew would be perfect for a book about startups breaking the status quo.

LET'S BREAK THE ICE

COLOURlovers lets people create and share color palettes.

HOW DOES IT WORK?

Anyone can sign up and start picking colors. Color palettes are searchable with a variety of characteristics, from keywords to hue to saturation. If you know a color is a given in your scheme, you can start with that and see what's been designed with that color. It can be a general as "purple" and as specific as HEX color "662D91."

COLOURlovers doesn't stop at pigments, as the website is a database for shapes and patterns too. They also track color trends by scouring color combinations in diverse sources, from wedding invitations to street fashion pics.

WHY IS IT COOL?

Show your true colors about color. It's patchwork for those born without the artist gene.

LET'S SAY...

You're the bridesmaid tasked with helping to pick out the colors for the wedding. That means it'll be seen on invitations, flower bouquets and even the dress you're getting from Rent the Runway (Chapter 22) for the big day. You guess the bride forgot about your horrific color choices from the high school prom committee, but with COLOURlovers, you can camouflage your less than perfect color choices with great taste.

SMOOTH SAILING

+ Design is becoming more important than ever. It's a way to differentiate yourself and your work from anyone else. COLOURlovers invites you to explore design's possibilities in a fun and easy way.

+ There could be an opportunity to bring in advertisers, especially if COLOURlovers can find a way to get visitors to indicate why they need color help. If they're building a website, COLOURlovers could show ads from Wix.com, GoDaddy or Squarespace.com. Whereas if a user is redecorating a room, COLOURlovers can show ads from Home Depot or Lowe's.

+ Millions of patterns, colors and palettes from which to choose, and thousands of community members with whom to interact.

CHOPPY WATERS

- COLOURlovers is built for inspiration. That's not a bad thing, but it's hard to monetize. Instead of forcing dollars from this site, the founders have turned to new and profit-driven ventures. In one, they built a product for professional color coordination. Another is a marketplace for graphic design elements called Creative Market.

GOT GOOSEBUMPS?

Check out the color combinations on COLOURlovers, and heart (the equivalent of a Facebook "Like") the ones that speak to you.

Chapter 64: IdeaPaint

BRAINSTORMING MEETINGS TYPICALLY revolve around trying to find the next million dollar idea using some pens and a slab of butcher paper. But everyone knows that the lightbulb can go off anytime, not just during a designated brainstorm sesh. Plus, keeping around rolls of butcher paper is not economical, environmental or practical.

In 2002, Babson College freshman John Goscha saw the writing on the wall (quite literally), and realized that having a perpetual dry erase surface in your work, home or school space could be both fun and productive.

LET'S BREAK THE ICE

IdeaPaint is a paint that transforms any surface into a dry erase board. Bye bye, chalk dust.

HOW DOES IT WORK?

IdeaPaint can be applied to walls, desks, doors, columns, old whiteboards, storage containers, or even garden gnomes. It comes in two forms, PRO and CRE-8, with a variety of colors from which to choose. Before you open the kit, you must first pick and prepare the surface you want converted to a dry erase surface. After using one of the approved primers, you sand the surface to ensure smoothness. Then, section the surface and begin painting, section by section. Wait seven days, and voila, get some dry erase markers and go nuts with your new white board. But remember, once you're done brainstorming, get out there and implement the best ideas beyond the board room!

LET'S SAY...

I. You're a Manager. You have a conference room in which you typically meet, brainstorm and give presentations. You decide to install IdeaPaint to facilitate innovative thinking, and help get your employees out of their chairs, moving around and collaborating with one another. After IdeaPaint dries, not only do you gain a large white board space for diagramming, drawing, planning, and exchanging ideas, but you also realize you can toss out all the laser pens in the office;

you can project presentations onto the IdeaPaint surface, and actually circle, underline and write on the projected slides with dry erase markers.

II. You're a math teacher at a middle school. You can install IdeaPaint on desktops to reduce the use of paper in the classroom and increase engagement with the lesson. Rather than doing exercises on sheets of paper, you can encourage students to scribble on their IdeaPaint-covered desks. You gain visual insight into the students' thought processes, and can make any corrections to their arithmetic right there on the table. And for them, it beats boring old paper.

WHY IS IT COOL?
Don't confine your thoughts to a piece of paper.

SMOOTH SAILING
+ IdeaPaint is a versatile product; you can apply it to any surface. There are lots of IdeaPaint product offerings to fit different needs, including a small kit for home which covers just six square feet. What remains constant across products is that IdeaPaint facilitates collaboration and communication at home, in school or around office spaces.

+ The paint for home use is sold at Lowe's, an incredible distribution channel for the company. It's comparably priced to typical indoor paint and the company offers long warranties. The paint is light to carry and ship compared to heavy traditional white boards. Ideapaint's distribution is also helped via support from Reebok and Breakaway Ventures.

+ The products have already won a handful of industry, green and consumer awards.

CHOPPY WATERS
- It smells stronger than normal paint. Ick.
- Because of the special nature of IdeaPaint, you don't have much time after you mix the paint to complete the job, and you're not able to do-over your work after you finish painting a section. You might incur a higher cost in materials, often replacing brushes and buckets due to the liquid's quick-hardening properties. IdeaPaint also has a rather long dry time: seven days after application.

GOT GOOSEBUMPS?

Liberate your dry erase pen-wielding creativity! Get a kit and slather the paint on one of the walls of your home or office. An innovative startup that supports innovation? That's cool.

Founders' Top 5 Tips for Better Brainstorming

1. Change your surroundings. "Get out of the environment that you work in everyday. If you stay in the same place, you'll fall into the same habits. Try some different places that get creative juices flowing," says Drew Johnson of SuperBoise, a mobile gaming agency.

2. Think for yourself first. Don't necessarily discuss as a group right off the bat. Coming up with your own ideas and then working as a team to improve the best ones can be ideal, advises Johnson.

3. Get exposed to new ideas, says Henrik Werdelin of Prehype, an innovation consultancy. Look beyond the web. "Read thoughtful books and apply the concepts," he says. Marc Brodeur of Brode (Chapter 29) says that "people who don't try new things are either content or they're afraid of consequences. You can never be satisfied with where things are—you don't need to be upset about the way things are, but be excited about the way things could be."

4. Diversity helps. Scott Summit says the team at Bespoke Innovations (Chapter 65) is varied in skill set, which helps with ideation. "It's all the ingredients of a good bite of Thai food. On the worst days it's like the UN because no one appreciates what the other does." But mostly the variety of perspectives brings forth innovative ideas, he says.

5. Do thought experiments. Sam Zaid, CEO of Getaround (Chapter 21), is a wiz at brainstorming, often thinking up extreme future situations and drawing out their implications. If everyone had a smartphone, would money still be needed? Credit cards? Smartphones could replace a lot of things. It's akin to "extrapolating scenarios like the military does with forecasting," he says. "Imagine the world in the future and backpedal from there. Getaround was self-driving cars to connected cars to mobile phones."

DEFROST: Startups and the Military

Military men and women are battle-tested, and can flourish as entrepreneurs who deal with proverbial battles daily. Grueling hours? The tireless pursuit of ideals? Fierce competition? Check. Check. And, check. Veterans may have more experience with these challenges than the rest of us. The leadership, organizational experience, and action-oriented work they espouse in the military can contribute greatly to the economy and startup ecosystem.

I was first exposed to the military personnel's penchant for business excellence as a high school student witnessing West Point grad Kelly Perdew win *The Apprentice*. There must be a movement to get more military veterans into startup culture. In fact, through the Small Business Administration, the US government now offers the Patriot Express Loan, which provides capital to military-affiliated entrepreneurs. The eligibility is broad, including spouses of veterans and active-duty military members.

"It's hard to uncover a heuristic around military and entrepreneurship because of the time perspective. In WWII, most healthy adult males served, so it's likely many of them later became entrepreneurs," says Christopher Michel, the serial entrepreneur behind Military.com, founding partner of Nautilus Ventures and former Entrepreneur-in-Residence at Harvard Business School. "There are leadership lessons in the US military. There's usually pollyannaish language around courage and integrity, but those aren't the most powerful ideas," Michel tells me. The most powerful is that "in the military we have to learn how to motivate and lead with tools other than money. People are motivated by personal needs like growth and respect. People aren't fundamentally motivated by money. It's about making a difference and being acknowledged. This is our bread and butter."

Chapter 65: Bespoke Innovations

MEDICINE IS CRAFT. Art is craft. Rarely do the two get matched in one startup.

LET'S BREAK THE ICE

Bespoke Innovations creates custom 3D devices with purpose. Their first products are beautifully designed prosthetic limbs for amputees.

BACKSTORY

Bespoke is a collaboration of art and science. One co-founder is a designer, the other a doctor. They saw an opportunity—nay, a need—for aesthetic design of prosthetics. Their approach is radical, and life-changing for those it affects.

"It's sad that anything with the slightest medical connotation falls into the category that it's okay if you tolerate it. Of all things you should love, it should be medical because it's personal," says Scott Summit, co-founder and CTO. "Prosthetics are the worst case because they're utilitarian and pragmatic. On the best day, you can only tolerate it. We say: this is a part of the human. You better make them love it, otherwise you're doing a disservice."

When I visited Bespoke, Summit was preparing for an upcoming TED talk. I asked if he already had his slides prepared. Not yet, he said, but he was thinking to address why certain products or conditions are sources of alienation. "We're surrounded by people who wear eye wear everyday," Summit tells me. "They have less than perfect vision but we never say, 'Oh my, I can't talk to them, they're wearing glasses.' That's because designers created glasses. More glasses are sold without prescription than with it because people like what it does to their face. Society rarely think of prosthetic devices as things that make you look good, but why shouldn't it fall into the same category?"

Sutha Kamal, CEO of the healthcare startup Massive Health, tells me that great design is usually ignored in medical systems. "The immediate response from the healthcare industry is that people in focus groups don't ask for design. Well, the iPhone wouldn't be built in focus groups. Beautiful design is something people are beginning to notice and love. That sort of love is missing from traditional healthcare."

Steven Dean, an entrepreneur who focuses on bringing design thinking and methodology to healthcare, says "What I've encountered with most product development is that it's not driven from the end user's needs. It's driven by technical and clinical requirements. It's not intentional, but it's how the industry was built. Now, there's an opportunity to bring user-centered design to healthcare products."

The co-founders of Bespoke are doing this through complementary skills. Summit says. "Artists create neat stuff that often has no value and doctors rarely imagine designing, but put them together and you have something really innovative like Bespoke."

WHY IS IT COOL?
Aesthetics + Practicality.

HOW DOES IT WORK?
For its prosthetic leg product, Bespoke employs a straightforward process. First, the client's intact leg is scanned. Second, Bespoke designs the prosthetic leg to match. Finally, the leg is 3D printed.

One of the first people Bespoke Innovations was able to help was a runner who had lost her leg. Rather than a standard replacement, Bespoke was able to create a unique leg for her. "It's her signature, like a fingerprint. How can you replace a leg with a carbon rod? It's absurd," Summit says. Bespoke performed a 3D scan of her healthy leg, mirrored it, and designed the prosthetic leg accordingly. The design attention didn't stop there. Bespoke chrome-plated the leg, "because chrome is sexy," says Summit. The results are stunning, I'll tell you. "People don't ogle amputees, but people tell her all the time what a beautiful leg she has!" says Summit. "People don't usually say that to amputees, and for the first time, it's part of the discourse."

The technology involved is equally stunning. According to Summit, no one had tried to print a prosthetic leg before Bespoke came on the scene. Summit figured that if a hinge could be 3D printed, a knee could be designed in a similar way. There's lots of machinery involved, but when the 3D printing is done, a leg comes out of the machine in one piece. It isn't "assembled," in the typical sense, and there are even a few pieces deep inside the knee construction that cannot be seen by a human eye. Summit says the leg is as complex as a car transmission due to interlinking and rotating pieces.

For all its technology, the 3D prints also happen to be "really strong, decently light, dishwasher safe and environmentally benign." Summit thinks it can be incredibly impactful in developing countries for these reasons.

The 3D printers Bespoke utilizes are located in South Carolina, and a team travels around the country with 3D mobile scanners of their own invention in order to service clients, including injured veterans.

The cost is a few hundred dollars for each 3D print. Bespoke has mastered efficiency in batching its print jobs because each run has a base cost. Ultimately, the company goes with 3D printing not because it's the cheapest manufacturing option but because "it's impossible to do it any other way." Summit says that a decade ago, Bespoke's products would be unmakeable since they can't be created with typical machines or by hand. A better option than prohibitively expensive objection molding, 3D printing allows Bespoke to simply print the individualized objects.

According to Summit, 3D printing devices have existed for about two decades. The first machines printed from liquid, which produced products that were accurate, but which became brittle and yellow over time. Next, power-based machines were invented. Then, adding a layer of metal to the objects for strength and beauty became a reality. Summit says "You can print metal very accurately. You can print rubber, glass, plastic, gold and silver too." At Bespoke, they're constantly experimenting. "What happens when you blast a laser into leather?" poses Summit. "We can laser tattoos. Chad who lost his leg, got tribal tats on his prosthetic leg."

Those design elements make a difference. "It's a life-shaking thing to have lost a limb," says Summit. "Why have the thing that replaces it make you wince? You've been through a lot so why not make it the coolest thing ever?"

This perspective changes the preconceived notions about amputees. "It shakes it up," Summit affirms. "Other people begin to ask, 'am I really feeling jealous?' They have this thing that's really cool. It's shifted social perception and consciousness. It was a source of misery and through design we can flip it on its head and make it a source of pride."

SMOOTH SAILING

+ Summit teaches at Singularity University, out of which several Coolest Startups came. I loved his description of the students. "It's like going to the pound and only dealing with the border collies. They're high energy and very brainy." SU invited Summit to teach in part because of his immense expertise in 3D printing. While the technology is 20-years-old, he's worked with it since day one.

+ Bespoke has all sorts of fun side projects, too. They've made a firefighter's "suit of armor of the future" for Discovery Channel, and "bling" (like rings and bracelets). Summit doesn't view Bespoke as a medical company. "In a way, we're a jewelry and fashion design company," Summit says. That's something that causes friendly banter with co-founder, Dr. Kenneth Trauner, who says Bespoke is a medical company first and foremost. Summit settles it by saying, "I consider us a new technology-design company." You can't put this Coolest Startup in a box.

+ Bespoke has contacts with many doctors and major hospitals who send the company new clients.

+ Environmentally, Bespoke is great. The company's products have an immesurably low carbon footprint, Summit says. "For the quality of life impact, I can't imagine anything having been created on par. It's good on every front and if we can make profit, that's great."

+ "Bespoke" literally means "custom-made." Individualization of products and services is a macro-trend we'll see more of in the technology industry over the next decade—a macro-trend that the company is already broaching, and with noble purpose.

CHOPPY WATERS

- This startup is exceptional from every angle.

GOT GOOSEBUMPS?

View the images of happy clients on Bespoke's website.

"The best way to predict the future is to create it yourself."

- Peter Diamandis,
co-founder of Singularity University

JOBFULL
Hire Me startups

Chapter 66: The Resumator

APPLYING FOR JOBS is less than thrilling, as any job seeker knows. But get ready for this revelation: dealing with applications is unnerving for *all* sides of the equation. HR people grow miserable over inefficient sifting of paper applications and candidate tracking. When both sides of a marketplace are down and out, therein lies a golden opportunity for a startup.

Add to HR another facet of an applicant for recruiters to consider: social life. Well, the online social network variety, at least. This Coolest Startup makes HR tools more efficient *and* more social media-savvy.

LET'S BREAK THE ICE

The Resumator makes it easy to promote jobs throughout the Internet, including social networks.

HOW DOES IT WORK?

Recruiting is hard work. It's about finding the right person for the right job at the right time doing the right tasks for the right price. It's like playing matchmaker, and if you've ever tried to set anyone up on a date, you know how hard that can be! The Resumator's idea is to mobilize your whole organization, and the social and professional webs that spin from them, to expand your recruiting reach. You're evolving the recruitment game and bringing in the best talent, all because the whole organization is getting involved.

But The Resumator doesn't stop there. With The Resumator, it's also easier for candidates to apply and for HR people to track applicants. "We want to be the ubiquitous HR product," says spokeswoman Laurie Barkman.

The Resumator does this with an incredible sleek interface that's easy for anyone to set up and implement. The first step is to input the open positions in the company. The jobs are then promoted on the company's website (through The Resumator's plug-in website module that works with just a few lines of code) and on social networks. As applications flow in, The Resumator's help doesn't end; it helps out with candidate tracking and evaluation too.

The most unique piece of The Resumator is its thoughtful usage of social networks throughout the company. What's in it for fellow employees to help promote jobs? Isn't that HR's job? Well, for those people who aren't incentivized by the pure passion of getting the best people into the firm to work alongside you, thankfully The Resumator also makes it easy for the organization to include employee referral funds. So if it's someone from accounting who discovers the next Chief Technology Officer for your firm, the accountant can add a few more debits to his/her name.

WHY IS IT COOL?
The Resumator's tool is Schwarzenegger-strong, so we hope they won't come up with an inverse product for firing or layoffs called The Terminator!

SMOOTH SAILING
+ It's definitely an evolution from the Monster.com era. The Resumator is designed with social media intimately integrated from the start.

+ The Resumator can accommodate extreme granularity, helping with interviews, too. HR can decide what factors are important in a job as well as the relevant scales and weightings for each factor, so that each applicant is rated on those same characteristics and on a comparable system during the process.

CHOPPY WATERS
- The Resumator competes with HR tools provided by professional social networks, like LinkedIn.

- The Resumator has a very startup-centric client list. Not bad, but we all know how insular startups can be! The Resumator needs to get out there to every business.

GOT GOOSEBUMPS?
Get the free trial. If your company is using one of those decrepit systems from 1999, throw a fit in the HR department and get them to change to The Resumator! Just don't go too crazy—HR has magic firing powers, you know.

Chapter 67: Brand Affinity Technologies

ADVERTISING IS EVERYWHERE. And we often like to see the faces of pretty and strong people in it. While the big campaigns (Cover Girl, pick me next!) are left to the A-listers, there are plenty of local and regional brands and products that would love to feature local hits in their branding.

LET'S BREAK THE ICE

Brand Affinity Technologies (BAT) is a platform for celebrities—no matter how small—to connect to brands and product endorsements, even at the local level.

HOW DOES IT WORK?

If you're a celebrity, you can expect to get signed to BAT with ease. The next step is showing up for a photo and video shoot. It's unclear if BAT provides free donuts and coffee, but by the end of the shoot, they'll have great footage of you to include in their databases.

Prospective advertisers can then peruse the databases and ask to use the provided footage, or they can pay for custom messages to be acted out by the pros to be used in advertising initiatives.

WHY IS IT COOL?

Peyton Manning shouldn't be the only celebrity to use his muscles for endorsements!

LET'S SAY...

You own a local bike shop and would love for a local bike legend to endorse your store in order to boost sales before the busy summer season. Tap into BAT for a great athlete to back you up.

SMOOTH SAILING

+ They are extending beyond their initial scope. Now BAT is about being a hub for better connecting celebs to their fans, too. One of their properties, Fantapper, is a massive database of celebrities that aggregates all of the celebs' web presences in one place for the benefit of fans. Fantapper has pretty strong usage from fans, so it's a great way for BAT to have expanded its product offerings by leveraging its proprietary information and celebrity domain expertise.

CHOPPY WATERS
   - BAT's database for its core product is highly sports-driven. Diversify!

GOT GOOSEBUMPS?
   Check out where in the world BAT's signed talent resides using BAT's online interactive map. You may discover a celeb in your neighborhood.

Chapter 68: Hire My Mom

BY THE 1970s mommies had entered the workforce in droves due to a variety of factors. Feminists cheer and businesses boom with women at companies, but many career ladies with offspring are torn by their lack of quality time with the kiddies. To balance work and home, Texas momma Lesley Pyle founded a company with a blunt name, "Hire My Mom."

LET'S BREAK THE ICE

Hire My Mom matches companies with work-from-home professionals (who happen to be mothers).

HOW DOES IT WORK?

Hire My Mom markets to businesses, encouraging them to list job opportunities that would be great for work-from-home moms, from data entry to blogging. Moms pay $99 per year to get a daily email and web access to the job listings. Companies aren't charged for listing their job opportunities. Moms directly apply to jobs that they find interesting and the companies decide who they want to hire.

According to Morgan Dierstein, CEO of RentAStudent (which connects students with companies for consulting work in a similarly high-quality way), the main trend helping companies like Hire My Mom or RentAStudent is outsourcing. "There are 21 million small businesses in the US that need in-house help because they don't have enough employees," Dierstein says. "You can't scale without help so you need to outsource some tasks you can't complete on your own."

While there are options to outsource the work abroad using Elance, Odesk or AskSunday (Chapter 46), Dierstein says those options can result in communication problems with workers which lead to lower-quality work. Using America-centric outsourcing firms like RentAStudent or Hire My Mom means reduced risk of a language barrier.

LET'S SAY...

You're the new mom -of a healthy, happy baby. Your maternity leave is up, but you decide that you want to continue staying at home with your newborn. You join Hire My Mom and find a slew of work opportunities. You apply and get one of the jobs, so you can now pay your bills and breastfeed.

WHY IS IT COOL?

Makes Moms happy (with work-life balance) all year round, not just on Mother's Day.

SMOOTH SAILING

+ Featured by Fox News, Entrepreneur.com, and many more media outlets, this startup has enviable brand recognition. Who could forget a name like "Hire My Mom"?

+ Hire My Mom has elegant execution of its business. It's an email listserv at its core, so the Hire My Mom business itself is low cost to maintain.

+ According to the Census Bureau, 5.4 million women are out of the workplace to stay home. At about $100 per year per member, these stats put Hire My Mom's potential revenues at over $50 million per year.

+ Hire My Mom creates a win-win-win. Moms benefit from flexible work opportunities. Companies benefit from being able to hire inexpensive labor (after all, they're not paying health insurance). And, Hire My Mom benefits with its cool business.

CHOPPY WATERS

- Data shows that men are hurting badly in the recession of the late-2000s. Maybe Hire My Mom should open another website: Hire My Dad.

- Charging members (instead of companies) for access to job opportunities is atypical in the jobs industry. Members may be concerned that they are paying to get paid.

GOT GOOSEBUMPS?

If a mom in need of a work-from-home arrangement, tell your mom to sign up, or sign up yourself. You can cancel membership at any time, though the company doesn't issue refunds. Even if you're not a mom you could sign up; they won't reject you from joining the site simply because you're not a child-rearing matriarch.

DEFROST: When Is a Startup No Longer a Startup?

There is little industry consensus on the timing or milestones that define when a startup shakes off the label. Many people considered Facebook a startup up until its IPO declaration, despite its seven years of age and roaring success (like you need reminding) that has made Mark Zuckerberg the world's youngest billionaire.

Was pre-IPO Facebook a startup or media mammoth? You could look at it from a few perspectives:

- Size of Consumer Base
- Market Share
- Number of Employees
- Prominence in the Media
- Self-Definition: Once a startup stops referring to itself as one, take it on faith that it has graduated
- Technological Development
- Exit Event

Any of the above, or a few in combination, can define the endpoint of a startup's life as such. But it's not quite that simple.

Starting from the top of that list, the number of customers to constitute critical mass varies by industry. For example, the customer base needed to deem car ownership successful is larger than that for video game console ownership, as the former is a necessity for many rather than a leisure purchase. Market share is similarly deceptive. For example, SecondMarket (Chapter 6) may be the most recognizable name in private company trading, but in the wider universe of illiquid assets, it still has room to grow. The vantage point makes a difference in the determination. Media prominence could be a measure of a startup's life; maybe a startup is deemed something greater once it becomes a buzzword. That too feels subjective. The number of employees in a startup's ranks could also be a valid metric, but whereas some successful startups grow to take in hundreds of thousands of employees, others defy this barometer of success by staying small. This fact throws another painfully convenient measurement out the window! As for self-definition, the problem is its subjectivity too. Maybe the shift happens when the company grows unwieldy, and is no longer able to define and push forward the cutting edge of technological development. But even that feels like a wrong definition, as not all startups are defined by their technological prowess.

The obvious determination may be the most touted one: the occurrence of an exit event like a Merger, Acquisition, or Initial-Public Offering (IPO). The implication of such a strict definition means that startups actually remain "startups" for quite awhile. M&As and IPOs don't happen overnight. The National Venture Capital Association (NVCA) says that in recent years, the median time for a startup to undergo M&A is seven years. For an IPO event, it's closer to 10 years. And, what if a startup decides to forgo an exit event and simply stay revenue-generating on its own for posterity? This possibility complicates an otherwise simple definition.

But at least it's a certain one. If anyone asks you, "when is a startup no longer a startup?" you can tell them that if the company goes IPO, gets acquired or merges, that's a certain endpoint.

This is a tricky question, startup experts agree. Brian Zisk, the founder of entrepreneurship conferences in the San Francisco Bay Area, says, "the lines have been blurred." Nick Ganju, CTO at ZocDoc (Chapter 55) says the definition may have to do with the disappearance of business uncertainty. "When the learning has decayed to a certain point, then you're no longer a startup," he responds. "Look at the airline industry. The key performance indicators (KPIs) are well-defined, like dollar per seat mile or capacity. All the metrics are completely standardized. It's common knowledge what the airline is doing. Whereas, startups are discovering how their business is done. I love coming to work because we're constantly learning, and as we figure out the business, the company grows in value and gets more attractive. When that stabilizes to the point that we know how to run the business perfectly, then it's a mature company. The rate of change is huge at ZocDoc so we're still a startup." Paul Murphy, Head of Business Development at Aviary (Chapter 61), reckons that may be right. "It has something to do with growth," he says. "When there's no longer exponential growth, people who were there at the startup's early days will leave." It seems the startup is then no longer one.

HEARD FROM A HOT SHOT

"I define end of 'startup' as when you 'invest with confidence.'"

- @JacobAldridge, a UK-based business coach, to @ASmartBear, Texas-based serial entrepreneur Jason Cohen

THEY SAY IT'S not what you know, but *who* you know that makes the (hiring) difference.

LET'S BREAK THE ICE

Turn your social network into a professional one.

HOW DOES IT WORK?

BranchOut is an application built within Facebook. It's Facebook's largest professional network, in fact. BranchOut was created by Rick Marini, who previously worked on Monster.com. Christopher Michel, a serial entrepreneur and investor who helped fund BranchOut, says Marini is an expert in the job space. "He knows how to help people leverage their network to get ahead," Michel says.

The concept is smart, and the application works as you would expect. After joining BranchOut, members can add information about themselves and connect with other members. The job search feature is one of the most valuable aspects of the system. Upon identifying an interesting open position in BranchOut, you can read more about the job and see the "inside connections" that you can tap at the firm. With another click, you can apply to the job.

WHY IS IT COOL?

Gets your friends to help you find a job.

SMOOTH SAILING

+ Alison Hillman, BranchOut's community manager, explains on Quora (Chapter 59) why Facebook is one of the best platforms for employment networking. First, the membership of Facebook is over 10 times that of the largest independent professional network, LinkedIn, so it's an ideal space online for networking of any kind. Second, LinkedIn focuses on white-collar jobs; utilizing Facebook would make the job types included more diverse. Third, Facebook has a high level of engagement, with many members logging in daily. Finally, networks on Facebook are typically more close-knit than on LinkedIn, where connections are often mere acquaintances.

+ In addition to BranchOut's app for Facebook users, BranchOut offers services for recruiters. Research indicates that almost half of all job seekers use social networks in their job search, so recruiters will go where the candidates are, and that's great news for BranchOut.

CHOPPY WATERS

- Not all Facebook apps have a hot layout. Using Branchout, or any app on Facebook, isn't as pleasant an experience as LinkedIn. Sure, the network is right there, but it's not a breeze to access.

GOT GOOSEBUMPS?

Join today. It's totally free. But you have to be part of Facebook first!

[NOT] MADE IN AMERICA

International Startups
Too Cool to Leave Out

FLUSHING A TOILET uses three gallons of water. When water is scarce, toilets seem truly wasteful. China-based entrepreneur Wu Hao figured that with current toilet technology, there wouldn't be enough water for everyone in the world to have waste management. With Landwasher, he's reinventing toilets to be more environmentally friendly and water efficient.

LET'S BREAK THE ICE

Landwasher toilets enable water-free flushing, ideal for places where water is scarce.

HOW DOES IT WORK?

A Landwasher toilet uses a unique flushing system that requires no water. Rather than water, the toilet uses urine and a patent-protected special agent to sterilize and flush away the matter in the toilet. Only a little bit of water is used in set-up for the first flush to operate properly, but otherwise, no consistent water supply is needed and little electricity is used to operate the outhouse.

Landwasher has already sold 10,000 portable toilets, and looks to expand geographically beyond China and into India and other regions. The system is particularly useful for developing countries where access to water may be scarce and piping infrastructure is lacking.

WHY IS IT COOL?

It may not be the sexiest product, but Landwasher leaves its mark with eco-friendliness and resource efficiency.

SMOOTH SAILING

+ Officials for the Beijing Olympics in 2008 selected Landwasher's product as the official mobile toilet vendor.

+ Because Landwasher's core product is the water-free flushing system and sterilizing agent, the toilets themselves can be diverse in design. Landwasher sells toilets in "modern urban" style to "antique" design. Landwasher can also design toilets that accommodate people with disabilities.

+ Landwasher toilets are eco-friendly. Not only do they

use little water or electricity, but the fluid used for flushing is made without those heavy chemicals that might otherwise bear negative effects on the surrounding communities.

CHOPPY WATERS
- This concept has been fully flushed out. No cons in sight!

GOT GOOSEBUMPS?
It's not easy to get in touch with this startup, stateside. Landwasher's official website is written in Chinese, but use Google Translate and you can at least figure out who to contact to order one of these revolutionary latrines.

Chapter 71: PrimeSense

REMOTE CONTROLS ARE last century. In the near future, we'll use our bodies to control space.

LET'S BREAK THE ICE

PrimeSense is a consumer electronics startup based in Israel that allows human gestures to direct devices, without the mouse or remote.

HOW DOES IT WORK?

PrimeSense's devices use sensors coupled with software. The sensor takes in the user's movements and environment, which the software interprets. What makes PrimeSense's technology unique, compared to Nintendo Wii, is that PrimeSense does not require the user to wear or hold any special device. There are major applications for this technology in gaming and virtual communications.

In the short-term, PrimeSense is looking to make TVs more engaging. For example, PrimeSense can recognize its users sitting on the sofa to enjoy some entertainment, and can then facilitate more advanced personalization of the TV set. The user could essentially be shown more customized experiences with the TV because PrimeSense identifies the user. This can facilitate new and faster visual information experiences. In the same way that tablets have enabled touch-screen technologies to wow consumers, PrimeSense is working in 3D to knock us off our feet. Controls are no longer just up-down and left-right—say hello to the element of depth.

PrimeSense is commercializing the technology primarily through licensing its concept to more mainstream brands and manufacturers. They could pursue a direct-to-consumer approach too. There are already thousands of developers building apps for the PrimeSense system.

WHY IS IT COOL?

Operating electronics with hand gestures is cool. Period!

SMOOTH SAILING

+ PrimeSense is positioning itself for a successful business because it doesn't take the risk of creating a new brand or manufacturing inventory. It's selling its technology to established players who can commercialize it.

CHOPPY WATERS
- Fun fact: PrimeSense made some of the 3D sensing technologies in Microsoft's Kinect product. With Kinect, after a rather easy initial setup, users can engage with games and software menus using their bodies. The stuff is somewhat buggy still, but hopefully PrimeSense will take the technology to the next level.

GOT GOOSEBUMPS?
Until manufacturers build the proper "ecosystem" around this product, PrimeSense is something you'll only be able to see in video demos. I can't wait to use it as soon as it's in my living room!

Chapter 72: Issuu

MAGAZINES HAVE GONE digital. Paperwork has too.

LET'S BREAK THE ICE
Issuu, a startup based in Copenhagen, Denmark, helps people keep documents beautiful and interactive.

HOW DOES IT WORK?
Journalism wasn't meant to be confined to plain paper, and online publishing wasn't meant to look like a boring old print-out. Issuu enables gorgeous and engaging publications for creative groups of all sizes—from a one-person writer in mid-America to a large team or brand. These publishers can upload any document (even a basic PDF) and use Issuu's tools to add links and other elements, like videos or slide shows. Publishers can then share the online publication with friends and subscribers, and consult in-depth analytics on what people read, clicked on and engaged with, completing an informative feedback loop for writers on what resonates best.

WHY IS IT COOL?
Issuu brings online publishing up to its full potential.

SMOOTH SAILING
+ While Issuu uses Flash-based tech, it is working on non-Flash technology to allow magazine perusal across devices.

+ Millions of people use Issuu monthly, but it's only just catching on in the US.

CHOPPY WATERS
- This could transform subscriptions for magazines, too. An option to charge for online publications would push Issuu to become a marketplace, not just an advertising business.

GOT GOOSEBUMPS?
Browse the magazine racks at Issuu.com. Have something to say? Make your own. We all have the power to create and it's never been easier to share your great ideas with the world.

APPENDICES
New Ways to See the Coolest Startups

A. By Funding
B. By Geography
C. By Age
D. By Incubators
E. By Type
F. Honorable Mentions
G. Resources

Appendix A: Coolest Startups By Funding

STARTUPS IN THIS volume of the book ranged in their funding levels from nearly $1 billion in investment money to none. The information provided in these Appendices comes from corporate websites and Crunchbase.com, a fantastic startup resource. Here's the list from big to penny-pinchedom!

20	Better Place	$950,000,000
17	Palantir	$245,000,000
1	Square	$168,000,000
55	ZocDoc	$95,000,000
2	Lending Club	$77,700,000
38	foursquare	$71,400,000
14	23andMe	$52,600,000
6	SecondMarket	$34,200,000
22	Rent the Runway	$30,000,000
48	TaskRabbit	$24,700,000
27	ViKi	$24,300,000
69	BranchOut	$24,000,000
62	Quirky	$23,300,000
54	Fitbit	$23,000,000
71	PrimeSense	$20,400,000
67	Brand Affinity Technologies	$20,000,000
53	Demandbase	$18,000,000
64	IdeaPaint	$13,300,000
19	Mission Motors	$12,400,000
15	Shapeways	$11,100,000
59	Quora	$11,000,000
61	Aviary	$11,000,000
3	Kickstarter	$10,500,000
13	Qwiki	$10,500,000
60	Disqus	$10,500,000
28	Turntable.fm	$7,000,000
12	Dwolla	$6,310,000
72	Issuu	$6,250,000
26	Fashion Playtes	$5,500,000
21	Getaround	$5,130,000
30	Khan Academy	$5,000,000

50	Quixey	$4,200,000
33	Skillshare	$3,650,000
36	HowAboutWe	$3,100,000
58	Oasys Water	$3,000,000
35	Codecademy	$2,500,000
7	AxialMarket	$2,000,000
39	ThinkNear	$1,630,000
65	Bespoke Innovations	$1,600,000
24	MoviePass	$1,500,000
49	Producteev	$1,310,000
57	Organovo	$1,000,000
63	COLOURLovers	$1,000,000
66	The Resumator	$875,000
41	Blueseed	$500,000
47	Boomerang by Baydin	$375,000
45	Tout	$350,000
4	StarStreet	$250,000
5	Segmint	$250,000
37	Sonar	$200,000
9	Hudl	$100,000
32	CourseHorse	$75,000
25	evoJets	$50,000
43	Snooze by LetGive	$25,000
51	iDoneThis	$25,000
40	Wello	$25,000
10	HaveMyShift	$12,000
70	Landwasher	-
34	Grovo	-
56	Asthmapolis	-
46	AskSunday	-
42	HealthMap	-
18	Dekko	-
11	Uppward	-
23	UJAM	-
29	Brode	-
16	Word Lens	-
52	RightSignature	-
31	Wolfram Alpha	-
44	Catchafire	-
68	Hire My Mom	-
8	FamZoo	-

COOLEST STARTUPS ARE all around us. Here's where the American companies in this volume of the book reside. Those with various locations around the US may be listed multiple times. Those with remote team members may not be listed.

Boston/Cambridge, MA
HealthMap (42)
Oasys Water (58)
StarStreet (4)
IdeaPaint (64)

Champaign, IL
Wolfram Alpha (31)

Chicago, IL
HaveMyShift (10)

Des Moines, IA
Uppward (11)
Dwolla (12)

Houston, TX
Hire My Mom (68)

Lincoln, NE
Hudl (9)

Los Angeles, CA
ThinkNear (39)
Brand Affinity Technologies (67)

Madison, WI
Asthampolis (56)

McLean, VA
Palantir (17)

THE OLDEST STARTUPS in this volume date back to 2004, the newest being born in 2011. The average age of a Coolest Startup from this volume is about three years. Here's the full list:

One year or under (Founded in 2011)
Dekko (18)
Turntable.fm (28)
Codecademy (35)
ThinkNear (39)
MoviePass (24)
Blueseed (41)
CourseHorse (32)
Snooze by LetGive (43)
iDoneThis (51)

Founded in 2010
Grovo (34)
Uppward (11)
UJAM (23)
Brode (29)
BranchOut (69)
Skillshare (33)
Tout (45)
Sonar (38)

Founded in 2009
Asthmapolis (56)
Word Lens (16)
RightSignature (52)
Square (1)
foursquare (37)
Quirky (62)
Quora (59)
Kickstarter (3)
Qwiki (13)
Getaround (21)
Quixey (50)

HowAboutWe (36)
Oasys Water (58)
Bespoke Innovations (65)
The Resumator (66)
Boomerang by Baydin (47)
Wello (40)
HaveMyShift (10)

Founded in 2008
Wolfram Alpha (31)
Catchafire (44)
Rent the Runway (22)
TaskRabbit (48)
ViKi (27)
Fashion Playtes (26)
Dwolla (12)
Producteev (49)
StarStreet (4)

Founded in 2007
AskSunday (46)
Hire My Mom (68)
Better Place (20)
ZocDoc (55)
FitBit (54)
Brand Affinity
  Technologies (67)
Mission Motors (19)
Shapeways (15)
Aviary (61)
Disqus (60)
AxialMarket (7)
Organovo (57)
Segmint (5)

Founded in 2006
HealthMap (42)
FamZoo (8)
Lending Club (2)
23andMe (14)
Demandbase (53)

IdeaPaint (64)
Issuu (72)
Khan Academy (30)
Hudl (9)

Founded in 2005
PrimeSense (71)
COLOURlovers (63)
evoJets (25)

Founded in 2004
Palantir (17)
SecondMarket (6)

SEVERAL DOZEN COOLEST Startups have enjoyed funding by startup accelerator programs. These are listed below.

500 Startups
Tout (45)
TaskRabbit (48)
COLOURlovers (63)
ViKi (27)

Alpha Lab
The Resumator (66)

Angelpad
iDoneThis (51)

ER Accelerator
Snooze by LetGive (43)

Neoteny Labs (Singapore)
ViKi (27)

SU (Singularity University)
Getaround (21)

TechStars
ThinkNear (39)
Boomerang by Baydin (47)
HaveMyShfit (10)
StarStreet (4)

Y Combinator
Disqus (60)

Appendix E: Coolest Startups
By Type

INNOVATION ISN'T ONLY online. Here is the breakdown of Coolest Startups by type of venture.

B2B
AxialMarket (7)
Segmint (5)
SecondMarket (6)

Biotechnology
Organovo (57)
23andMe (14)

CleanTech
Getaround (21)
Oasys Water (58)
Better Place (20)
Mission Motors (19)

Communications
iDoneThis (51)
Producteev (49)

Consumer Web
Turntable.fm (28)
Codecademy (35)
Grovo (34)
BranchOut (69)
Quora (59)
Kickstarter (3)
Qwiki (13)
HowAboutWe (36)
HaveMyShift (10)
Wolfram Alpha (31)
Catchafire (44)
TaskRabbit (48)
ViKi (27)

StarStreet (4)
ZocDoc (55)
Disqus (60)
HealthMap (42)
Lending Club (2)

Design
Quirky (62)
COLOURlovers (63)

Device
Asthmapolis (56)
Bespoke Innovations (65)
FitBit (54)
PrimeSense (71)

eCommerce
CourseHorse (32)
Snooze by LetGive (43)
Fashion Playtes (26)

Education
Skillshare (33)
Khan Academy (30)

Entertainment
MoviePass (24)
UJAM (23)

Incubator
Blueseed (41)

Mobile
Dekko (18)
ThinkNear (39)
Uppward (11)
Sonar (38)
Word Lens (16)
Square (1)
foursquare (37)
Aviary (61)

Product
Landwasher (70)
Brode (29)
Wello (40)
Shapeways (15)
IdeaPaint (64)

Search
Quixey (50)

Service
Rent the Runway (22)
AskSunday (46)
Hire My Mom (68)
Brand Affinity Technologies (67)
evoJets (25)

Software
Tout (45)
RightSignature (52)
The Resumator (66)
Boomerang by Baydin (47)
Dwolla (12)
Demandbase (53)
Issuu (72)
Hudl (9)
Palantir (17)
FamZoo (8)

Appendix F: Honorable Mentions

THERE ARE SO many upstarts out there, so many that I could only have discucsed them all at the cost of overwhelming my dear readers. Plus, many startups aren't quite developed enough yet to warrant a place on my main list. But some show promise. Here is the list of startups I have my eyes on:

1. **Xtranormal** - Videos are becoming all the more important as people's attention spans shrink. Xtranormal has really awful voiceovers and super gimmicky interfaces to create video memes, but it could get more sophisticated.

2. **Authenticate It** - Helps get rid of the phonies in your life. Never buy a fake again.

3. **Melon Card** - "Most people don't know that there are dozens of companies tracking info on everyone," says Drew Gilliam of HaveMyShift (Chapter 10). "99% of it is harmless, but sometimes bad things surface." Melon Card helps you know what's out there about you. Some people say that the Internet is written in ink, not of the erasable variety.

4. **Timehop** - "At a time when so many apps encourage users to send more and more information out into the Internet, Timehop invites introspection," says Samara Trilling, a Coolest Startups online reader. "Timehop sends you an email every day with all of your foursquare, Instagram, Facebook and Twitter posts from one year ago that day. It's my favorite email to receive every morning!"

5. **AirBnB** - I know they're a huge startup, but they're just an honorable mention to me. They've have some hard times due to allegations of shady advertising, to homes occasionally getting ransacked... but a nice vacation house for a week on the cheap? Still sounds like a deal.

6. **Coffee Joulies** - Like the Baby Bear, your beverage won't be too cold or too hot.

7. **Voxy** - It's difficult to learn a language by studying it just one or two hours a day. Studies show that it's best to immerse yourself in the language to really get your tongue sharp. Voxy is a mobile app that "brings language learning into daily life," says Jeremy Johnson of education-based startup 2tor. For example, if you check in to a bank or

restaurant, the app would provide you with handy words that apply to your immediate environs.

8. Zivelo - Ever wonder who makes those touch-screen kiosks at the mall? Well, Zivelo makes the best and brightest.

9. GiveForward - Healthcare in this country is brutal, and this startup isn't waiting for legislation changes. Now people can help out others directly.

10. Reflex Edge - Us Americans love our men (and women!) in uniform. Military folks make great entrepreneurs seeing as they've already been battle-tested in the realest sense. Check out the Reflex Edge team, military veterans building military things.

11. The Shirt - I wish I had thought up this startup; for years I never bought button down white shirts because the bust button would always pop! No more problems now with this Oprah-endorsed product, The Shirt.

12. Mequilibrium - This startup gives you tools to reduce stress.

13. The Greatist - They're making the "gymbase," a database for gyms. The Greatist has an awesome brand, fantastic blog, and fun team too.

14. GoSpotCheck - Businesses pay people directly to be their eyes and ears on the ground.

15. SoundCloud - We have search engines for videos and words, but what about search engines for sounds? That's the tune that SoundCloud is humming.

16. Visual.ly - The world is getting more visual and data-rich. Browse and share infographics with this startup.

17. Nest - Nest evolves the thermostat to be eco-friendly and gorgeous. Michael Sinanian, a reporter at VentureBeat, says, "Nest redesigned the thermostat, a long neglected but super important piece of home comfort. It's a magical product. It just works."

18. GreenGoose - The technology in this startup is a collection of accelerometers that measure motion. It's useful for collecting data about your offline activities so you can optimize them and constantly improve.

IF YOU LOVED reading about *The Coolest Startups in America* and have a hankering for more, read on to find resources that are updated multiple times daily with startup-related content.

For specific information about a featured startup, I recommend visiting the startup's Twitter profile as well as checking the company's Press or News pages on their websites. Both are great resources for hearing the latest straight from the galloping horse's mouth.

TechCrunch (www.techcrunch.com) is a good startup news outlet. It was acquired in 2011 by AOL and continues to be one of the top destinations for content about startups. Know, however, that the writers on the site have big personalities and sometimes do angel investments themselves, which can certainly affect their motives.

This Week In Startups (www.thisweekin.com/startups) is an excellent video series hosted by startup veteran Jason Calacanis. Entrepreneurs are interviewed and great new startups are highlighted and discussed.

Startup Digest (www.startupdigest.com) is an email newsletter service that aggregates startup events, jobs and articles. Every Monday, Startup Digest sends out its events newsletter, curated by city, to subscribers. On Wednesdays, the startup jobs list is emailed. On Fridays, the best articles and blog posts about startups are curated, with topics ranging from Mobile to Retail.

Mashable (www.mashable.com) is a news source focused primarily on social media innovation and companies. Like TechCrunch, it is updated by startup journalists throughout the day and provides another voice in startup news, especially for the digital centric.

GigaOM (www.gigaom.com) was started by former Forbes writer, Om Malik. It is a website for tech analysis, trends, and news. They also have an offering called GigaOM

Pro, which provides research for industry professionals who need access to the latest data and insights on tech companies and trends.

Hacker News is a social news website run by Y Combinator, one of the US's most prestigious incubator programs. Members of the community can submit articles, and others vote them up or down, adding to the intelligent conversation all around these interesting pieces of content. Michael Sinanian of VentureBeat, another great startup resource, says he reads it religiously. It's a great reference not only for Technology discussion but for conversation around startup culture too, Sinanian says.

VentureBeat is a high-quality blog on technology and technology leaders. The resource includes many articles that don't just report news but also provide thoughtful analysis on innovation.

Wired Magazine is one of the best consistent publications around for technology—on and offline. The monthly magazine showcases cool gadgets and explores macro technology trends. The mag has even coined new terms, like "crowd sourcing." It's an institution as a technology resource.

VC Bloggers

Many startup founders and CEOs blog, but venture capitalists provide an interesting, broad view of the startup landscape and their opinions are particularly well-regarded. Two of the best VC bloggers are Steve Blank at www.SteveBlank.com and Fred Wilson at www.AVC.com. Keep your finger on the pulse with them, as these VCs are unusually open about trends they see.

Startup Rage (www.StartupRage.com) is a fun resource in which one picture tells it all. On this website, one startup at a time is featured in a comic strip that explains the startup's mission and model. Startups are depicted in picture form so they're easier to understand than ever, and humorous too!

Epilogue

I **HOPE TO** publish many volumes of *The Coolest Startups in America*. And *The Coolest Startups in...* Mobile. Africa. China. Cleantech, you name it! Let me know what you loved about this book, what you loathed, and with what you resonated. Contact us via the book's website at www.CoolestStartups.In.

And remember, be open to new people and ideas. Progress is made through reception. I encourage you to root for the innovations that create wins for us all.

Acknowledgements

THANK YOU FIRST to my former professor and always-mentor, Dr. David Owen Robinson. With his belief in this project, I went for it.

Thank you to my dear friend, Polina Minkin, who has put up with Square-filled dinner party conversations too many times. You were my inspiration—nay, my light bulb!—for this book.

Thank you to my dear friend and talented designer, Julie Friedenberg, whose creative execution for my vision for the book design—"They must see the cover from across the airport terminal!"—has been lauded by publishers and readers alike. Thank you to Jeff Fan and Ryan Van Dyke for designing and creating the website for *The Coolest Startups in America*. This book would be nothing without the forward-thinking web presence you helped create.

Thank you to the book's interviewees: Alex Taub, Alex Budak, Ed O'Boyle, Henrik Werdelin, Dan Dascalescu, Rob Heiser, Dr. Fuyuen Yip, Keith Murphy, Greg Meier, Jeremy Johnson, Leah Busque, Marc Brodeur, Michael Sinanian, Nick Friedman, Ronnie Cho, Steven Dean, Jason Shen, Brian Zisk, Michael Karnjanaprakorn, Gulam Sarwar Ansari, Drew Gilliam, Julie Sygiel, Ilya Sukhar, Eric Slaim, Jordan Lampe, Zach Hamilton, Will Curran, Jeff Fernandez, Morgan Dierstein, Adam Dopplt, Drew Johnson, Bill Dwight, Brian Shields, Nihal Parthasarathi, Christopher Michel, Pravina Raghavan, Hagi Schwartz, Aaron Schildkrout, Jeremy Levine, Nick Ganju, Daryl Bernstein, Sutha Kamal, Sarah McIlroy, Dr. Kenneth Trauner, Sam Zaid, Scott Summit, David Van Sickle, Ilan Abehassera, Adrienn Wanner, Liron Shapira, Josh Abdulla, Iz Derdik, Jim Bruene, and Paul Murphy.

Thank you to my former managers at Yahoo! Inc., Havi Hoffman, Nicki Dugan, Jason Anello, who infused me with a love of new technology and neat ideas at an early age. Thank you greatly to my peers and superiors at SecondMarket (Chapter 6) for accelerating my intimate understanding of startups and the entrepreneur ecosystem.

Thank you to my agent, Matthew Carnicelli of Carnicelli Literary Management, who promoted me and *The Coolest*

Startups in America to publishers with an exuberance I never before knew could be. I'm grateful for your belief in this project, and happy to have worked with you in this process.

Thank you to my friends-cum-editors, Anne Eidelman, Tai Vardi and Virgilia Kaur Singh. Thank you to my editor Pierre Bienaimé for your wisdom and words. I could not have finished this volume and to this great caliber without your aid. You have been such a pleasure to work with you, on and off the Google Doc.

Thank you to my family. Bro and sis, Michael Bloch and Adele Bloch, shine on. Thank you Simon Bloch for being a fellow entrepreneur and an advisor to me. And thank you especially to my mom, Sophia Bloch, and my boyfriend, Evan Plous, who read through my many drafts and encouraged me to wake from slumber the hibernating entrepreneur within.

BEYOND INTERVIEWS AND corporate websites, the following sources were used in writing this volume of *The Coolest Startups in America*.

CHAPTER 1

Butcher, Dan. (March 21, 2011). PayPal mobile transactions exceed $6M per day: CTIA keynote. Mobile Commerce Daily. http://www.mobilecommercedaily.com/2011/03/22/paypal-mobile-transactions-exceed-6m-per-day-ctia-keynote

Nocera, Joe. (March 15, 2008). Credit Cards Are Frothy, Not Bubbly. The New York Times. http://www.nytimes.com/2008/03/15/business/15nocera.html

Schonfeld, Erick. (May 21, 2011). Mo' Money: Square Now Processing $3 Million A Day In Mobile Payments. Schonfeld, Erick. TechCrunch. http://techcrunch.com/2011/05/21/square-3-million-day/

Morris, Cheryl. (July 5, 2011). Mobile Transactions to Hit $1 Trillion by 2015. BostInno. http://bostinno.com/2011/07/05/mobile-transactions-to-hit-1-trillion-by-2015/

CHAPTER 2

Nardi, Ugo. (November 10, 2011). Bring Back That Old-Time Banking Religion. American Banker. http://www.americanbanker.com/bankthink/bring-back-old-time-banking-religion-1043977-1.html?zkPrintable=true

Paulson, Matthew. (January 1, 2012). Prosper and Lending Club Facilitated $40 Million in Loans in December. P2P Lending News. http://www.p2plendingnews.com/2012/01/prosper-and-lending-club-facilitated-40-million-in-loans-in-december

Google. Web Advertisements by Lending Club.

CHAPTER 3

Jeffries, Adrianne. (December 20, 2011). Caveat Backer! Vere Sandals, Overfunded Kickstarter Project, Fails to Deliver. BetaBeat. http://www.betabeat.com/2011/12/20/caveat-backer-vere-sandals-overfunded-kickstarter-project-fails-to-deliver/

DEFROST: CAN'T ANYONE BE AN ENTREPRENEUR?

Kent, Steve L., The Ultimate History of Video Games. Roseville, California. Prima 2001

CHAPTER 5

Schwartz, Nelson. (October 15, 2011). Online Banking Keeps Customers on Hook for Fees. The New York Times. http://www.nytimes.com/2011/10/16/business/online-banking-keeps-customers-on-hook-for-fees.html

McMillin, David. (September 10, 2011). Boomers move to online banking. Bankrate.com. http://www.bankrate.com/financing/banking/boomers-move-to-online-banking/

CHAPTER 6

Rusli, Evelyn. (June 29, 2011). Unprofitable Square Valued at $1.6 Billion. The New York Times. http://dealbook.nytimes.com/2011/06/29/unprofitable-square-valued-at-1-6-billion/

CHAPTER 9

Barnouw, Erik. Tube of Plenty: The Evolution of American Television. Oxford University Press. 1990.

CHAPTER 12

Salmon, Felix. (May 25, 2011). Why clearXchange is great for payments. Reuters. http://blogs.reuters.com/felix-salmon/2011/05/25/why-clearxchange-is-great-for-payments/

CHAPTER 13

Gantz, John. IDC. http://www.emc.com/collateral/demos/microsites/emc-digital-universe-2011/index.htm

CHAPTER 14

Noble, Ivan. (April 14, 2003). Human genome finally complete. BBC News. http://news.bbc.co.uk/2/hi/science/nature/2940601.stm

Harmon, Katherine. (June 28, 2010). Genome Sequencing for the Rest of Us. Scientific American. http://www.scientificamerican.com/article.cfm?id=personal-genome-sequencing&offset=2

Wikipedia.org. Individual genome sequencing from Illumina, Inc. Everygenome.com. Retrieved 19 October 2011.

Darce, Keith. (May 9, 2011). Illumina drops sequencing price to $4,000. UT San Diego. http://www.utsandiego.com/news/2011/

may/09/illumina-drops-human-sequencing-price-4000/

Hall, Yancey. (March 7, 2006). Coming Soon: Your Personal DNA Map?. National Geographic. http://news.nationalgeographic.com/news/2006/03/0307_060307_dna.html

Baertlein, Lisa. (November 20, 2007). Google-backed 23andMe offers $999 DNA test. USA Today. http://www.usatoday.com/tech/webguide/internetlife/2007-11-20-23andme-launch_N.htm

Pollack, Andrew. (June 26, 2008). Gene Testing Questioned By Regulators. The New York Times. http://query.nytimes.com/gst/fullpage.html?res=9501E1DB1238F935A15755C0A96E9C8B63

CHAPTER 15
Wall, Mike. (November 10, 2011) Print Your Own Space Station — in Orbit. Space.com. http://www.space.com/9516-print-space-station-orbit.html

Kaufman, Rachel. (June 21, 2011). 3-D printers launch small businesses. CNN Money. http://money.cnn.com/2011/06/17/smallbusiness/3-D_printers_small_business/index.htm

CHAPTER 17
Savitz, Eric. (October 17, 2011). Web 2.0: Twitter Seeing Nearly 250 Million Tweets/Day; Over 100 Million Users. Forbes. http://www.forbes.com/sites/ericsavitz/2011/10/17/web-2-0-twitter-has-nearly-250m-tweetsday-over-100m-users/

Multiple authors. Quora. http://www.quora.com/Twitter-1/How-many-tweets-per-day-are-there-on-Twitter

Rudegeair, Peter. (September 23, 2011). Yuri Milner on the future of the internet. Reuters. http://blogs.reuters.com/chrystia-freeland/2011/09/23/yuri-milner-on-the-future-of-the-internet/

Basulto, Dominic. (October 7, 2011). Innovators, data will set you free. The Washington Post. http://www.washingtonpost.com/blogs/innovations/post/innovators-data-will-set-you-free/2011/10/06/gIQAhidPSL_blog.html

CHAPTER 19
Backer, Patricia Ryaby. Industrialization of American Society. http://www.engr.sjsu.edu/pabacker/industrial.htm

United States Department of Transportation. Federal Highway

Administration. http://www.fhwa.dot.gov/interstate/faq.
htm#question3

Environment America. (September 21, 2011). Danger in the Air:
Unhealthy Air Days in 2010 and 2011. http://www.
environmentcalifornia.org/reports/clean-air/clean-air-program-
reports/danger-in-the-air-unhealthy-air-days-in-2010-and-2011

CHAPTER 20
Yarow, Jay. (April 21, 2009). The Cost Of A Better Place Battery
Swapping Station: $500,000. Business Insider. http://www.
businessinsider.com/the-cost-of-a-better-place-battery-swapping-
station-500000-2009-4

CHAPTER 21
Clayton, Mark. (September 24, 2007). The hidden costs of free
parking – one space at a time. USA Today. http://www.usatoday.
com/tech/science/discoveries/2007-09-24-free-parking-research_N.
htm

DEFROST: WHY IS MOBILE CRITICAL?
BBC News. (July 9, 2010). Over 5 billion mobile phone connections
worldwide. http://www.bbc.co.uk/news/10569081

Shiels, Maggie. (June 1, 2011). Cisco predicts internet device boom.
BBC News. http://www.bbc.co.uk/news/technology-13613536

CHAPTER 22
Wikipedia. Wedding industry in the United States. http://en.
wikipedia.org/wiki/Wedding_industry_in_the_United_
States#cite_note-0

Silicon Alley Insider. (October 7, 2011). The 100 Most Valuable
Startups In The World, Revamped And Revised!. Business Insider.
http://www.businessinsider.com/2011-digital-100?op=1

CHAPTER 23
Founded Project. (January 7, 2011). UJAM: Founded to prove
everyone can be a musician. The Founded Project. http://www.
foundedproject.com/2011/01/ujam/

CHAPTER 24
Motion Picture Association of America (MPAA) Industry Report.
2010 Theatrical Market Statistics. 2010.

Biagi, Shirley. Media/Impact: An Introduction to Mass Media.

Wadsworth Publishing. 2006.

Tyson, Jeff. (September 18, 2000). How Movie Distribution Works. How It Works. http://entertainment.howstuffworks.com/movie-distribution2.htm

CHAPTER 25
Wutkowski, Karey. (November 19, 2008). Auto execs' private flights to Washington draw ire. Reuters. http://www.reuters.com/article/2008/11/19/us-autos-bailout-planes-idUSTRE4AI8C520081119

CHAPTER 27
Camarota, Steven A. (October 2011). A Record-Setting Decade of Immigration: 2000-2010. Center for Immigration Studies. http://cis.org/2000-2010-record-setting-decade-of-immigration

The Economist. (November 19, 2011). The magic of diasporas. The Economist. http://www.economist.com/node/21538742

Kristof, Andras. (November 17, 2011). What is ViKi?. Quora. http://www.quora.com/What-is-ViKi#ans819720

CHAPTER 30
Cregets. (June 19, 2007). Dramatic Chipmunk. Youtube. http://www.youtube.com/watch?v=a1Y73sPHKxw

The Huffington Post staff. (January 27, 2011). President Obama Takes Questions From YouTube (LIVE VIDEO). The Huffington Post. http://www.huffingtonpost.com/2011/01/27/president-obama-youtube-live-video_n_814955.html

CHAPTER 32
Myers, Courtney Boyd. (July 21, 2011). In NYC, CourseHorse is changing the way you search for classes. The Next Web. http://thenextweb.com/apps/2011/07/21/in-nyc-coursehorse-is-changing-the-way-you-search-for-classes/

CHAPTER 34
Miniwatts Marketing Group. (Last Updated: February 6, 2012). INTERNET GROWTH STATISTICS. http://www.internetworldstats.com/emarketing.htm

CHAPTER 35
Wadhwa, Vivek. (September 1, 2011). Mr. President, there is no engineer shortage. The Washington Post. http://www.

washingtonpost.com/national/on-innovations/president-obama-there-is-no-engineer-shortage/2011/09/01/gIQADpmpuJ_story.html

CHAPTER 36
Match.com and Chadwick Martin Bailey. (2010). Recent Trends: Online Dating. http://cp.match.com/cppp/media/CMB_Study.pdf

DEFROST: INCUBATION NATION
Kincaid, Jason. (May 24, 2011). Y Combinator's Paul Graham: We're Looking For People Like Us. TechCrunch. http://techcrunch.com/2011/05/24/y-combinators-paul-graham-were-looking-for-people-like-us/

CHAPTER 40
Schwartz, Ariel. The WaterWheel Makes Clean Water Cheaper, Easier To Carry. Fast Company. http://www.fastcoexist.com/1678162/the-waterwheel-makes-clean-water-cheaper-easier-to-carry

Koenig, Cynthia. (August 15, 2011). hello wello. Vimeo. http://vimeo.com/27724804

CHAPTER 41
Official Press Release. (March 14, 2011). Kerry-Lugar-Udall Visa Bill Will Create Jobs in America. http://kerry.senate.gov/press/release/?id=4e6a51f6-fb2b-4212-b299-b0c46c7e6b58

CHAPTER 48
Delio, Michelle. (April 13, 2001). Kozmo Kills the Messenger. *Wired*. http://www.wired.com/techbiz/media/news/2001/04/43025?currentPage=all

CHAPTER 56
Ressi, Adeo. (May 28, 2011). Is There A Peak Age for Entrepreneurship?. TechCrunch. http://techcrunch.com/2011/05/28/peak-age-entrepreneurship/

CHAPTER 61
Snow, Shane. (June 2, 2011). 6 Factors Behind the Mobile Photo Sharing Boom. Mashable. http://mashable.com/2011/06/02/mobile-photo-app-trends/

CHAPTER 68
Jayson, Sharon. (December 1, 2004). Census: 5.4 million mothers are choosing to stay at home. USA Today. http://www.usatoday.com/

news/bythenumbers/2004-11-30-census-momshome_x.htm

DEFROST: WHEN IS A STARTUP NO LONGER A STARTUP?

Jones, Del. (March 5, 2008). 'Forbes': Facebook CEO is youngest self-made billionaire. USA Today. http://www.usatoday.com/money/2008-03-05-forbes-billionaires_N.htm

Tunguz, Tom. (January 2012). Where We've Been & What's To Come. Redpoint Ventures. http://redpoint.posterous.com/where-weve-been-whats-to-come

CHAPTER 69

Hillman, Alison. Quora. http://www.quora.com/Alison-Hillman/answers

Protalinski, Emil. (November 17, 2011). 48% of job seekers have used Facebook to look for work. ZDNet. http://www.zdnet.com/blog/facebook/48-of-job-seekers-have-used-facebook-to-look-for-work/5486

CHAPTER 70

U.S. Geological Survey. U.S. Department of the Interior. How much is your daily indoor water use?. http://ga2.er.usgs.gov/edu/sq3action.cfm

Abrar, Peerzada. (January 13, 2012). Why India's clean tech sector is attracting US, Europe and Asia Pacific entrepreneurs. The Economic Times. http://articles.economictimes.indiatimes.com/2012-01-13/news/30623761_1_solar-power-india-s-national-solar-mission-harish-hande/2

CHAPTER 71

Crook, Jordan. (January 16, 2012). PrimeSense Demos A Gesture-Based Next-Gen TV Interface. TechCrunch. http://techcrunch.com/2012/01/16/primesense-demos-a-gesture-based-next-gen-tv-interface/

CHAPTER 72

Ferro-Thomsen, Martin. (January 13, 2011). With which Slideshare, Scribd, or Issuu alternative is it possible to view PDFs with your iPhone and in Facebook?. Quora. http://www.quora.com/With-which-Slideshare-Scribd-or-Issuu-alternative-is-it-possible-to-view-PDFs-with-your-iPhone-and-in-Facebook

Index

2, 70, 76, 94, 226

about the author

Doreen Bloch is a former Analyst at SecondMarket, the largest marketplace for private company stock trading. She is a graduate of the University of California, Berkeley's Haas School of Business undergraduate program, and a Jack Larson Fellow for Entrepreneurship & Innovation from the Lester Center at Haas.

Doreen is the CEO and Founder of Poshly.com, a big data company working on Internet personalization. She is also a self-publishing expert, through her imprint Building Bloch Books.

Doreen is an avid writer and speaker, whose work has been featured by *The New York Times*, Fox Business, Under 30 CEO, *Forbes*, The Daily Muse, Feministing and more. She is also a member of the Young Entrepreneur Council. Her website is www.DoreenBloch.com.

Made in the USA
Lexington, KY
22 April 2012